Politics, Power and Revolution

Politics, Power and Revolution

An Introduction to Comparative Politics

Peter Calvert

READER IN POLITICS,
UNIVERSITY OF SOUTHAMPTON

Wheatsheaf
Books

A MEMBER OF THE HARVESTER PRESS GROUP

First published in Great Britain in 1983 by
WHEATSHEAF BOOKS LTD
A MEMBER OF THE HARVESTER PRESS GROUP

Publisher: John Spiers
Director of Publications: Edward Elgar
16 Ship Street, Brighton, Sussex.

British Library Cataloguing in Publication Data
Calvert, Peter
   Politics, Power and Revolution
   1.   Political Science
   2.   Comparative government
   I.   Title
   320.3   JF51

ISBN 0-7108-0167-X
ISBN 0-7108-0196-3 Pbk

Photoset 10 on 11 point Times by
PRG Graphics Ltd, Redhill
Printed in Great Britain by
The Thetford Press Ltd., Thetford, Norfolk

Contents

Preface   vii

1 The Study of Politics   1
2 Origins of Government   18
3 System, Development and Modernisation   37
4 Communication   54
5 The Struggle for Power Resources   67
6 How Demands are Presented   87
7 How Support is Shown   99
8 Inside the Black Box   117
9 Maintaining the System   132
10 Force and Political Stability   145
11 Violence and Political Change   160
12 Government vs Politics   171

Notes   175

Index   192

Preface

We live in an age in which it simply is no longer possible to do without a knowledge of politics. It is through politics that the principal decisions in any society are taken. These decisions involve the reconciling of many different points of view, and the more different the points of view, the more important it becomes for the understanding of the final outcome that we have a knowledge of politics. So the subject, although a very old one, is attracting new interest, and we are rapidly learning more about it.

This is just as well, for there is more to be learnt. No longer is it possible to get by with a knowledge of the politics of one's home town, or even of one's own country. We live, politically speaking, in a shrinking world. In this world more states interact than ever before, and many decisions taken for internal reasons have wide international repercussions. Furthermore, as we shall see, though people in different countries are motivated − driven to act − for much the same reasons, they do not act in the same way. There are many reasons for this. The study of these similarities and differences is known as 'comparative politics', or sometimes, to avoid repetition, as 'comparative government'. But though government is the more noticeable part of politics, it is not all of it, and the wider term is more accurate. The purpose of this book is to give a general introduction to the main themes of comparative politics, as they are at present understood, which will be of use to any person wishing to make use of it, whether in study, travel, trade or negotiation with a country or countries other than his own.

In shaping it, I have drawn freely on my experience of lecturing to second-year students of the University of Southampton since 1965. Though it is based on those lectures, it does not reproduce them, though I have tried, for the reader's sake to retain something of the discursive style. Like them, it is intended to be truly comparative. It is not a series of studies of governmental institutions of specific countries: there are numerous such studies, and some are very good indeed. Secondly, I have written to convey to others the essence of a wide range of literature, as I see it, and am not therefore 'plugging a line' – at least I hope not.

My thanks are especially due to Karen Dawisha and Joseph Frankel who read and commented on the typescript draft: and to Alan Brier, Frank Gregory and John Simpson, who gave advice on specific points. They are in no way responsible for what I have made of their advice.

1 The Study of Politics

Politics, the 'master science' of Aristotle,[1] is, on account of its importance and complexity, most difficult to define. Its field of interaction is to be found in every aspect of society where decisions are to be made, and nowhere more so than where the most fundamental and crucial questions have to be resolved. But the principal institution of any society dealing with political matters, and the key to understanding its politics as a whole, is its government.

By government we mean an organisation composed of individual people, men and women, who collectively, though in different degrees, participate in the making of decisions. However, we must always remember that, even if government is their full-time job, it is not the only thing they do. Like all other people they are also private individuals who play other roles in society, including those of the governed. This is a distinction which we shall find useful to remember during the discussion which follows, for politics is seldom a major activity in the life of someone who is not a member of a government or closely associated with one, and, though it is an essential activity for the community at large, it is not essential for any given individual – an important point in explaining why inadequate governments get into power, and others stay when they are so manifestly incompetent at their job.

But what is their job? What, to begin with, is politics?

Politics can be defined as the art of getting others to do the things you want them to do. The distinctive structure associated with it is the government, or more accurately, governments, because there may well be more than one in any community at any given level, and there are always several levels at which governments exist anywhere: national, regional, local – even personal. But politics is not action, but interaction; it is both what governments do to rule people, and what people do to try to influence their government.

POLITICS AS SCIENCE

I have defined politics as an art, because for those who practise it that is what it is, a skill which they generally learn by trial and error, and not by study. The study of politics we term political science, and those who study it professionally are known, correctly, not as politicians but, in a rather cumbersome phrase, as political scientists. This term has given rise to a lengthy, but nevertheless rather absurd argument about the appropriateness of the word science. In its original sense, the literal translation of the German *Wissenschaft*, it means both what we now understand as science (e.g. physics, chemistry, biology) and more generally knowledge. But as the so-called 'exact' sciences have become more exact, so their practitioners have become, if anything, more intolerant of the claims of other disciplines to the use of the word, despite the fact that in their own fields they have increasingly had to recognise the limitations of measurement. In what respects, then, can political science be regarded as a science?

First, it will not be seriously disputed, I think, that it has a defined and unique field of study. It is not, for example, history, sociology or philosophy, though it has both borrowed from and contributed to each of these disciplines in what has been a fruitful interchange for each.

Secondly, it seeks to build up a body of knowledge of politics which is as comprehensive and exact as techniques permit. In comprehensiveness it suffers from two problems. Political phenomena are very short-lived, and it requires very intensive study to keep up with a developing political situation. Indeed, if you are actively involved in it, it may occupy all your working day for several days, or even weeks. On the other hand, if you are seeking to examine it from outside, you encounter a unique obstacle: the problem of governmental secrecy.

Exactness, on the other hand, is an essential requirement of the *art* of politics. In so far as political activity is to be realised in the form of decisions, it involves the amassing of a given number of votes, whether in committee, in a meeting, or in an election. The stock-in-trade of the successful politician, therefore, is the recollection from moment to moment of the balance of advantage or disadvantage to his side, together with the tally of obligations amassed in the course of bargaining for support. However, this knowledge is in itself a valuable part of his bargaining ability, and so is jealously guarded. Hence the political scientist in this respect too is aware of a barrier of information. Other difficulties exist too. With many actors come problems of collecting, maintaining and above all recalling large amounts of information culled from many different sources. This information has to be reduced to a standard form. Much of it is not numerical, but in nominal form, that is to say, certain information is either present in a given category or it is not. This restricts the range of possibilities for analysing it. But in themselves, none of these problems is strange to the exact sciences.

Thirdly, political science seeks to analyse the information obtained in order to discern regular laws. It has been argued that we cannot hope to do this, since in dealing with human beings as opposed to natural phenomena, knowledge of the results of an investigation into a pattern of behaviour will lead to changes in that behaviour pattern in the future. This is assuming one were able to discern a pattern, much less a law, in the first place. One such example is the prediction of Marx that bourgeois governments would be overthrown by the organised force of the proletariat. Knowledge of this prediction, taken in conjunction with the example of the fate of governments that have disregarded it, have led to counter-measures being taken against the possibility by other governments. Statements about social phenomena, then, cannot be predictive in the 'If A then B' sense.[2]

So political science cannot hope, then, to be truly scientific? No, because not all sciences can make such predictive statements, and, in fact, the belief that they can stems from a quite inadequate knowledge of the nature of the so-called exact sciences. Medicine, for example, is undeniably a science, yet many statements in medicine about the effect of one or another treatment can only be couched in terms of probabilities. It can be said that a treatment usually helps patients with a certain condition to a complete recovery, but it cannot be certain that it will help any *one* patient to whom the treatment is administered. As in medicine, too, the weighing of probabilities in politics is seldom a simple matter; the more serious any problem is, the less likely that it will occur on its own, and the more likely that it will occur in conjunction with other problems to which it is closely related. In such circumstances, a decision on one problem will necessarily have consequences for the others which may well make their solution much more difficult, and in extreme cases it may seem very difficult to make any useful decision at all.

Just as the exact sciences (including medicine) have had to build up their basic store of information over many generations, and often by trial and error, so too political scientists are doing the same. The fact that the road may be a long one is no excuse for not setting out on it boldly. As the Chinese proverb has it: 'The journey of a thousand *li* begins with a single step.'

METHOD

We study politics comparatively because there is no other way in which to obtain the raw data on which to base informed judgments. It is certainly possible and, indeed, most desirable for political philosophers to think constructively about how people ought to act in ideal situations. It is, in fact, the only way to explore the full range of possibilities implicit in any given situation to think about it as an abstract problem. But this can only be done in the light of general principles about human behaviour which are derived from experience, as is the problem itself, so at best that necessary experience will be a broad one. In one sense, then, there is no study of politics that is not comparative. All political science, as all other sciences, involves learning by measuring and examining events which are comparable, so that our first ideas of how the results should differ from one case to another (hypotheses) may be tested, and, if supported, gain acceptance as regular statements of future probability (theories).

The difficulties of information outlined above dictate our choice of method. Our method is the clinical one: to examine cases in such numbers as we can find of the phenomenon which we wish to investigate; cases which will be complicated by irrelevant information and misleading statements by the participants involved, and by a wide range of other differing factors which we must learn to live with as best as we can. And it is this that demonstrates just how much the political scientist can help the practitioner of politics, namely the politician.

Like many other professionals, politicians over the years develop abilities to size up and guide a situation. These abilities, which, as I noted above, are generally self-taught, are often of a high order, but they are not without their faults. Apart from those errors which creep in unconsciously over the years, as the politician grows tired or careless, he has a specific limitation to his knowledge in that he is trained to think in adversary terms, and a general limitation that the deeper his knowledge in his chosen field, the less adequate his knowledge will be in others. These other fields the political scientist has the freedom to explore, and in other countries or in other times he can seek out and examine patterns of behaviour generally rare or unknown in the politician's society, but ones with which – in changed circumstances – the politician may some day have to deal.

And the political scientist, while he cannot answer all the questions a politician might wish to put to him, and may well not be able to answer some questions which would be most useful, can answer, or help to answer, some very useful questions. How can we choose a leader who will have the support of most of the people? How can we devise an electoral system for a given desired result? How can we decide a difficult political issue and avoid responsibility for the outcome? These are only a few of the questions the comparative study of politics helps one to answer. It is obvious how practical they are.

THE ASSUMPTION OF UNIVERSALITY

The study of comparative politics rests on a fundamental assumption, the importance of which we should be aware. It is that human behaviour is broadly speaking constant; that it will be the same in the same circumstances, regardless of time and space. Without this assumption the philosophical problems of studying politics in a comparative context would be immensely complicated if not, indeed, rendered impossible. However, this is not in itself sufficient reason for making that assumption. We do so because the overwhelming weight of evidence is that mankind is biologically a very homogeneous species.[3] Such differences as exist between the populations of different parts of the world are trivial, and such as exist are in any case easily accounted for by accidental factors, such as the relatively temporary isolation of small units of population on remote islands. And between the sexes such differences as exist appear minor compared with those of many animal species. We may deduce from this that variations in fundamental behaviour patterns between different communities in different parts of the world are likewise to be considered very slight, and hence may be safely ignored in our general working assumption.

SOME DEFINITIONS

Before turning to the question of how far we may learn from man's origins about the nature of variation to be expected in his political behaviour, it will help to define some more useful terms. *Government* is that part of the political system which successfully claims to have the legitimate monopoly of the use of force.[4] Once secured, this monopoly is merely a sanction, the ultimate sanction that the decisions of government can be made effective. But the sanction is never completely, and often very incompletely, secured. Though most writers have assumed that some form of organised government is essential to the maintenance of society, this is not an assumption which we find either necessary or helpful to make. As we have seen, there are always a number of levels of government in any society; there is not, indeed, any such thing as an absolute dictatorship. Nor should we assume that there is, even at the highest level, only one government in a given society at any one time, since the claim to monopoly may be successful and yet be challenged, and in any case successful is a relative term, since there seems to be always an irreducible level of unregulated force in any society. However, when we are making comparisons in comparative politics, we shall normally be making them between the national or central governments of different countries.

The national level is, in theory, the highest level of government possible, owing no obligation to any higher level. The organised community within which a government claims obedience as of right of all citizens, has traditionally been known as a *state*: sometimes they are termed nation states. Originally, this was to distinguish them from earlier forms of political organisation, such as tribes or city states, since modern states cover a relatively wide area within which the majority of inhabitants identify themselves with one another, by the possession of a common language, religion and/or culture, and to this sense of identity we give the name *nation*. However, the term is a misleading one, for there is no exact correspondence between state and nation; there are states with more than one nation (Britain), nations with more than one state (Germany), states without substantial national identity (Chad) and nations with no definite state at all (the Palestinian Arabs).

The study of the relations between states is commonly known as international relations, and forms an academic discipline so closely allied to politics that the two are normally taught together. Indeed, the fact that the disciplines have become separated is largely fortuitous, and there is everything to be gained by bringing the study of comparative politics and international relations as closely together as possible. The fact is that the practice of international relations was established in a political climate which established the belief that states were in every sense quite distinct and separate from one another, treating with one another as equals, and owing no duty to any outside earthly authority. This notion, which is termed *sovereignty*, is often said to be one of the attributes of a state.[5]

However, the concept of sovereignty is not a real attribute, simply a convenient, and indeed very important, legal fiction. In fact ever since the concept of the state emerged, in or around the sixteenth century, states have interacted with one another and so at least to some minor extent have been dependent on others. By the time of the Treaty of Westphalia in 1648 there had grown up a substantial agreement on certain basic principles of international law which all states should obey. And in the twentieth century, and especially since 1945, states have given up substantial proportions of their former freedom of action to transnational and supranational organisations and, indeed, to one another. Yet this should not lead us to believe that we are witnessing a decline of the state. On the contrary, there are more states now than ever before, and in almost all of them the spirit of nationalism seems as strong as ever. And, since the whole inhabitable world is now parcelled out between them, it is quite impossible for anyone to ignore their existence, or escape from the influence of one or another of them.[6]

Our primary subject of study, then, is the state. There are quite a number of them – 161 have varying degrees of relations with the United Nations (1982) – and this number is in theory quite large enough for meaningful analysis in statistical terms. However, the universe of states is not a random sample, and its members in fact differ drastically in all kinds of most obvious ways. At one end of the scale there is the gigantic Union of Soviet Socialist Republics. It stretches across eleven time zones, and covers 8,599,806 square miles (22.4 million square kilometres), or one-sixth of the world's land surface. In 1980, it had a population of 264.5 million. At the other end, at least as far as the 161 agencies in relation with the United Nations in 1980 were concerned, is the Pacific island of Nauru, with an area of 8.2 square miles (2130 hectares), most of it covered with guano, and a population in 1977 of 7254.[7] Clearly, moreover, any comparison between the Soviet Union on the one hand, and Nauru on the other must be almost meaningless, even if the formal legal status of each is the same. The disparities are, in fact, so great that a small handful of cases – the superpowers, for example – invalidate the generalisations about the rest. We do not therefore like to try to compare states, unless they are in some respects reasonably comparable – at least not to begin with – or until we have built up a sufficient general body of knowledge to compensate for the obvious differences of size, population, climate, natural resources, and so forth. In other words, having first defined our unit for study, we observe the second general principle of comparison, which is to ensure that as many variables are held in common as possible.

We compare, for example, the two superpowers, the United States and the Soviet Union. We compare those states which have had recent experience of being great powers, which are in one or another respect on the bigger end of many scales of comparison. We can compare Britain (area 93,323 square miles, 241,705 square kilometres, population 55.93 millions (1976)), France (area 210,038 square miles, 543,965 square kilometres, population 53.59 millions (est. 1980)), and West Germany (area 96,005 square miles, 248,667 square kilometres, population 61.44 millions (1979)) because they are, by world standards, very similar in size and population, occur in the same temperate region of the world, have many similar geographical features, share a common historical tradition, exhibit rather similar economic and social structures, and have banded themselves together in a regional association called the Euopean Community. But we run into considerable problems if we try to make comparisons between widely separated examples of whatever kind. Political scientists, therefore, have suggested a number of possible strategies or 'approaches' to the general problems of comparison, and one of these may well have advantages over all the others in considering any given problem.

The examples I have given so far are those normally given a whole unit approach. By this we mean that writers try, more or less successfully depending on the space available, to compare all relevant structures in two modern states that have important aspects in common. Literature of this kind usually falls into one of two categories: the 'big fat book' on the principal countries of the world or the countries of a given geographical area, and the series of books organised on a common basis, with or without an introductory text or texts. Each has its disadvantages. The former tends to be over-condensed and unwieldy, while the latter seldom extends to more than one or two dozen of the principal countries of the world before the editors' zeal or the publishers' money runs out. The fact is that unless you stick to comparing two countries at a time, the whole unit approach generates so much information that handling it can be very troublesome.

Other writers have borrowed from anthropologists the technique of comparing different societies known as the competing power centres approach. This involves, for politics, identifying centres of political power in given societies, and finding out with whom they compete and for what. Certain patterns recur again and again, the best known of which is generalised in Galtung's terms as the conflict between the centre and the periphery.[8] Conflict between centre and periphery is the basic pattern operating whenever political unification takes place, whether this is by the voluntary linking of states in alliance or confederation, the federation of states of common heritage, or the conquest of imperial possessions by a colonising power. Generally speaking, the stronger the resistance put up by the periphery to the pretensions of the central authority, the weaker the structure of the whole. Hence, by examining more closely the nature of the competing centres, we can for example gain greater insight into the special conditions that gave rise to federalism in the

United States or Germany, as opposed to its abandonment in Brazil or Venezuela; federalism being, in fact, a very special case of a stalemate in the conflict between centre and periphery. The European Community is the product of a very different sort of balance in which the bulk of the strength of the institution continues to reside with the periphery.

Another level again is the local community approach. In this, reasonably sized areas defined as forming communities with some sort of individual coherence are compared across national boundaries. Rokkan and Valen used this technique to identify differences in size, scale, potential for political organisation, specialisation, etc. which have obvious implications for the comparison of the countries concerned.[9] Studies of towns in different countries have been made for various purposes, usually by geographers or town-planners, and these too have obvious value for the understanding of comparative politics.[10] An obvious weakness, however, is the very different nature of units in different countries.

To remedy this, Neundörfer proposed the use, already known in economics, of a standard unit approach. This involves the definition in each of two countries of a statistically defined standard unit;[11] for example, one might take an area of population 50 million people living in an environment with a comparable working environment and degree of industrialisation and find out how political arrangements differ – compare, for example, England and Wales with a comparable slice from the East Coast of the United States, somewhere between Massachusetts and Maryland, or the Ukraine in the Soviet Union. If you can find two statistically comparable units which are also politically comparable this approach may have its virtues, but there are in fact considerable problems involved in finding such areas, as the above examples will have shown. England in area is comparable with New York State in the United States, but New York's population is much smaller, and it plays an even smaller role in the political structure of the country of which it is a part. And an exact comparison in statistical terms could give one, in political terms, a miscellaneous and so meaningless slice of jurisdictions and responsibilities which could be given little or no political meaning.

From whatever aspect we begin, we expect ultimately to aspire to combine our material into a whole unit study of two states, and thereafter to increase the number of states studied, though this necessarily entails reducing the amount of information about each country that can be handled. Some such overall surveys, which have only become possible in the last fifteen years with the development of adequate computing facilities, have been made, and the multi-country survey was first used on a grand scale in *A Cross-Polity*

Survey (1964) by Banks and Textor.[12] A similar approach was used for the study of revolutionary incidents in my own *A Study of Revolution* (1970).[13] The principal limitation on the technique is that, as applied to the overall structure of states, it gives a static picture, a snapshot in time as it were, which needs comparison with earlier and later studies to be developed effectively.

It should be noted that this sort of cross polity survey has nothing in common with the technique of interviewing people in various states used by Almond and Verba in making comparisons of political behaviour.[14] That technique has, of course, valuable possibilities, but students of comparative politics point out that linguistic differences are such that there must be considerable doubt whether a questionnaire administered in more than one language may not, by unintended differences of meaning, create excessive additional differences in interpreting the results.

Finally, it is, of course, quite legitimate to study any one country or any one aspect of politics on its own, in the hope that one's findings may be interesting in themselves. But such studies will be much more valuable if they are done in the awareness that there is value to others in recording results in a form that will make later comparison easier, while there is also an advantage to oneself in using knowledge of other countries to formulate a wider range of questions to ask your material. There is no advantage to anyone, either, in piling up so much material that no one handling it can do anything useful with it, or, on the other hand, spending so much time deciding on one's approach that one never arrives.

To sum up, therefore, there are many possible approaches to the problem of studying governments and politics. Where you begin is largely a matter of individual choice – the subject matter is, after all, the same whichever direction you choose to approach it. To be fully effective, however, any study must seek to take place in an informed knowledge of the range of possible variation that can take place. Study must embody a sufficient depth of historical knowledge to show us how the society and its political system have evolved and are evolving, and this means awareness not only of the techniques of the political scientists but also those of the historian. This done, we may then tidy up our ideas by the use of shorthand expressions for general concepts such as are implied by the use of technical terms and systems of classification. These are useful only provided that we remember that they are there to help us, and not to force our ideas into a rigid mould, for modern states are both too complex and too unstable for us to be confident that any very rigid system of ideas is going to have lasting value.

Thirdly, what value our research may have depends entirely on the adoption of a satisfactory research design. This has a number of stages: we first formulate clearly what it is that we wish to investigate. Next, we establish hypotheses that we wish to test; these hypotheses, moreover, must be capable of being analysed in terms of the data we have obtained and will seek to obtain. In political science we can normally not use either of the two methods by which validity can be ascribed to scientific research. We cannot do experiments, and we cannot arrange for our observations, other than in surveys of individuals, to be randomised. So our choice of analytical techniques must reflect the limitations of our material, though this does not mean that we should not at all times strive for greater accuracy. In the end, the results of our work must then be set out clearly and made available to other researchers, showing how and why those conclusions have been obtained.

Lastly, we must avoid using our categorisations to stultify the further development of thought, by labelling societies, institutions or people instead of examining them, and filing them instead of examining them. In this sense, as we shall see, many popular political words familiar from newspapers and television – like democracy and dictatorship, socialist and capitalist – serve to arrest and not to further the development of a true science of politics, unless their historical limitations are both realised and transcended.

SCHOOLS OF INTERPRETATION

Political scientists have prejudices like other people, and the most persistent of these are their own political views. It comes as no surprise to find, therefore, that their writing on politics can be grouped in the main in one or another of three competing schools of interpretation.

1   Historical / descriptive

Despite criticisms that have been levelled at the historical/ descriptive method by the supporters of other schools, it lies still at the basis of all work in political science, and, it may be said with confidence, provides 90 per cent of the information on which all the more ambitious approaches in each of the schools depends. Work that neglects the basic principles of historical research produces valueless data, so the political scientist, if his work is not to be helplessly dependent on others, must understand the value and significant features of different historical sources. And he will learn from the best historians three things: to take account of all the information available to him, even if he does not agree with it or it with him; to give due weight to the factor of time in the development of events; and to show clearly to the reader the source of his ideas.

The weakness of historical studies, on the other hand, is the tendency to historicism, which is the explanation of events in terms of themselves. And, as I have already indicated, political scientists must go beyond the historians and translate their works into a set of common concepts before they can hope to make meaningful comparisons. Interestingly enough, in the historical/ descriptive tradition, such common concepts have most often been supplied by lawyers, though legal terminology was in the first instance developed for very different purposes.

2 Marxist

Marxism contributes to modern intepretation the powerful and seductive idea of a common path of development for all societies. This is not an original idea, but it was one which gained considerable impetus from the onset of the industrial revolution, since Marx himself, who asserted the primacy of economic causes in determining human behaviour, was the first to seek to explore these in relation to an overall philosophy of history, which he hoped – and repeatedly asserted – had in itself a predictive value. Though where they were not so vague as to be meaningless, Marx's own predictions have consistently been proved wrong, his own emphasis on two points is of the greatest value to the study of comparative politics: the fact that the political cannot be detached from the economic and social aspects of a community, and the need for hard data as the essential foundation for any serious future research.

The weakness of the Marxist approach is the undue respect his disciples continue to attribute to the diverse writings of a mid-nineteenth-century writer, and the trivialisation of his most interesting propositions by the unthinking repetition by the so-called vulgar Marxists. Where Marxism is most fruitful is where it has been incorporated into the general body of human knowledge, of which no one school of thought has a monopoly.

3 Behaviouralist

The adherents of this school derive from the natural sciences an emphasis on clinical study of behaviour in very small groups and in the individual. This fills an essential void in Marxist theory, which is concerned above all with very large groups and movements. As has been demonstrated by biologists, propositions derived from the behaviour of one size of group are simply not valid for other sizes of groups (the so-called ecological fallacy). And, as much of politics involves small-group behaviour, the political scientists' use of the work done in this area, which has been slow to be accepted other than at the most superficial level, is hardly excessive, though it is also true to say that obsessions with methodological purity have had a stultifying effect on actual research.

Biology has also contributed to political science the concept of social entities as systems performing specified functions. Again this is not a new idea, for the notion of the 'body politic', familiar in medieval times, is but an earlier version of the same idea. The expansion of the concept of system in political science has, however, as in biology itself, been much aided by the cybernetic revolution and the successes of engineers in developing artificially intelligent machines.[15] The system concepts can be applied on a large scale, even to a whole nation state, utilising the concepts of regionally or functionally distinct subsystems within one common whole of interrelated parts.[16] Increasingly, therefore, political scientists have come with advantage to talk of political systems and not of states or governments, as we have done hitherto.

Systems analysis has contributed to political science in addition three essential ideas. The same functions may be performed in different systems by different structures – a worm, for example, 'sees' with its skin.[17] It is function that determines structure, though it has too readily been assumed from this that all structures will have useful functions. In fact they do not necessarily do so, since they may merely represent the residual traces of a function that is no longer performed, as in the case of the vermiform appendix in human physiology, and the American Electoral College in politics. Thirdly, they offer a possibility for research which unfortunately is difficult, if not quite impossible, to apply to political systems; that of feeding in a known input and observing what comes out the other end.

But before we go on to consider the implications of these and other developments to the study of the political systems of today, there are some other questions of definition we should consider.

CONSTITUTIONS

When the study of comparative politics began with Aristotle (384-321 BC), it began in very favourable conditions. As a Greek, Aristotle was dealing in the main with states of roughly comparable size, and all very small by today's standards. They were limited to the effective size of a city and its rural hinterland; they had very similar economies and social structures; and there was a large universe of them available for study – 146 in all. He could therefore compare them with relative ease, and so we need not be surprised that he did so with great sophistication, nor that his empirical observation of politics on a small scale has continued to be of great practical value to politicians ever since, despite the very different context in which the observations were recorded.

Aristotle himself would have said that he had studied the 'constitutions' of the Greek city states. But the English word constitution is used in politics in two senses. In its general sense, with a small 'c', it means the way in which a state is organised, and with a capital 'C' it means a written document setting out the way in which the state *should* be organised, a meaning which goes back to the legal bargains embodied in the Constitutions of Clarendon (1164), and was revived and extended by the framers of the fundamental laws of the United States to refer to the document they wrote in 1787.

Today when we use the word it is this second sense that is most often intended, and no confusion can occur in writing provided we remember to use the capital 'C'. Nor does the fact that the English word has so recently obtained its meaning as *the* fundamental document setting out the way in which a country is to be governed mean that such documents were unknown in ancient states. Quite the contrary, they were perfectly normal and written on wood, cast in bronze or carved in stone, were set up in the meeting place of the Council or the principal temple of the patron deity of the city, where Aristotle (or anyone else, for that matter) could have consulted them for the price of a small offering. In a similar way the Constitution of the United States is enshrined in a stone hall in the National Archives Building of that country, hermetically sealed in a vacuum and capable of being lowered within thirty seconds by 4½ tons of machinery into an atom-bomb-proof shelter.

But, of course, it is not sufficient to look at the Constitution of the United States to find out how the Americans run things. There are many things that it does not say – no mention is made, for example, of political parties – and there are some parts of it that today would be downright misleading. Everyone knows that states do not operate according to their written Constitutions, and an extreme case was the first Constitution of a united Italy, which had no amending procedure written into it, so that politicians there, long before Mussolini, had simply got into the habit of ignoring it if it did not agree with what they wanted to do.[18] We are interested in Constitutions, of course. But we are far more interested in the constitution with a small 'c', or what, with the French socialist writer

Ferdinand Lassalle, we may perhaps call the 'real' constitution.[19]

To preserve the analogy of Ancient Greece or Rome, for a moment at least, the real constitution is not found in the temple, but in the market-place. And it is clearly in the market-place that Aristotle learnt much of his information, in conversation with informants and, to put it bluntly, in gossip. Aristotle, is full of gossip; it is a pity that some of it is now too old for us to find it as amusing as the Greeks must have done. There is no need to abandon your sense of humour when you study politics; in fact, there is probably no subject for which a sense of humour is more necessary. It was clearly through gossip that Aristotle learnt not just who was supposed to be in charge of the state, but who was actually boss; not just how the elections were held, but how they were fixed; not just who was the heir-apparent, but what his opponents were doing to dispose of him as tidily as possible.

If these things are all well understood, and the basis of government well established, there is little or no need for a written Constitution at all. After all, a written Constitution is a document describing an historical situation, a restraint on the too rapid change of government. If it is to work as such, it must be made by a special process, one that is more comprehensive and hence more complicated than the normal process by which laws are made. Such a process, however, is only possible where a substantial measure of agreement on the fundamental values of society already exists. One country in the world that has never had a written Constitution as such is the United Kingdom, but even the United Kingdom has produced not one but several documents which are accorded a special status as landmarks of constitutional agreement: Magna Carta, the Act of Settlement (1701), the Acts of Union (1707, 1801), the Parliament Acts (1911, 1949), and so forth. [20] This is not to say that Britain could not have a written Constitution, for the Belgians wrote it down as long ago as 1831, so that in turn the British Government, as Verney has pointed out, could copy it for the benefit of Canada, Australia, New Zealand and other countries too. [21] But as the example of South Africa, Ghana, Nigeria and later examples shows, the existence of a written Constitution is no guarantee that that form of government will be maintained, or that, as with the Stalin Constitution, it will be a fair reflection of how government functioned at that time. And it is a sad fact that it is just those nations which have been most assiduous in providing written Constitutions for themselves – nations such as Venezuela, France or the Dominican Republic – which have, in historical times, least often been governed on a basis of general agreement, and most used to having their constitutional government set aside.

The comparative study of government, therefore, must be conducted in the context of politics. It comprises: (i) institutions – the legal basis for government and the Constitution; (ii) functions – what the government does and how it is influenced; and (iii) the context of government – the history, geography, economy and society of the country concerned.

TIME

I have already mentioned in this context the need to study events across time, or as some writers paraphrase it, in a 'diachronic perspective'. For reasons which will become clearer in chapter 3, discussion of political matters frequently ignores the time dimension, so that the diachronic perspective is not something that comes naturally, rather it is something that has to be achieved. How often do you hear British politicians say something like this: 'We don't want coalitions in this country because they lead to weak, unstable governments like they have in France'? But weak, unstable governments are not typical of France in the Fifth Republic (1958-) at all. As a current example Italy would be much better, and France is only used because a memory survives of the rapidly changing administration of the French Third and Fourth Republics (1871-1940; 1946-58). Secondly, coalition governments in Britain in the twentieth century (1916-22, 1931-45) far from being weak, were in fact exceptionally strong. Why then is this not recognised? Partly at least because Victorian writers, with a different historical perspective again, said coalitions would be weak, and this has become accepted wisdom, partly because it suits some politicians to preserve it.

To introduce the time element, then, is at the least to multiply the number of variables involved. Much as we may wish to avoid this, we simply cannot do so. So we then have to accept that this perspective may be very difficult to make precise, since a science of politics that simply dealt with the immediate instant – what we may call the anthropological present – would be seriously limited. The safest way in which to handle comparisons across time is on the same principle as we handle comparisons across space, namely by holding as many variables in common as possible, and this means comparing events and structures where possible in close temporal proximity. If we have to range farther afield we shall need some means of linking the time periods involved; in other words, not just a diachronic perspective, but a developmental perspective.

At this point you may reasonably feel: this is all very well, but where is it all going to end? It is hardly helpful to say that it does not, though this is to a considerable extent true. In practice, as with any other field of study, we have to set defined boundaries to work in comparative politics. These boundaries are not and cannot be definite, however, since the definition of what is political is one of the things that varies from society to society. On the other hand, comparative politics is not the all-embracing study of politics either. For the sake of convenience it does not pursue the theoretical speculations which we associate with political philosophy, nor on the other hand go into the close detail of human action which is subsumed under the study of political behaviour. Each sub-group of the discipline of political science contributes to the whole, but it is not the whole, though each contributes something to the others. Writers of the past, in particular Aristotle and Montesquieu, have contributed to political thought concepts which lie at the base of the work we do today. Conversely, what we discover in the course of our examination of comparative politics must necessarily form part of any future body of theory about politics. We have, after all, many advantages over our predecessors. If only Montesquieu had had, for example, the opportunity to travel to the South Seas and examine society there, his generalisations about the effect of climate on behaviour might have been very different.[22] If Rousseau had lived in the time of Gauguin, and made the same journey, he would hardly have formed the views he did about the idyllic quality of the state of nature.[23] And it is with primitive government, and political anthropology, that I propose to begin our more detailed examination of comparative politics.

2   Origins of Government

The origins of government and of the state lie at a time so remote in human history that we are still unable to resolve many important controversies which knowledge of them could clarify. We begin with pre-human society.

To some people, a reminder of their animal nature is seen as impolite, though they do not go so far as those North American Indians who knocked out their canine teeth because they reminded them of it. Others regard any comparison between man and animal as an insult to the animal. Comparisons are, of course, impossible without some knowledge of animal behaviour. The study of this is the subject of the new academic sub-discipline of ethology, derived from both psychology and biology, both of which are well established sciences in their own right. The literature is extensive, but only a tiny proportion of it is relevant to the political scientist. As far as its impact on politics is concerned it is, of course, the works of the popular writers that have transmitted it to a wider public, and in so doing may indeed have created new and strange misconceptions about politics. It is to the works of these writers, therefore, that I shall primarily refer.

AGGRESSION

Since government concerns the establishment of a claim to monopoly over the use of force in a human society, it seems prudent to begin with the question of whether or not there is any natural predisposition in man towards the use of force. Among philosophers, Thomas Hobbes in particular claimed that there was, but few modern psychologists would agree with the argument of Konrad Lorenz that man, in common with other animal species, has an innate instinct of aggression. Lorenz argues[1] that the observation of animal behaviour shows that the human being is the only species (apart from the rat) that kills its own kind. Some animals that have the capacity may do so by accident, and there are few species for which this is not possible. Others, such as the fox, may deliberately kill their offspring if there is not enough food to go round. But only man among the higher animals has elaborated it into a full-time activity, with rewards for those who practise it most successfully.

What has gone wrong, Lorenz suggests, is that we are failing to control our basic instinct or drive of aggression. Aggression is, he suggests, an essential drive which defines the community and protects it against outside attack. In other words, if the community has a boundary (and it may be a highly mobile boundary), that boundary is defined as the line at which the aggressive response is triggered off by an intruder. It is a fail-safe mechanism in that it is safer to respond aggressively to someone who turns out to be a friend, than it is to accept as a friend someone who turns out to be an enemy. This seems a highly plausible argument, and we may reasonably accept that a simple mechanism of this kind could be a reasonable explanation of the aggressive actions we do in fact see in animals as well as in human beings. The advantage of the explanation is that it also accounts for the ritual element in our societies. Rituals are the means by which the aggressive response is inhibited, so that human beings, as well as animals, can live together in large communities for safety, and above all mate and rear children.

The opponents of the idea of the aggressive drive usually base their case on the argument that aggression is socially conditioned; that it derives from an unfavourable environment, and in particular from overcrowding, which leads to conflict, child battering, crime, and ultimately war. A recent popular study of man's social development stated bluntly that there was no such thing as an aggressive instinct in man, because war as such was an activity which began only with the introduction of the horse. Unfortunately, in the case of ancient Egypt, where the written records go back well before the arrival of the horse (c 1600 BC) it is quite apparent that very bloodthirsty wars were fought on foot at least 2000 years earlier.[2]

Many of those who reject the idea of an aggressive drive follow the view of John Dollard and colleagues who in 1939 asserted that 'aggression is always a consequence of frustration'. The frustration-aggression thesis is still widely popular, and among political scientists in recent years Ted Gurr has made use of it to develop a theory of how internal conflict arises in a political system.[3] Though such lines of research still look promising, they present in fact considerable difficulties, since the concept of frustration is a very subjective one. Circumstances which one person finds frustrating may strike another as perfectly reasonable. In any case, why should overcrowding and bad social conditions necessarily lead to the aggressive response? Withdrawal, or in extreme cases population collapse, would seem on the face of it to be equally likely responses. The point is, surely, that people do behave aggressively in certain social conditions, and the relevance for us is that these are the conditions in which modern societies have to function. And aggression begins with their personal relations with one another, so the ways in which those relations may be modified are of fundamental importance to their political development. If 'an Englishman's home is his castle', does the separation from his neighbours which this brings help him to develop a society in which his level of aggression is relatively low? Or can he shrink his horizons to the walls of a French, American or Soviet apartment and still get on well with the people next door, and vote accordingly? If so, the ability to do so consciously must depend in part on a greater understanding of the nature of ritual. For it appears that there are indeed universal ways in which man indicates that he is not hostile, and these include, for example, making oneself smaller, smiling and indicating that one's hands are empty.[4] These are formalised and ritualised in different ways in different societies. The French, for example, shake hands every morning before breakfast to indicate that they are not going to kill one another; the British find it necessary to shake hands only once in a lifetime, or thereabouts.

Similarly in Britain people drive on the left-hand side of the road so that they can have their sword arm free, and the man coming in the other direction can see that it is not holding a sword. The French, on the other hand, drive on the right, so that the sword arm is as far as possible away from the person on the other side, and that too indicates a peaceful intention. These two apparently diametrically opposed patterns both stem from past experience of the same kind. And Americans take it so seriously that they not only drive on one side of the road, but even tend to walk on one side of the sidewalk. This never happens in Britain or France.

Hence, though we cannot deduce from the general patterns of behaviour universally applicable rituals, we can identify rituals which do perform the same functions in different societies, and the basic effect of the most fundamental of these is to inhibit hostility and aggression within the society, and to delimit its bounds.

TERRITORIALITY

This brings us to the second great debate, the question of whether or not man is a territorial animal. Many animals do have a territorial

instinct, that is to say, their entire social pattern depends on defining a strip of territory for themselves. The red deer buck, as Ardrey
points out, cannot mate until it has first found a patch of territory
and then successfully defended it against all comers. And deer that
lose their territory lose their place in society, and become isolated
individuals separated from the rest of the herd. But there is a furious
debate about whether or not human beings have the same instinct.
Opponents of the idea point out that many animals do not have a
territorial pattern of organisation, and that among these animals are
some of man's nearest relations; that man's own ancestors were
probably forest-dwelling primates who were constantly on the move
in search of food, and that consequently they probably would not
have needed or wanted a territorial space.[5]

There are two simple pieces of observation which anyone can
make which suggest that despite these and similar excellent arguments, man does have some form of territorial motivation. One is to
travel by train. When you get into a train, into an empty carriage,
and watch the other travellers you see a very interesting pattern
develop. People arrive bearing a number of possessions of various
kinds and shapes – the umbrella and briefcase of the commuter, the
bags and parcels of the shopper, or the suitcases of the holiday-
maker. Each finds a separate compartment, and puts a coat on the
seat next to him, a bag on the seat opposite and an umbrella
blocking the way in from the gangway. In no time at all they have
defined a territorial space. Soon each compartment contains one
person (or group) with their territorial spaces all defined. Then one
more person gets in. At this point, with much begrudging muttering
and signs of irritation, someone moves, usually only when challenged by a direct question, one or two of his things, and they split
the compartment sideways and each piles his belongings on the seat
beside him. And so it goes on until the railway carriage is filled up.

Secondly, when an audience comes into a lecture room, they dot
themselves all round the room. They do not all sit in the corner next
the radiator, even when it happens to be under the window which
forms the only source of fresh air. So it can be neither the lure of
warmth nor ventilation that defines where they sit. Again, they
begin sitting all over the place and only fill in the interstices as the
room fills up, and the one thing they all have in common is that they
will all sit a long way back from the lecturer, so that he may, in a
large hall, have to shout VERY LOUDLY to make himself heard,
the reason being, it seems, that they are not really there to listen to
him, but to partake in a social ritual in which they define their
territorial space.

If, then, man is a territorial animal, that has very important political significance. It means that property is the foundation of human society, that the instinct to go out and get a house and a mortgage, before getting married, is correct, and that it is not the other way round. Property, in that case, would not just be an economic problem, as everyone has realised at least since Marx, but a biological one, and the important role played in politics by the regulation of property rights within the community could have very much more far-reaching consequences than we can see in a generation, or even in a century.

But many psychologists strongly reject the idea of a territorial drive in man, pointing out that for all but the last 12,000 years or so of his evolution he has been a hunting and gathering animal to whom the idea of territory would have been useless, and that no other primates are territorial animals. The everyday manifestations of the train and the lecture room they would agree, do show that human beings engage in the 'maintenance of personal space', but only to a very limited extent. The fact is that the modern phenomena of competition for the control and use of territory are to a great extent man-made and can be explained under the frustration-aggression thesis by competition for food in conditions of growing scarcity and serious overcrowding. Overcrowding in giant cities has been the most striking development of the twentieth century as the continuing growth of Tokyo, Shanghai and Mexico City bears witness, and overcrowding, we now know, may lead to sudden complete biological collapse in some species – rabbits for example. The correction of such problems is a vast political problem, with implications for government control and use of land throughout the community. Most developed countries have however now developed elaborate systems of planning and control of development, or zoning as it is known in the United States.

Some have gone further: in the Soviet Union agricultural land was, under Stalin (1924-53), reorganised into collective farms under state ownership. Great suffering was occasioned to millions of peasants, and a catastrophic drop in production followed, bringing hardship and even starvation to many parts of the country. Peasants living on collective farms were, however, permitted to retain a small plot for their own use, and today these private plots contribute a disproportionate amount to the overall level and variety of production. In China, however, during the Great Leap Forward (1958-61) private property in agriculture was wholly abolished by the formation of communes, only to be restored by allowing private plots openly from 1961 to 1966. During the Great Proletarian Cultural Revolution 'rectification campaigns' were used to induce the peasants once more to surrender their plots, with some success, but evidently not without cost in terms of economic disruption. In Cuba no allowance was made for private plots, and the country has conspicuously suffered from a serious decline in levels of pre-revolutionary production which has led it even to have to import black beans, a staple food in the Caribbean area.[6]

On the other hand, when a community's property rights are infringed by another community, as we know all too well from the history of Europe in this century, the aggressive response that follows may not be confined to the communities concerned. Obviously, for the sake of the survival of the human race as a whole, it is essential that we should face up to the problems involved. And the problem will arise, for we are now faced on a global scale with a conflict which has been the common property of mankind for thousands, if not millions of years, and that is the conflict between those who have food, and those who want to get hold of it.

There are two points in pre-history at which this was important. One, the better known one, is very recent. Following the last ice age (c 10,000 BC) an accidental mutation between two wild grasses gave rise to the primitive wheat, the cultivation of which is the basis of the civilisation of the Mediterranean basin. Somewhat later, a similar mutation and crossing of strains gave rise to maize, the foundation of the civilisation of the New World.[7] Both developments, quite independent as they were, created a possibility for static communities engaged in common tasks over a considerable period, and, by giving in return the potential for a considerable surplus of food which could be stored (and indeed had to be stored during the winter), brought about the need for large-scale storage and the defence of the supplies thus won. These large-scale communities became the basis of one of man's most important social and political inventions: the city.[8] Indeed the word city – *polis* in Greek – gave its name to politics.

As had already been said, since cities came into existence they have had to live in conflict with their envious neighbours, who have always tried to subject them, and what they saw as their independence, to their overlordship or political control. But we are concerned for the moment here with something more fundamental. Was there, as Morris suggests, an earlier stage of man's development at which a more important conflict developed in him; a conflict which made him use earlier aggressive responses in the new situation?[9]

Morris argues that man's primate ancestors were, as we have seen, originally largely vegetarian food-gatherers, eating principally roots or nuts eked out with occasional worms, grubs or beetles. His best argument here is our teeth, which are those of a primarily vegetarian creature with powerful jaws for grinding but not much in the way of teeth for eating meat. During the ice ages, his argument continues, it became very dry in Africa, and the vegetation became very thin; there were, however, still a substantial number of large animals around, and with the power of his developing brain it occurred to man to copy the carnivorous animals and kill and eat large prey, for which purpose he developed tools. But the problem is, Morris suggests, that having learnt to kill very recently in biological time, man has still not learnt how not to kill. In other words, as he is still a rather mixed-up primate, he lacks the biological restraints which stop carnivores such as lions, tigers and wolves from killing one another.

This alone would create inbuilt conflict and cause problems. But Morris argues that the problem goes deeper; for him the conflict between the vegetarian and the carnivore goes to the root of human political organisation. The typical organisation of the vegetarian is a mixed community of both sexes arranged in a strongly hierarchial pattern around a single dominant figure, male or female. The typical organisation of the carnivore is a divided community in which the dominant form of organisation is the association of equals; for the male the hunting band and for the female a nuclear family unit each dependent on a different member of the male community. The human being, Morris suggests, is divided between these two forms.

Although male dominance has undoubtedly been a dominant feature of the political organisation of most advanced societies for most of recorded human history, it is not fashionable at the present time in western or Communist societies – though it is noticeable that in practice, politics is one of the last areas of human activity in both parts of the world where women have succeeded in obtaining anything more than token integration. Consequently the idea of the hunting band, and the strong evidence from writers such as Lionel Tiger, that the monopoly of political power by the male involves something more than an accidental by-product of his greater physical strength, has been strongly challenged.[10] One of the most interesting challenges has come from a rival interpretation of the same crucial stage in man's evolution.[11]

According to this view, when Africa became arid, man did not take to hunting, or at least not immediately (since he undoubtedly did at some time, as witness the discoveries of bones at Olduvai Gorge). Instead he, or rather she, migrated to the sea-shore, and settled down in the water to become a semi-aquatic animal and live on fish. In this view, women did most of the food gathering, and the stones on the sea-shore formed ready made tools. Furthermore this theory, better than any other, accounts for that peculiar feature of human beings, the absence of hair, which is of course quite characteristic of animals that dwell in the water. Better still, it accounts for why hair survives on the top of the head, and why it falls out in men but not in women; it survives to keep the sun off the head as it sticks out of the water, and it does not fall out in women because children need it to hold on to when their mothers are swimming.

All this is very plausible, but as man undoubtedly did become a hunter, it seems likely that the marine stage in human development, if, indeed, there was one, came rather earlier in evolution and was quite separate from the late introduction to the large-scale hunting of meat. Many argue that all such theories are misleading, since the characteristic of the human being which has ensured his survival has been an unspecialised digestive system capable of tackling most foods that come to hand. But the one thing that is clear is that man's pre-human ancestors, whether vegetarian or carnivorous by habit, lived in very small communities. The size of these communities is certainly disputable; they were probably bands, that is to say groups, not as small as the nuclear family units of gorillas, nor as big as the tribes of baboons. The government of the band, therefore, was not a specialised function, and we can discern no easy difference between the family and the community.

Secondly, it appears that different bands must have interacted with one another, for it seems likely that mating between individuals of different bands was normal. The complex rules needed to secure this in primitive communities survive in a number of forms, and they form the basis for the incorporation of new members of the band and hence its possibilities for growth into a tribe by the fictitious incorporation of unrelated individuals or bands, such as appear to have taken place in most historical communities, for example Israel, shortly before the beginning of historical records.

Thirdly, war seems to have been a characteristic feature of human organisation from the earliest times, and a great deal of his social and all his political organisation is strongly conditioned by it. It is possible that at least at first it had a eugenic effect in that the accidents of evolution had eliminated many of the creatures who might have become man's most persistent natural enemies, and the few who were left were just dangerous enough to require co-operation to tackle them, and just not too dangerous to eliminate the human race entirely.

Fourthly, the development of larger-scale forms of social organisation derived from a number of sources. Conquest was one, but it was not the whole story. The attraction of greater food resources, the fame of a successful leader, and the endless growth of towns, all played a part. To see how this affected the structure of present-day societies, however, we now have to make a tremendous leap and come down to the present. We have to deal next with the question of primitive government and government in primitive societies.

PRIMITIVE GOVERNMENT

The reason for this tremendous leap is an interesting and important one. The fact is that we who live in developed modern states know very little about the pre-history of our own societies that can help us bridge the gap between pre-human society and primitive government. The problem is one of archaeology. Archaeology deals with material remains, preferably of stone, brick, metal or bone. Other organic remains are very rare, and owe their preservation only to exceptional circumstances, for example when the soil is completely waterlogged and never dries out, as with the bog remains of Finland or the Swiss lakes. Of many primitive cultures which depended almost entirely on organic materials in their daily lives we have only the sketchiest knowledge. Even estimates of population in such circumstances are very dubious.

And, of course, in the absence of written records or inscriptions we have no direct first-hand evidence, even in the most advanced cultures, for politics. We have to *infer* political development from what details we know of the economy from its material remains. And such inferences depend too heavily for comfort both on the prejudices of the investigator and on his own knowledge of primitive cultures. This knowledge he can only get from present-day societies, and it is therefore important for us also to know something about what modern anthropology has to tell us about primitive government, always remembering that there is no guarantee that it is directly applicable to the past history of the modern states we shall later be dealing with.

Our problems begin with the term primitive government itself.[12] To begin with the term primitive. This, which is not, unfortunately, a word which is entirely value-free in the ears of the hearer, implies here no criticism. It is used specifically to refer to the study of pre-industrial societies by anthropologists. But the real irony of the term comes in the second part, for, as we shall see, there are primitive societies which do not have a distinguishable government. So this is sometimes referred to by anthropologists as 'government without the state',[13] but this merely compounds the difficulty.

The study of primitive government has had a chequered history. Most of the people who in recent years have studied at first hand are anthropologists. But the study of political anthropology, properly speaking, is very recent, and only really began in 1940 with the publication of Meyer Fortes and E E Evans Pritchard's *African Political Systems*.[14] Before that time, anthropologists, it seems, were not much interested in politics, and even they recorded that they had not learnt much from political philosophy,[15] obviously unaware that though political philosophy covers many things, it does not cover the whole of political science.

However the point they were making was a serious one. One of the basic problems with many earlier writers such as Montesquieu, Rousseau and Marx, was that none of them had ever seen a primitive society; their knowledge of them was based on travellers' reports. And those travellers were not trained investigators, but seamen, merchants and conquerors, and in their reports they quite naturally tried to fit everything they saw into their own rather limited experience. Thus every tribe had to have a chief, and if it did not some hapless individual was singled out as the most likely candidate. Women, as sailors are inclined to find, were always complaisant; food, as compared with the arid wastes of bully-beef and ship's biscuit, was abundant. Moral lessons were always available for those who, as Montesquieu did openly in the *Lettres Persanes*, sought to criticise their own society by skilful comparison with the alleged features of another exotic one.

The one thing that all these views have in common is that they all sound good from a long way away. Rousseau could talk about the naturally peaceful state of mankind in a state of nature: it was Captain Cook who was actually killed. Marx praised the state of primitive communism in Russia; his own economic position was adequately sustained by donations from friends and admirers for him not to have to work. Even in our own time, feminists have made much of primitive societies such as the Tchambuli, where the female is dominant and the male waits upon her, without having to consider whether the Tchambuli's superstition and fear of the powers of unseen spirits might not have its disadvantages.[16]

What, then, do present-day anthropologists actually teach us? To begin with, they tell us that no society, however primitive, lacks politics. There may be, as the Nuer of the Sudan illustrate, no actual discernible government as such,[17] yet decisions are made. They may not be made through the setting-up of a distinct separate organ of decision-making, but they are made nevertheless. And it is significant, perhaps – the Tchambuli apart – that they are ascribed to the male members of society. This is not to say that there are not decisions of political importance made among the female section of such communities, and it may mean only that they are not noticed by anthropologists, who are mostly male.

Secondly, they tell us that there is no one form of development followed by all primitive societies. The emergence of the state, as they tend to call it, or government, as we would call it, does not follow an identical pattern. As a matter of fact, the very idea of a state is historically peculiar to Europe; there is no exact parallel to it in Islamic thought, where the identity of state and belief was originally seen as axiomatic.[18] And there is no exact correspondence with it in China either, for Chinese thought only allowed for one universal society focused on the Emperor.[19]

CHIEFDOMS AND LINEAGE

The most general form of government adopted, however, is that of the tribal chiefdom, which, as we have seen, has different origins. Modern tribal societies purport to be based on kin groups, but we do not know whether these correspond to real relationships or not, and we strongly suspect they do not on the grounds, as already stated, that inter-marriage is one of the fundamental characteristics of human societies. Even where conquest seems to have been responsible primarily for the unification of tribes into societies, as in Ancient Egypt, this conquest was ratified by formal bargains including marriage. And in fact down to the Second Dynasty there is evidence that the formal unification of Upper and Lower Egypt through the marriage of the two royal lines, represented symbolically by the God Horus and the Goddess Neith, was repeated in each generation, and that it was the foundation of the peculiar custom of brother-sister marriage in the Egyptian royal family in later generations.[20]

What complicates the question is that in other cases we do not know how far the concept of kinship was a retroactive fiction. As Henige convincingly shows in *The Chronology of Oral Tradition*, kinship is primarily a ceremonial relationship, and is normally adjusted to allow for political changes.[21] Most important is the fictitious incorporation into the kin structure not just of individuals but of groups. When the tribe goes to war and fights another tribe and the other tribe is beaten then the lesser, defeated tribe tends to be incorporated over a period of time into the structure of the state. We find it not only among primitive communities in the sense which anthropologists study them, but historically, for example in the *Anglo-Saxon Chronicle*, where the West Saxons incorporated the followers of Withgar in the Isle of Wight and of Port, the eponymous founder of Portsmouth.

Before we arrive at the emergence of the tribal chieftain under a single lineage group, that is, before we get to the stage at which a decision is taken that political activity is primarily vested in one family following a pattern of inheritance from one generation to the other, which is not completely indisputable but somehow regulated by custom, we do come across some tribes, and in particular the Nuer, who have in fact no form of political structure as such, and have nothing corresponding to a chieftancy as we know it. They do have officials whom the anthropologists called 'leopard-skin chiefs', not because they were chiefs but because they did wear leopard skins as a badge of their activities and of their position. A leopard-skin chief, though not a chief, is in fact something rather more interesting, and even very modern to our eyes, namely an arbitrator.[22] He is a person who is recognised by the rest of the tribe as being the person you go to if you have an intratribal dispute, and he will hand down some kind of decision which is binding on the people who have agreed to accept his arbitration. This process, as far as we can see, pre-dates the emergence of a single lineage in temporal development. But this is not, of course, to say that there was ever an exact stage like this in other societies. If man was, as we now suspect, always an hierarchical animal by instinct, trying to replicate in his tribal social structure the basic concept of the family, then there probably has been, since pre-human times, some kind of surrogate head of the family, and given the biological basis of human society this post was almost certainly hereditary in some shape or form.

THE RULES OF THE GAME

The last concept that we have somehow to relate to these different primitive structures is that of law. The idea of the state is inconceivable without a body of law. Indeed, until comparatively modern times the law was regarded as being a fixed, indivisible entity, something given, something of divine order and divine sanction. The lawgiver, the man who codified law, the Solons of this world, did not, on this view, invent laws. They were people who declared the existence of the law which already existed and had always existed and would always exist.[23] Arbitrators simply work on basic principles of fairness which they determine in a given situation. Law, on the other hand, means a continuity through time over a much longer period and, more importantly, it is necessary for the extension of the tribe beyond a certain point. In other words, there becomes a time at which the geographical area over which a tribe operates is so great that, unless there is some common decision as to the principles to be applied over this area, then decisions are taken which contradict one another, and hostility is generated.

The prime function of law is to regulate disputes. Inside the tribe war is regulated by law of some kind. Outside the tribe there are, in primitive circumstances, no laws of war as such. There may be customs which hold good at certain times and certain places. But between tribes war has always been a bloodthirsty affair. Only inside the tribe does it appear that fighting was inhibited, and necessarily so; in other words, the structure of a community cannot long survive if people spend all their time fighting each other. The war of all against all is in fact completely contrary to the maintenance in practical terms of all orderly society, and the only result of it is that the tribes split up.

What then does the law consist of? First, it consists of rules, and primarily of rules governing the maintenance of three properties of the tribe: people, pigs and gardens, to borrow a striking phrase from the anthropologist Roy Rappaport.[24] (By pigs we can understand herd animals of all kinds, such as goats and cows.)

These rules are the rules of a game, the game of politics. The game is a complex one, for it consists of competition within the tribal boundaries for access to each of the principal resources. Part of the complexity stems from the nature of the resources themselves, for it is necessary to point out straight away that the first has a unique property – that people are divided into two groups each in competition for the other. From a male point of view, women are resources, but they are also players; and to women, men are not only players, they are also resources, much as men may find it beneath their dignity to think so. It should not be assumed, either, that there is any universal order of priority between these resources. In pre-conquest Ireland, for example, men regarded cows as considerably more valuable than women, and this is one of those things that depends, it seems, on the law of supply and demand.

A second complication arises from the fact that the various resources may be traded off between players, not according to their 'intrinsic' value, but according to the saliency of the need for each felt by the players in question, in each of the series of transactions of which the game of politics consists. Since the game of politics lasts a very long time – much longer than any human lifetime in fact – there develops a very complex awareness of the network of bargains and consequent relationships involved which acts as the fundamental underpinning of all other human relationships within society.

And why does the game take so long? It is tempting to answer: Because without it life cannot go on, or the species be reproduced –

but that seems too great an oversimplification. In pre-modern times I find little evidence that people had to participate in politics simply in order to live. This is not to say that politics did not intrude itself upon them, and the more frequently the nearer we come to modern times, but simply that unless one lived in a city there seems to be have been little need, simply to earn one's livelihood, to take part in politics at all. Nor, for the reproduction of the species to have been quite effective over a space of more than two million years, was it necessary, it seems, for mankind to develop settled communities. One is forced back to the explanation that people take part in politics not because it is essential to them, but because they like it; that, in short, it enables them to structure time. We are a long-lived species, and we are already forgetting how hard we had to work to structure time before television was invented.

For politics is not just a game, it is the ultimate game; a game played with real people and real things. Consequently, as Bailey points out, its rules are different in nature from other games in that you have three options as a player in how to treat them. You may play according to the rules and seek to win that way. You may seek to bend the rules in your favour, or even to break them when others are not looking, for there is no umpire to tell you you can not. Or, you can work to change the rules, so that you can make the game more congenial.[25]

If this is so, the inhibitions which restrain behaviour contrary to the rules, even within the tribe, can never be absolute. Their effectiveness depends on the extent to which they have been effectively implanted and reinforced by ritual, and the evolution of human society resembles that of animals themselves only in this respect; that societies that fail to develop effective inhibitions against self-destruction simply cease to exist as such. We have to be careful here about the apparent range of choice offered by modern anthropological example, since in many cases the fact that a society is still distinguishable as different is a sign that it has already ceased to evolve.

The result is that the state, however sophisticated, reproduces the structures of the primitive community through two devices familiar to anthropologists: replication and encapsulation. By replication, in this case the acceptance of an hereditary ruler or father-figure, the emergent state replicates the pattern of the extended family. By encapsulation it then seals itself off from the outside world by defining a social boundary which distinguishes itself from all other social functions. In other words independent states in some kind or form existed before there emerged the modern concept of the nation state – the state inhabited by only one nation, with conter-

minous boundaries and identical aspirations. The state emerges at
the point at which the decision is taken, agreed, conceded, or grows
up somehow, that one lineage has a specific claim to political
authority. Political authority rests with one lineage, and law is the
foundation of its claim to do so.

By lineage we mean descent within a family, broadly considered.
And in some modern states, for example Saudi Arabia where the
state takes its name from the ruling family, Qatar with the al-Thani
family, Bahrein with the al-Khalifa family, Kuwait, Nepal and
Bhutan, membership of a lineage still confers access to political
power. They vary, however, in the extent to which the rules of
succession are defined; in Saudi Arabia, for example, a family
deliberation can alter the order of succession. And this should
remind us that in all states in which the order is not defined – in
republics as much as if not more so than in monarchies – the rules
still have to be settled afresh at each transition of power. The way in
which this is usually done is by armed conflict.

Similar conflicts lie at the heart of the constitutional order in all
countries. In the United Kingdom, for example, where force has
not been used to alter the disposition of political power for over 150
years, the fact that Queen Elizabeth II is descended from King
Alfred through a roundabout route is misleading. She is also
descended from Charlemagne, Louis IX and Rodrigo the Cid, but
she is not Queen of Germany, France or Spain, and in constitutional
theory her position in England (though not Scotland) depends
ultimately on William the Conqueror and his forcible annexation of
the country.

Today, of course, many lineages have lost their powers. In
western Europe and Japan their survival has depended on the
willingness of their incumbents to play a constitutional role as heads
of state. Where they have recently disappeared, in Iran, Greece,
Afghanistan and Ethiopia, they still had, or claimed to have, power.
As Aristotle put it, 'the less the area of the prerogative, the longer
will the authority of a king last unimpaired,'[26] and today, as in his
day, monarchy is not fashionable. Nevertheless, the fact that almost
all modern states have passed through a period of monarchical rule,
and this has been very much longer in sum than any period of
republican rule, is bound to be significant. It is from this age that our
modern heads of state, now generally called presidents, inherit the
reserve powers of their office, which is, in turn, as we have seen,
bound up with the notion of *sovereignty*.

Nor are presidents of most modern states presidents in the sense
we would attach to the chief officer of a golf club, or a debating
society. They are often – very often – men like the Sforza, the

Visconti or the Medici of the time of Machiavelli, who owed their control of state power to the direct or indirect use of force. Within the sphere of sovereignty their control of state power depends, certainly, on their ability to get it recognised; but the power we are referring to is, once successfully secured, nothing less than the power to imprison, banish or, if necessary, execute individuals who are contravening the law, as interpreted by other people who have the power and the authority. The idea of sovereignty, therefore, is that there are no practical limits to the ruler's power; not just that there are no practical limits to the amount of punishment he can inflict, but that there are no practical limits to anything that he can do within the defined area for which sovereignty is claimed.

Sovereignty, for obvious physical reasons, is not a fact but a fiction, which is retained because it is convenient from the point of view of governments and lawyers. It is intimately bound up with two other ideas – those of legitimacy and authority, with which it is often confused.[27]

Legitimacy is the term we use to refer to the fact that a government is generally recognised to have the right to do what it does. It depends, therefore, not on what the government claims, but whether or not that claim is recognised. The fact that a government is recognised as legitimate, whether by its own citizens or by its peer states, gives it authority, which is the assurance that its commands will be obeyed.

Authority itself, however, is not absolute or unlimited. To have authority to do something is the right to do that thing, and to be obeyed; it is not a general grant of power to do anything you want. Authority, therefore, can be delegated, divided or shared. In fact, all operation of complex governments depends on this fact, since the delegation, division or sharing of the tasks of government depend on it.

The question of authority was treated by Max Weber as being central to the evolution of the modern state.[28] Originally, he believed, the authority of government stemmed from what he termed charisma; that is to say, the outstanding personality or personal qualities of an individual. In more developed societies, charisma was 'routinised', or subjected to legal forms and controls. It could be either traditional – accepted because it had always been accepted – or legal-rational, which is to say, accepted as being conferred by formal rituals involving some kind of choice or recognition by or on behalf of the society as a whole. Weber therefore distinguished these three types of authority, charismatic, traditional and legal-rational, from one another, while treating them as 'ideal types' which were not necessarily found in pure form. Thus a man of outstanding personal qualities may legally be elected President, which gives him legal-rational authority; while if his family has long been prominent in the society in question, he will therefore have traditional authority as well. An interesting example of this duplication was Prince Norodom Sihanouk as Prime Minister of Cambodia.

The fact is that, in all modern states of which we have knowledge, we can identify a specific moment in time when a government has seized power, and all other governments after that time claim part or whole of their authority by virtue of being successors to that government. All Weber's forms of authority, therefore, amount to the same thing, the habit of obedience, or, to put it another way, the inertia of social systems. Social systems, once established, will tend to continue unaltered until either the society decides to change them or it discovers that it has forgotten any need for them. By extension, the longer a social institution continues in existence, the longer it is likely to continue. So it is with the key social institution, that of government itself. The habit of obedience is perpetuated the more easily since very few people, if any, see or are in the habit of seeing the government as a whole, and thus may be, and frequently are, protected by encapsulation from the attentions of the government. All that is not central to them is regarded as being peripheral. So the bulk of governmental operations survive war, invasion, revolution, civil war, earthquake, flood or pestilence, joining together after the event to repair the damage as best as possible in the accustomed mould. And changes of major importance in government only take place either incrementally, by slow changes over a long period of time, or, as in the case of Japan or eastern Europe after 1945, by imposition from without.

It is important to stress that the initial seizure of power does not confer either authority or legitimacy. Nor are the motives relevant. Governments which seize power always claim to be acting under the authority of some superior law – be it divine right, the will of the people, or the mission of the armed forces to protect the state. But such arguments have to be recognised as fallacious. A man who steals a loaf has still committed theft whether he eats it himself or gives it to his aged mother. In this sense, then, no modern government has legitimacy from the fact of its past history, and all governments depend on the active or passive consent of their subjects to their actions, which gives them a lot of scope to coerce their subjects into accepting those actions.

Sovereignty, then, is the claim to the highest authority within a given area. When Henry VIII in England proclaimed his independence of papal supremacy in matters of religion, he described, or permitted his agents to describe, in an Act of Parliament of 1534, the realm of England as 'an Empire'.[29] When he proclaimed it an empire he was proclaiming that he owed no allegiance to any higher authority. Though the terminology strikes us as strange (we would now describe such a document as a Declaration of Independence), he made use of an instrument which is inseparable from the idea of national sovereignty, namely, he made use of an assembly, which in England happened to be called Parliament. It was Parliament which declared on his behalf that the realm of England was an empire, and the concept of sovereignty in the modern sense, therefore, is inseparable from the idea of the representation of the people as a whole. In other words, right from the beginning of the claiming of unlimited sovereignty by states we also have in historical terms the emergence of an assembly as the representative of the people. The same is also true of the Netherlands, Switzerland, France and the United States.

In using the term 'assembly' we are including congresses and parliaments of all sorts, but it refers to a particular aspect of them, distinct from the parliaments and congresses we actually see sitting today. It refers to a grouping together of people representing the nation as a whole. They do not have to be elected by any specific system of election. There only has to be general acceptance that the assembly as constituted represents the nation as a whole; it stands for all classes and all interests and it acts on their behalf – and, they must obey it.[30]

The other important point that we can identify in the development of the concept of sovereignty is the emergence of the *levée en masse*. This can be dated to 23 August 1793, when the infant French Republic was confronted with simultaneous invasion by Britain, Holland, Spain, Prussia and Austria. For the first time in modern history, its government responded by calling up the entire male population of military age to fight on behalf of the state, drove the allies back across the Rhine and captured Belgium. Militarily it was obviously a great success, but in the neo-classical context of the late eighteenth century we have to see the *levée en masse* as something more, as a political innovation of profound significance. The French citizen, like the Roman citizen before him, was called upon to fight for his country or state.[31] It is an association of ideas which the twentieth century has found very hard to get away from, but get away from it they must if women are to continue not to have to fight. In Israel, where they are, they have only been called up once. This is not because women do not fight; in Dahomey the celebrated Amazons were not only much feared by their neighbouring states, but much more so than the armies of their all-male rivals.[32] But when the significance of the exclusion is explored, it will be seen that it goes back to the classical definition of the idea of 'citizen'. The citizen in politics was not just a person who lived in a city, but one who had to take part in all the duties of state, and the most important of these duties is defending it in an emergency, when you have to rally round and be prepared to fight.

Conversely when the Romans held elections they voted in the military order in which they were supposed to fight – by regiments, in modern terms.[33] And the revival of the concept of universal military service at the end of the eighteenth century is a very important development in the idea of the nation state, because for the first time in modern times war stopped being something that happened mostly somewhere else, and became something which the whole nation was engaged in in some way. Once the whole nation was being called up for military service, it was only a few very short years before it was agreed that the whole nation must also vote. So the emergence of the concept of the *levée en masse* brings the automatic assumption that those involved will then have a say in whether or not the state goes to war. The nation-at-arms, then, is the other turning-point in the history of the nation. The result is the nation state, not just the nation sovereign, but also the nation-in-arms.

So we end where we began, with mankind as an aggressive species, organised in hunting bands of theoretical equals, each threatening one another's property in people, pigs and gardens. The next question is, assuming we do still want to compare these hunting bands, how are we going to do it?

3   System, Development and Modernisation

Modern states are so large and complex that we have to be selective, to draw some limits to the amount of comparison needed between them. It would be a lifetime's work to make a comparison between the entire cultures of two modern states in the way that anthropologists can do with those of two primitive tribes, and at any given moment our information would always be incomplete. We therefore isolate for attention those aspects which are most important, and for this purpose we have to define the political system; that set of interconnected interactions which controls society as a whole.

The political system might be regarded, as Talcott Parsons did, as one of a number of subsystems of the overall social system; or, with Easton, it can be distinguished as an entity for study on its own, engaged in transactions with the social system which constitutes the nearer part of its environment.[1] The choice is ours, and for reasons which I shall give in a moment, I prefer the second approach. But whichever we choose, we must at all times remember that the political system is not a real entity, but a conceptual one. The political system is not a group of people, a huddle of buildings, or even a carefully constructed machine. It is a set of social relationships, and its boundary is set by the limit of those relationships, wherever that happens to fall.

It is partly for this reason that the broader concept of political system is attractive, since that way its boundary appears to coincide with that of the state, and from the point of view of a student of international relations this would seem to be convenient. But unfortunately it is misleading for the student of comparative politics, and in two ways.

On the one hand, the political system of many states – for example, Brazil – does not impinge directly on the lives of a significant fraction of its inhabitants. They live their lives in what, as we have already seen, the anthropologists call an encapsulated society: one which exists within the territory of the state without forming part of it.[2] Such encapsulated societies exist on a different time-scale from the 'modern' society of the state as a whole, so that studies of them have a value for students of primitive societies over a relatively long time, and a number of such studies co-exist in the 'anthropologists' present' which we have already mentioned, though the societies of which they form the principal significant trace may now be much modified, or even, as in the case of the Brazilian forest Indians, destroyed. We must take account of such descriptions, therefore, in our efforts to understand the political systems of the societies which encapsulate them, but we have to remember that they are in no way reliable descriptions of life in the political system as a whole.

On the other hand, the boundary of the nation state of today, as we have also seen, is penetrated from outside by many different influences.[3] Indeed, many international-relations theorists regard domestic and international politics as only aspects of one inter-related whole. One cannot understand the political system of the United Kingdom without at least taking account of the view that since 1967 its financial arrangements have been dictated by the 'gnomes of Zürich', or the United States without considering its insatiable need for oil which has become noticeably more expensive since 1973. Our delimitation of the political system and its inter-actions must take account of these influences.

The political system – this abstract concept made up of inter-relationships with a definable boundary – is political because it is concerned with the making of decisions about the allocation of power resources. And this allocation is disputable because power resources are limited. By power resources we mean those things which people want, which if controlled by governments enable them to maintain their power over those they rule. In material terms this means food, clothing, housing and energy, or the equivalent cost of those items, the supply of which is, at any given point in time, itself limited. But such is the indefinable nature of political power that it also means the ability to use force to control them, the habit of exercising authority which we call *status*, and the limitations on access to authority which are often loosely and inaccurately termed *class*.

The reason is that, given the finite nature of resources, the ability to control them without the constant use of force depends on the inherited authority of government. Inherited, that is, in the sense that no one is ever born into a society which is going to wait until he is grown up to settle its political organisation. Every human being always finds politics waiting for him, with the rules already settled in favour of the incumbents and with a corresponding advantage for those on whom they confer favour. Those rules, which are designed to maintain the existing order, are in the first instance directed towards one prime aim – to minimise conflict. And the most important of them, the fundamental rules that underpin all the others, are the rules governing the constitution and operation of the political system.

Now it is possible, and entirely meaningful, to describe a political system in terms of its rules, in its own legal language.[4] Ask someone in Britain how the country is governed and he will describe the rules and the way in which they are made and changed: Magna Carta, the Act of Settlement, the Great Reform Act, the Statute of Westminster and the relationship of the monarch, Parliament, the law courts, and the county councils. Ask an American and she will talk of the Constitution, the President, Congress, the Supreme Court and the states.

Separately, each description will be quite clear and easy to understand. Put them together, however, and problems of comparison will not take long to emerge. Britain has no president; the United States no prime minister. Congress and Parliament are clearly both some form of elected assembly, but they are very different both in appearance and procedure. And Americans not only do not hold elections in the same way as the British, but not exactly in the same way from one state to another.

Over the past twenty years, therefore, many political scientists have been trying to develop a common language to describe the political systems, not only of the United States and Great Britain, but of all other countries as well. To do so they have tried to return to first principles and consider what it is that the abstract political system must do in order to exist at all.[5]

First and foremost it is a decision-making process. It exists to make decisions, and to do so it must receive demands on which to act, and information on which to decide. It must also receive personnel to make the decisions, and it may also (and in practice always does) receive a great deal of resources, both material and moral, with which to enforce its decisions. These we can collectively designate as *inputs*. Its decisions, the rules by which they are enforced and its interpretation of them, are its *outputs*.

The first attempt to label these inputs and outputs for the purposes of comparative politics was made in 1960 by Almond and Coleman.[6] Outputs were already familiar as the powers of government set out by the makers of the American Constitution, and since followed by most other constitutional lawyers. However to distinguish the functions from the bodies set up to embody them, Almond and Coleman labelled them, rather than the legislative, executive and judicial powers, the functions of rule-making, rule-application and rule-adjudication. By doing so they made it easier to discern that, for example, when Congress impeaches the President of the United States, it is, although formally designated a legislature, actually exercising the function of rule-adjudication, and there are many other such examples of overlapping functions in all constitutions, some deliberate and some accidental.

Almond and Coleman broke new ground when they turned to the inputs, as these had been largely ignored by earlier writers. One of them they termed political communication.[7] This strictly speaking, however, is not an input, but a method by which inputs and outputs are conveyed, and I therefore propose to treat it separately in chapter 4.

Almond and Coleman's other three categories are: (i) Political socialisation and recruitment; (ii) Interest articulation; and (iii) Interest aggregation.

Political socialisation and recruitment, which are rather odd but not incompatible bedfellows, consist of the process of education forming citizens' attitudes to politics; and those structures that exist for the recruitment of people into political or administrative office.

Interest articulation refers to the process by which people express their needs and wishes. They can be divided into demands upon the system and expressions of support for it.

Interest aggregation means the process of linking together various interests into a more or less coherent programme of action on which a decision can be taken.

Almond and Powell, adapting the earlier classification, have distinguished interest articulation and interest aggregation, together with political communication, and the three output functions of rule-making, rule-application and rule-adjudication, as *conversion functions*, that is, those processes which enable the political system to convert demands and supports into political decisions. Among these decisions are some, undoubtedly, affecting political socialisation and recruitment, which are seen by Almond and Powell as *pattern maintenance functions*. The efficiency of the system in doing each of these things they describe as its *capabilities*.

What is not at all clear, however, even in the revised model, is just why these, *and not any other categories*, should have been chosen. This leads such writers, moreover, in their earlier work, often to equate greater efficiency with greater technical complexity, and at the same time to obliterate what seems to be an essential distinction between demands and supports, for it is impossible to imagine a control system that does not convert one, demands, into the other, supports. Certainly they do recognise that inputs may arise within the ranks of the decision-makers themselves. These they term variously 'withinputs' and 'intraputs'. But there remains an impression that the initiative for political action comes in the main from outside, and that is something which this categorisation does not enable us easily to determine.

Approaching the problem of steering mechanisms from the viewpoint of cybernetics, Deutsch identified other important properties which we should seek to identify in any political system. A cybernetic system is a self-steering mechanism guided by analysis of consequences of its own decisions. Knowledge of these consequences, which is termed *feedback*, is literally fed back from the output to the input side of the process. Hence just as inputs are converted into outputs, in turn the outputs are monitored for specific inputs. Using the analogy of a gunsight, Deutsch reminds us that such a mechanism will have to have the capacity to anticipate what the future course of events may be, and to modify the information received by the input side accordingly. The gun must fire, not at the aircraft, but in front of it, so that by the time the shell arrives the aircraft will be at the correct position in space to be hit by it. In this instance this correction is known as *gain*, an allowance for the delay in response to a decision which is known as *lag*[8]

I propose, therefore, in using the term 'political system' to use it as equivalent to government, that is to say, that system of interaction which forms the fundamental control mechanism within a society. The boundary between it and the rest of society, as I have already said, is not a clear-cut one. It runs not between individuals, but between the different roles they play. Most people do not participate in making demands in politics most of the time. But they cannot opt out of it when it makes demands upon them, at a minimum when they are called upon to pay their taxes. Politics is an essential part of modern societies; it is certainly never absent.

I would further argue that there are only two main types of inputs to the political system: *positive* and *negative*.[9] Positive inputs, which enable the government to perform its functions at all, include support in the widest sense, but more particularly the resources to make decisions. Negative inputs are demands on government for action or payment.

There are also only two main types of outputs. Political decisions as such are not outputs, any more than a tap is water, or a switch electricity. Positive outputs are rewards; negative outputs are sanctions or punishments.

The prime purpose of the political system is to survive. Like any other system, it can either adapt to changes in its environment, it can change its environment to suit it, or it can, and usually does, do both. It utilises its outputs to maximise support for it, and to minimise the demands made upon it, within the parameters of the society in which it operates, and under the general constraint of the principle of economy of effort. Given unlimited resources there would be no problem in maintaining support indefinitely. Scarcity, population growth, natural disasters and international influences, however, limit resources in almost all modern political systems, so that the allocation of resources is the fundamental task they face. It is the curious characteristic of politics that a very small amount of power, correctly used, can be sufficient to gain control over a very large quantity of resources, both physical and human. To understand fully how any individual government is actually operating, therefore, it is necessary to trace the direction and intensity of all the possible functional flows, and of their interactions – a simple equation of power between government and society would not only be misleading, but meaningless. To trace them, we must first label them.

The government puts *out* resources to perform the function of *power resource extraction* by which, in turn, it takes in necessary *support*.

Being challenged continuously concerning its right to do this, it puts *out* more resources in *input control* in order to regulate and where necessary screen out *demands* coming *in*.

It will, further, regulate society in its own interests, through the general function of interest arbitration which can be either positive or negative. By *positive* interest arbitration it strengthens interests and thus attaches them to itself, at the same time depriving the society at large of the resources implied; by *negative* interest arbitration it does the reverse. However, the strengthening of interests soon implies a challenge to the authority of the government itself and will lead to corrective action being applied, so that the two processes are in fact continuous. The principal means employed can be simplified into taxes on the strong and subsidies for the weak, but since the resources for the maintenance of the system in each case are drawn from the social system and the political system of itself produces nothing, the maintenance of the political system in its existing form is only possible for so long as sufficient groups within the society have an expectation of getting something out of it.

In Table 1 the symbols P and F refer to inputs to and outputs from the political system respectively; Q and E to inputs to and outputs from the social system with which it is conterminous. The symbols + and − (read positive and negative) identify the direction of flow.

Table 1   The political and social systems

Input		Output	
P+	support	F−	power resource extraction
P−	demands	F+	input control
Q−	taxes	E−	negative interest arbitration
Q+	subsidies	E+	positive interest arbitration

The principle of the economy of effort goes right to the heart of the system, however. Thus though all governments owe their origins at some time, and their continued maintenance ultimately, to their faculty of coercion, they do not choose to operate in the coercive mode for most purposes because it involves a disproportionate drain on their resources and weakens them for their ultimate task, their own defence against an external attack or natural disaster. What happens when they do will be the subject of a later chapter. Basically, however, the principle is very similar to that on which banks operate. No government has anything like enough force at its disposal to subdue all its citizens if they all rise in revolt simultaneously. But since they rarely, if ever, do so, governments can continue to operate for very long periods of time with very small reserves, and the longer they have operated, the greater the confidence that they will continue to do so, and the greater the degree of actual positive popular support on which they can count.

Popular support will be maximised if, in addition, the government can be seen to be doing visibly useful things for its citizens. However to do so requires a great deal of money, and in consequence the first task of government is to extract from the society it governs the resources it requires for its chosen programme. The principal way in which this is done is by taxation, which in the modern state has almost completely superseded the system of individual fees and charges for specific services which earlier governments used. Taxes are not paid voluntarily; they are extracted from citizens more or less painlessly with the aid of a series of bargains to supply remedies for specific demands which the citizens or their representatives present, but they are extracted nevertheless, and the first task of a successful government is to maintain the function of power resource extraction.

Given adequate resources, the government can then embark on a strategy of maximising supports and minimising demands in which its use of positive and negative outputs is very keenly attuned to the needs of the situation. A government which in this way is keenly aware of the desires of its citizens we often term a democracy; one that does not is loosely termed a dictatorship, particular if coercion is used to limit demands upon the system. But before using these or any other terms, we must be careful that we really understand what we mean by them.

We have now considered the principal aspects of the theory of system which has been used as the basis for the study of comparative politics. Clearly the identification of a political system, or even the identification of certain functions performed by the political system at one time, is not enough.

We have to do three things more. First, we have to learn to classify within the structure we have developed so as to use the variables we derive to show up useful and interesting differences between states. Secondly, we have to be prepared, as I said in chapter 1, to view the political system across time and developmentally, so that we see the system not just as it is, but as it has come to be, and how we expect it to develop in the future. History is part of this, but political science differs from history in striving to derive predictive models. We are therefore concerned not only with the maintenance of the system and its adaptation, and with the nature and efficiency of the communications on which it depends, but with the capabilities of the political system, its capacity for change. Thirdly, we have to go out to find the information we need, and to start work.

Classification as a means of organising information is essential, and the first system of classification propounded for states was that used by Aristotle himself, who divided them between those ruled by the One, the Few, and the Many.[10] This distinction, even though it was not developed for use on modern complex states at all, is still useful, but as we shall see, only in a limited sense. It appeals to the most important of our popular feelings about politics, the sense of how far – if at all – the system appears to respond to our own individual wishes, and in an age when democracy is almost universally espoused as the ambition of each and every political system, it still operates as the chief criterion for determining just how far any given state or political system can be truly regarded as democratic.

But the mere number of the rulers (read decision-makers) in a modern system is not an adequate guide to the way in which the system as a whole actually operates, even assuming that we could determine the exact number. For one thing, the capacity of the ultimate decision-makers is determined by their effectiveness. This depends both on the amount and accuracy of the information that reaches them, and on their capacity to implement their decisions once taken. Even the Caribbean ruler who in 1962 personally shot his political prisoners with a machine-gun had in other, more complex respects, to depend on others to act on his orders.[11] Once a ruler depends on others, his autocracy is qualified, and so, in practice, the rule of the One becomes the rule of the Few. Not only must the others continue to render their services, but they may and do act in his name, and place the responsibility on his shoulders.

Concepts such as the Few and the Many, on the other hand, are irritatingly imprecise. One of the few definite things that can be said, for example, about the fourteen families traditionally said to control El Salvador is that intermarriage and breeding combine to make the actual number quite meaningless. Moreover, the overwhelming majority of modern states have what Aristotle would have called 'mixed' constitutions; that is to say, they combine elements of monarchy, oligarchy and democracy in differing proportions. Rule application is vested primarily in the hands of one person (a president) or a few (a cabinet, a praesidium or a junta); the need to sanction rule-making in many (a popularly elected legislature). Not only are the structures of such systems overlapping and complex, but, as we have already noted, they exist in an evolutionary context and may well have diverged considerably from the ideal types they profess to represent.

Consequently, various modern writers have sought to identify a number of criteria by which to distinguish two or more broad types of political system. This process has taken place under the influence of cold war thinking and the rivalry of the superpowers, each of which professes a belief in their system, which excludes enthusiasm for that of the rival system. It is scarcely surprising, therefore, that such classifications tend to emphasise the differences between what may most neutrally be termed the liberal democracies of western Europe and the peoples' democracies of eastern Europe; Europe being, in intellectual terms, still the principal arena in which this competition is manifest.

Thus Dahl, who in his *Modern Political Analysis* began with the Aristotelian criterion as his point of departure,[12] has come to distinguish two broad types of political systems which he has termed *polyarchies* and *hierarchies*, according to such criteria as the existence of a separation of powers, the independence or otherwise of the judiciary and civil service, the existence or otherwise of the judiciary and civil service, the existence or otherwise of competitive parties, and formally organised pressure groups with open access to the decision-makers.[13] This distinction draws in turn on Friedrich's distinction[14] between *totalitarian* states and others, according to six criteria:

(i)   an official ideology, to which everyone is supposed to adhere;
(ii)   a single mass party usually led by one man, organised hierarchically;
(iii) monopoly of the effective use of all weapons by party and bureaucracy;
(iv)   monopoly of the means of effective mass communication;
(v)   a system of terroristic police control; and
(vi)   central control and direction of the economy.

In recent years the concept of totalitarianism has come under strong attack, both from eastern Europe and from specialists on eastern Europe. The former point out that the six criteria link together three principal historical instances: Mussolini's Italy (1922-44), Hitler's Germany (1933-45) and the Soviet Union under Stalin (1928-53), and they reject this linking as propagandist, principally (though not entirely) because they see the purpose of the Soviet Union as being entirely opposed to that of the other two instances. The latter, on the other hand, have failed to find evidence that the overwhelming control claimed for the state by the proponents of the model does in fact exist in the Soviet Union today. They identify competing power-centres and interest groups within Soviet society, and dismiss the 'rational actor' model of Soviet decision-making in favour of a 'bureaucratic politics' interpretation (see chapter 8).[15] Other eastern European states, notably Poland and Hungary, have diverged from the model substantially on the criteria of centralised control of the economy, and acceptance of the ruling ideology.

By loosening the definition of totalitarian somewhat, Crick extends to eleven the number of criteria by which he distinguishes between *autocratic, totalitarian* and *republican* regimes.[16] In theoretical terms this seems a retrograde step. Understanding of the underlying processes can only be reached by establishing a framework within which the underlying relationships between the criteria can be understood. Extending the number of criteria may *in itself*, therefore, not be particularly informative, and in any case even those who adhere to the totalitarian model have never been able to argue that there are very many of them in the world at large.

Blondel has proposed three axes of classification which could enable us to link all such criteria.[17] These are the radical-conservative dimension, the democratic-monarchical dimension, and the liberal-authoritarian dimension. These are helpful distinctions which we shall find it useful to bear in mind in what follows. For I propose to take an approach which is rather different, but is, nevertheless, based on the same imperative, to relate the universe of states to underlying processes. All classifications, however detailed, will be actively misleading in so far as they distinguish categories at one moment of historical time. For within the universe of states we can find order only if we recognise that we are looking at an evolving pattern, and that the confusion stems from the conflict of two principles:

1 Each political system has some freedom to evolve according to its own internal political dynamics; and
2 All political systems have been shaped by the influence of two periods of political evolution which have occurred in the last 200 years, each of which has altered (in ways that are not wholly compatible) prevailing ideas about the relationship of the individual to the state.

Thus most states today wear a formal aspect of government which is of one of two types: the parliamentary or the presidential state.[18] Both are historical variants of what Verney has called the 'Convention Theory' state.[19] 'Convention' refers to the fact that in it all conversion functions are exercised by an assembly (alternatively termed a Convention), and 'Theory' to the fact that in all states this form of government either never has existed at the national level, or it has never existed for very long when it has existed. It is more a theoretical model of what government ought to be like; a transplantation of the principle of direct democracy into modern dress.

The relationship here between Verney's view and Aristotle's on the one hand, or Almond and Coleman's on the other, is through this differentiation between the executive and the legislative powers, which we originally owe to Locke, and its more sophisticated transplantation into the notions of rule-application and rule-making. Locke however also spoke of a third power, one which has scarcely ever been specifically incorporated into the Constitution of any modern state, but which is implicit in the structure of all states, namely the federative power − the power to conduct relations with other states.[20] An exception is the USSR, which amended its Constitution after the United Nations was created to give individual Union Republics the right to conduct direct relations with other states. The federative power was never found very attractive by other theorists who were very reluctant in applying it to the actual study of states. It appeared that the federative power, such as it was, was exercised either by the executive, or, worse, by the army. And the eighteenth-century solution to the problem was to reject the notion altogether and to replace it by the concept of a discrete judicial power. The judicial power, under the functional name of rule-adjudication, has been transplanted into modern terminology without necessarily getting away from the fact that, by and large, with the possible exception of the United States, the executive branch of government is that branch which in most states exercises the judicial power. We cannot easily distinguish the judicial from the executive in most states, even where the belief exists that there is an abstract entity called law existing independently of the power of government.

The effectiveness of power can be tested, in Dahl's terms, by the degree of subsystem autonomy and the number of subsystems within the political system as a whole.[21] It is clearly very relevant to any assessment of the power of central government to determine the extent to which the state is differentiated into subordinate units, or the extent to which it is centralised.

The majority of states are strongly centralised. Some, but by no means all, have a considerable degree of regional autonomy, and in a few this is so great that the formal state is little more than a confederation of competing areas or tribes. Dahl's interest in this range of possibilities is natural enough, since, being an American, he lives in a federal state — one in which the balance between central power and regional autonomy is very carefully fixed. However federalism is the product of a political compromise, and so very unusual — a compromise between centripetal and centrifugal forces, the demands of central power and the demand for independence.[22] But this compromise is inherently unstable, with a tendency towards greater centralisation; and there are very few states in the world that are federal states at any one time. It just so happens that in our own time most of them happen to be rather important, and therefore we have to pay more attention to federalism than perhaps its historical existence might specifically warrant.

MODERNISATION AND DEVELOPMENT

Before leaving Aristotle, we might note that he did not just classify states by the rule of the One, and the rule of the Few and the rule of the Many. He also classified them as good and bad. Nowadays this is called a value-judgement, and we are taught by some writers to shun it like the plague. If we describe a state as being good or bad it indicates we are contaminated by some kind of ideological viewpoint. Well, people will have views on whether states are good or bad, and these do creep into their views of the world, so we must face up to the problem. The whole attitude of many people to the world is characterised by the distinction, for example, between what is and what is not democracy; the notion of the 'totalitarian model' of states in reality, as opposed to the concept of totalitarianism in theory. All this derives from a very clear ideal of us and them; they do things differently from us, and we do not like the way they do it, and therefore advance from their type of system to our type of system is just that – an advance. It is not just simply a shift sideways to them; it is a stage in progress.

Hence, when one turns to discussing the development of political systems it is tempting to discuss them in terms of something called modernisation.

But political modernisation is a very troublesome concept to identify, let alone to apply systematically. Perhaps as you read this you are looking out on the glass, steel and concrete of a college, factory or block of flats which represent, in visual terms, a stage of modernisation of building techniques. As you look, you are aware that in turn this depends on a process of economic modernisation, if you will, involving such trends as the growth of corporations, economies of scale, mass production, greater use of machinery, and substitution of natural products by synthetic ones. But it is not clear that the government of the town in which that building stands, or indeed the political system of any country in the world, has changed in the sense that builders have changed from the use of stone and wood to the use of concrete and glass, and the growth in size of political units is not in itself a guarantee of greater political effectiveness, and may well be the reverse.

As you will see, one of the constants in human nature is the inclination to take oneself too seriously. This means that in every age thinkers have instinctively thought of themselves as being the climax of a process of discovery, without realising adequately that they in turn will be superseded by others. And modernisation, therefore, is only the process of arriving at the present which itself is only a brief moment before the future. Not only may it not represent an improvement, it may, as our own century has shown, sometimes represent a giant leap backwards.

This problem is well illustrated by the well-known developmental model of Edward B Shils, which formalises concepts widely used in speech and in the press.[23] He distinguishes, on the one hand, the rule of the Few, which he calls oligarchy, from the rule of the Many, democracy. He then proceeds to sub-divide these types by two different criteria: what he takes to be the actual effective degree to which the concept is applied, and for what purpose the government concerned advocates it.

He thus derives two types of democracy: *political democracy*, such as exists in western Europe and the United States, characterised by free elections, competitive parties, pressure groups, and so on; and *tutelary democracy*, such as was characteristic of Pakistan under Ayub Khan (1958-68), where the government holds many rights in abeyance on the pretext that the people need to be educated before being ready for political democracy. This category might include many military governments that, as in Bolivia, Ecuador, Peru and Brazil in 1978-9, promise free elections once they have ended illiteracy, taught everyone who to vote for, and given them an official party to support – but there must surely be serious doubts whether democracy is the right word for it.

And it is in fact very difficult to distinguish tutelary democracy from the first of Shils' three categories of oligarchy, which he calls *modernising oligarchy*. This is where the rulers justify their restraint on public self-assertion on the grounds that to do so will promote economic development.

Naturally modernising oligarchy can be made to look attractive, particularly if judiciously contrasted with its old-fashioned counterpart, *traditional oligarchy*, where nothing is ever done because the rulers like things the way they are.

Lastly, however, Shils offers a third category, that of *totalitarian oligarchy*. This is rule from the centre directed by an ideology which justifies it on the grounds that it is in the true interests of the masses and backed by a coercive apparatus which demands positive and not merely negative acceptance.

Although these three types correspond to popular ideas of differences between states – and especially to types which were fashionable in the 1950s when the scheme was outlined – the way in which the differences are drawn is not really up to the strain of actual classification. Was Brazil under General Medici (1970-4) a modernising oligarchy, as it professed to be, or a totalitarian oligarchy as Amnesty International tended to regard it? Not only is there, it seems, no very hard-and-fast line to be drawn between democracy and oligarchy, but the divisions between the subtypes are just as uncertain. And the scheme makes no mention of perhaps the most fruitful subtype possible, that of totalitarian democracy, which in the hands of J.L. Talmon did so much to illuminate the way in which earlier ideals found a logical development in the so-called people's democracies of eastern Europe after the Second World War.[24]

The problem is a basic one, and it is that we can only go so far, when dealing with the modern, complex political system, with whole systems, and nothing at all if we are shackled by a time-bound concept of modernisation. Though it is undoubtedly difficult to do so, we have to think in terms of a continuum of historical development stretching past us into the future. And we have to be very much more precise about details, and ask ourselves what kind of structures this political system has developed in order to carry out the functions it purports to be serving.

Almond and Powell's[25] development model rests in the first instance on the concept of authority, following the distinction made by Weber between patriarchal, patrimonial and feudal authority.[26]

Patriarchal authority is authority vested solely in the representative of the lineage; patrimonial authority depends on the possession of goods, or lands having value; feudal authority involves a bargain between the holders of each of these concepts for a series of reciprocal obligations of service and protection. The most decentralised of the lot, is the *feudal* system of authority, where there are two types of patrimonial authority in conflict. In other words the representatives of the lineage in the first instance hold centralised authority which is, however, counterposed by other people who have a right to authority within their own areas and over whose traditional rights he has no authority at all; the differentiation of subsystems, to use a more modern terminology.

Out of the patrimonial states there has been developed, in turn, what has been called the *historical bureaucratic* state. This is the kind of state and others described in Eisenstadt, the state in which the system of government itself becomes so formalised that it operates whether or not there is a competent representative of the lineage actually in charge.[27] In other words, every so often, human inheritance being what it is, either the inheritance fails or there is a 'time of troubles' when there are many contenders for the throne. But the bureaucratic structure by that time is such that decisions continue to be made, that the system continues to work; the field boundaries are still delimited; the harvest is still gathered, a tenth is dished out to the priests, and a pittance is dished out to the poor, if they are lucky. The whole system continues to work on the basis that it always has worked, just because the degree of sophistication of the system has become sufficiently elaborate for the system itself to continue in a state of equilibrium, regardless of dynastic considerations. And it is out of this historical bureaucratic system that modern states have derived.

It will be noticed that Almond and Powell do not, as I have sought to do, stress the duality of the origins of government. They accept the fact of government, and with it, implicitly, the assumption that it is beneficial to society. I want to stress that there are always two elements in conflict in government: government and the people, the claim to power and its acceptance, or reward and punishment. Government is interaction, not action.

Almond and Powell provide a special category for the *secularised city states*: very small states such as Liechtenstein, San Marino or Monaco, but probably not Andorra or Luxembourg. Secularisation refers simply to the fact that the religious element has, in modern times, been taken out of their government, which presumably excludes the Vatican City State, but it is very hard to see why.

From this point onwards Almond and Powell view development as a process of *political mobilisation*; that is, the bringing of more and more people into the political life of the community. Certainly the mobilisation of individuals does mean at the same time taking account of their interests. To bring them into the political system, they have to be getting something out of it if they are going to be required to continue to put something into it. It is, of course, possible to find, even today, systems in which large sectors of the population are not incorporated in the structure, and so a category is provided for *pre-mobilised modern systems*.

Finally, they conclude with two categories of *mobilised systems*, in which mass participation is both required and encouraged, and so is qualitatively different. One is the *democratic* state in which the desire of the people to produce inputs is fully accepted and channelled, even when it is a question of demands rather than supports. The other is the *authoritarian* system, where the support is wanted but demands are not.

To summarise, therefore, Almond and Powell see the evolution of modern states as following an historical path from the patriarchal-patrimonial level, through the feudal states and the historical-bureaucratic states, to the pre-mobilised modern states; modern, that is, in that they still exist in today's world, but are not mobilised in the sense that the mobilised modern state requires or permits. And in these mobilised modern states, the common factor is that people participate widely in politics, some because they want to do so, some because they are made to do so, and some for both reasons.

For me the possibilities are somewhat more complex (see Table 2). The distinctive features in which I differ from Almond and Powell and, indeed, from most of the authorities which I am going to discuss are two. First of all, the dualism which they discern as coming into evolution of states at the division between the authoritarian and democratic states of today I see as running throughout the whole course of human history. Indeed, this conflict, natural because politics is institutionalised conflict, provides the basic dynamic, as I see it, for all experimentation with political forms. We may have forgotten, or become habituated to the essentially violent and self-imposed way in which we have acquired our governments. But the facts are still fundamental to our understanding of how they work today. All governments exercise just as much power as they believe they can get away with. It is in the extension or, conversely, in the limitation of these powers that all modern governments have been shaped.

Secondly, precisely because this dynamic is continuous and fundamental, I have no difficulty in accounting for the ways in which the process of political change ebbs and flows. It does not follow a cycle of change from one form of government to another, returning to the beginning, as Plato and later Polybius suggested;[28] nor, as the Victorians (among whom I count Marx himself) would have it, is there an irresistible progress in the sense that political systems evolve along a single line towards a predictable future state. Of course, human beings learn by experience, but even with books to aid them, memories grow cold and old men die.

Table 2   Varieties of government

Primitive	Agrarian	Imperial	Assembly	Apparat
tribe	kingdom	empire	presidential	party
band	theocracy	dictatorship	caesarism	praetorian
	horde	feudal	federal	
	city	anarchy	parliamentary	

What above all makes it difficult to identify discernible categories of states is the fact that, however complex they are, they are made up of very simple assemblages of horizontal and vertical links, replicating the tribe and band of primitive times. It is easy to make fun of this idea, for the notion of modern man as an ape in spaceman's clothing is richly comic. But it is, none the less, uncomfortably true. It follows that the replacement or mutation of a relatively small number of links in the system by which interests are balanced, amounts to a fundamental change in the system as a whole. In this respect at least, the industrious Constitution-makers of the nineteenth century, with their obsession with detailed legal checks and balances, were not misguided, though they failed to allow for the realities behind the systems they sought to construct.

4 Communication

Throughout the last chapter we have come closer to seeing the political system as a cybernetic model. That is to say, that it is self-steering, existing within its environment by monitoring responses from it, including those resulting from its own actions.

Such a process, and the process of interaction generally between government and environment, implies the existence of forms of communication. Indeed, in the exposition of Almond and Coleman the role of communication in a political system has been separated out as a distinct function of that system: that of political communication. It is extremely unlikely, on *a priori* grounds, that this concept has any value within the scheme as it stands, as the nature of communication is not the same thing as the thing to be communicated.[1] All social interactions depend on communication, and there is therefore no such thing as political communication, only communication employed for political purposes.

What is communication? Communication is the transmission of a signal through a channel from a transmitter to a receiver.[2] The signal, which is generally in the form of an economical statement known as a code, need not be consciously transmitted, but it must be recognised and interpreted by the receiver into a pattern of actions or statements. Communication therefore includes a process of coding, and a process of decoding, as well as the act of transmission, which may be either direct or through third parties. An essential prerequisite, therefore, is that the code should be known to the parties at both the sending and receiving end, if only by inference from other circumstances. Lastly, a communication may result either in action directly by the receiver, or in action by a relay or servomechanism communicating or creating the conditions for communication to one of more indirect recipients.

Communication in the proper sense cannot be accidental, then. However it does not follow that all communications can be easily understood or accurately interpreted. Many political messages are sent for the purpose of deliberately confusing or misleading the receiver, or, in other words, from preventing him from drawing the correct conclusions from a pattern of actions or statements.

Communication is the foundation of society. Sophisticated means of communication distinguish human society from that of the animal world, as in advanced human societies from primitive ones. It is known that there are parallels to human communication among dolphins and others of the cetacea, but no land-based animal appears to have a 'vocabulary' of more than about twenty different types of signal. What is interesting for our present purpose, about these signals is that relatively few actually consist of grunts, squeaks, whistles or indeed noises of any kind, but of ritual complexes of sound and action, and that these complexes represent whole chains of actions for a whole species. Examples are ritual mating dances such as that of the peacock, or the peace dance of the goose.[3]

There are severe limitations on this kind of expression: it is mainly restricted to direct confrontation; it is complex and time-consuming; most importantly, however, it is a dead-end in the development of language, the essence of which is that the most complex language is built up out of simple and interchangeable building blocks, namely words, each of which has a simple restricted meaning. It is the use of languages of this kind that distinguishes the pattern of communication in human organisation.

Nevertheless, the existence of simple communication systems among animals shows that they fulfil the needs of the animals using them. Much the same kind of lesson can be drawn for human society. For each type of society, good communications are appropriate communications. A small rural community can be well integrated and interact fully by direct speech and occasional, short written notes for the milkman or baker: a city such as New York or Tokyo would disintegrate under the same conditions. But conversely the same number of farmers deprived of direct speech and dependent for integration on television and radio would not be a community at all. In fact it is just this reliance in modern states on the mass media which leads to decentralised and demoralised urban as well as rural life, where no one knows what is going on in the house next door, but no one cares either.

The fact is that communications in modern times cannot only be too dispersed to be effective, they can also be too rapid. An aspect of this which has been of the most profound significance in shaping our present historical age (including two world wars), has been the enormous gap for more than a hundred years after 1844 between the ability to transmit information, which was virtually instantaneous, and the ability to transmit people, which was not. Although this differential has been reduced nowadays to a very small amount, it has still, for physiological reasons, more importance than the physical facts would seem to warrant.

Decision-making is done by individuals, and individuals simply cannot cope with huge quantities of information on all levels simultaneously. The problem of mass communication is a simple one: the difficulty of processing raw information into meaningful statements on which decisions can be based. This applies to the citizen as much as to the decision-maker. How each deals with it depends much on the options open to him. This depends in turn on an understanding of the nature of the different types of communication available.

At the simplest level of understanding there is face-to-face communication, that is to say, direct speech between two human beings. It is at this level that government alone becomes truly real to the individual person. Therefore it is not surprising to find that the essence of government to the man in the street very often is a visit from his local councillor or his MP, perhaps; the directions of policemen, or the observation of postmen or refuse collectors about their daily tasks. These are the people with whom the citizen deals directly, and, as they know to their cost, it is on them that his resentments tend to get discharged. The fact that a motorist is charged for speeding means that he momentarily develops a much more acute awareness of the punitive aspects of government than of its beneficent ones, though receipt of government pensions or government aid make him correspondingly sympathetic.

Face-to-face communications are direct, real, present. They are the necessary foundation of systems in which interaction, characteristic of them, is replaced by action. The only other means of communication with the characteristic of interaction is the telephone which transmits speech directly, and which like direct speech leaves no written record. It is difficult to say what the political consequences of widespread distribution of telephones may be – the leading telephone nations, New Zealand, the United States and West Germany having little enough in common, except prosperity. But two characteristics have become very clear. On the one hand, it is difficult for a society to be a completely closed one if its citizens have telephones. In the USSR this feature of the telephone is minimised as far as possible by the absence of a satisfactory telephone directory. Yet even with this limitation men like Sakharov have, through the use of the telephone, retained access to the outside world and to world public opinion as long as they have not been in prison. On the other, in open societies, telephones have a great advantage for the citizen over physical presence: properly used, they enable him to penetrate to a much higher level of decision-making than would otherwise be possible. As in face-to-face discussion, too, refutation can be advanced directly, specific points confronted, and statements demanded which cannot easily be evaded.

When interaction is replaced by action, a whole range of communications is opened up which is generally cheaper and has other specific advantages and disadvantages. They can be divided broadly as between voice and visual means, on the one hand, and between mass and restricted communications on the other; but to some extent these attributes are interlinked. For example, interaction is not a feature of a mass meeting, even though communication is by voice, and even face-to-face. Questions may be offered, but even when answered immediately need not be revealing: the continental practice of gathering questions together and answering them in a supplementary oration gives all the advantage to the speaker. Heckling, as it is known in England, is forbidden in many countries; in others, such as South Africa and Australia, it is much more vigorous and inclined to cause physical harm to the speaker.[4]

Mass communication by voice, the radio broadcast, is now proportionately very cheap and has extensive uses in spreading government propaganda both at home and abroad. The role of Radio Cairo in inflaming opinion in Algeria in 1954-6 is considered to have been a major factor in the response of the Mollet government at the time of Suez, but it was undoubtedly just as important in integrating post-revolutionary Egypt itself.[5] With the added effect of television, it was extensively used by Castro in Cuba to communicate the views of his regime, but in the nature of mass communications this could not, as was then thought, perform the function of informing the government on the views of the people.[6] And the East Germans can receive not only radio but also television broadcasts from West Germany.

Visual communications apart from television depend, except in rare instances, for most of their effect on the use of writing. Writing is a code for expressing on paper or other material the sounds of the code that is language. Knowledge of this code is however not a normal part of each individual's basic home instruction, and is imparted by specialists as the first part of a process of formal education. Literacy is therefore not a political attribute as such, but it does arise only as part of the attribute of formal inculcation in the values of society. This point is important, since the existence of such values determines the interpretation of written material as certainly as they do the interpretation of photographic or pictorial material, a classic instance of the ambiguous interpretation resulting being the

'Chinese slavery' poster used by the Liberal Party in the United Kingdom general election of 1906.[7]

Individual visual communications are primarily letters and similar messages; mass communications include, apart from posters and handbills, newspapers and even books, all forms where the same text is multiplied by printing press or photographic means.

Mass communications by their nature can be monopolised almost completely by governments. Even clandestine printing presses are of little avail if the supply of newsprint or ink is a state monopoly, as in the USSR and all other socialist countries, or as in Chile under Allende, or Peru under Velasco Alvarado.[8] Fortunately, in modern times the particular appeal that television has to members of governments attempting to put over their point of view to the largest possible number of people means that these controls are suitably neglected. The immediacy of television has given it a special place in the folklore of politics, perhaps not entirely justified by the facts. Direct personal conversation may increasingly be invaded by shared television experiences, but equally the same experiences facilitate the education of young children and provide topics of conversation for people of all ages who hitherto might have had nothing in common.[9]

Each of these three categories is subject to unconscious influence from a fourth, that of unintentional communication, or metacommunication – information gained from signs.[10]

Signs are easy to understand in theory, but difficult to interpret in practice. The idea that one can walk down a street in a strange town and look at it for the evidence it gives on the lives of those who live there is not a remarkable one. Whether the street is swept, what sort and size of houses it contains, whether they have gardens and what sort of plants they have in them, whether the houses are well painted, what sort of curtains show at the windows, the presence of garages, lawnmowers, scooters, bicycles, cars and children's toys – all these, given experience of that society, inform the passerby of the social standing, income, occupation, taste and even the political sympathies of the residents.

In a society in which governments are on the alert for manifestations of discontent, of course, people may take great care to assume a uniform outward appearance. Besides they may, and frequently do, live in flats or apartment blocks; the presence of a concierge, security guard or electrically-operated door here can be a sign of the degree to which those within feel it necessary to defend their position against the outside world or, as with the Russian *dezhurnaya*, a sign of the degree to which the state may wish to keep an eye on the residents.

So it is not necessary for a conscious act of communication to occur. All action or inaction implies communication for those able to decode it. Some individuals find this very irritating when they try to profess political opinions at variance with the message presented by their life-style, and, not surprisingly, fail to convince.

The way in which communications are used in the political process can be dealt with under three headings: those of inputs, communications between decision-makers, and outputs.

Inputs can in turn be divided into two categories: input communication in general – that is, all influences from the environment; and feedback, the response monitored to actions by the decision-makers themselves. The first step is regulation of the input, both to reduce the pressure to manageable proportions, and to distinguish the first from the second. The effect upon decision-makers of wholly unregulated input communication can hardly be imagined. It has occurred, however, for only brief periods, as in the case of the revolutionary government of students in Cuba under President Grau San Martin in 1933.[11] Sufficient to say that no one – no individual or group – could possibly exercise any functions of decision-making if exposed to a continuous unregulated flood of inputs. It is all one whether they are pestered by people with demands, or by people with offers of support, since the one generally turns out to be conditional on the other.

For this reason, the development of modern government meant, early on, the development of a staff. Through the staff communications can be channelled according to forms which reduce the amount on which the decision-makers are called to operate, so that the total volume each has to handle is reduced to manageable limits. This of itself, in all but rare cases, screens out the use of face-to-face communication; indeed, of reciprocal communications of any kind, for the volume is controlled in time as well as extent most manageably by being converted into written memoranda.[12] The citizen is thus restricted in fact, if not in theory, to written communications which reduce both the urgency of his request and the subtleties implied by its individual circumstances.

There are basically three types of decision which decision-makers can choose. They may choose to continue a policy, to initiate a new policy, to compromise between an existing policy and a new policy, or between any two or more policies.[13] The choice between these depends not only on the content of the cases presented to them, however, but also on the force with which it is presented, for it is this that acts as index to the quantities of demand and support engaged in its behalf. The effort to press a new policy on decision-makers is likely to be handicapped as against pressures for the *status quo* or compromise in any screening process, therefore, and broadly speaking the more effective the staff the less effective the forces for change. In such circumstances the suppliant may well feel the urge to circumvent or to destroy the screening process and to engage the attention of the decision-maker at first hand. Riots and demonstrations are the result.

Clearly it would be fatal for governments to be so effectively screened. In particular, a government must have information on the effects on the environment of its own actions. Unlike an organic body, it has no other compulsion than conscious choice to do so, but equally so its actions could be taking place in a void. For this purpose, therefore, governments find it necessary to devise systems by which they can admit the inputs they wish to admit, while continuing to exclude unregulated calls upon their time. Such role-bearers have been termed by David Easton the 'gatekeepers'.

Part of these can be specialised organs of the staff; such are statistical services and their ancilliary collectors, such as registrars, notaries, customs officials and treasury agents. Part can be *ad hoc* mechanisms for specific tasks, such as royal commissions, assises, delegations or committees of inspection. In a democratic society, the decision-makers themselves will be expected to be seen going among the people; in President Johnson's words, 'pressing the flesh',[14] and obtaining apparently spontaneous responses of joy to the presence of someone associated with government policy as a whole, or a crucial sector of it. This is certainly useful as far as it goes, but as an output of government enabling a higher level of extraction of effort rather than a genuine input mechanism.

Assuming that the process of regulation of inputs has been assessed, we next have to look at the means by which the decision-makers handle communication among themselves. Decision-makers are people. Decisions are made by people, even if they are made by omission more often than by commission. And these people may, and often do, form a particularly close group. In our discussion on élites we shall notice that the élite might be identified either subjectively or objectively. If the latter, the decision-makers themselves will communicate essentially as do non-élite members of society. But sections of them, and in the case of subjective élites perhaps the whole group, can compensate for the greater mass of information they have to handle by making use of more direct means of communication, by abandoning the written record and resorting to voice or face-to-face means. This gives them not only an advantage against the mass of society, however, which is not necessarily a good thing, but also against the bureaucracy which may otherwise all too easily overwhelm them with its rigidity and resistance to change.

It is particularly at this level that we must take into account the fact that all communication is subject to distortion, specifically of three types.[15] It may be subject to bias, which is selectivity to certain signals rather than to others; to interference, the effect of the general mush of noise, coming in this case from the social environment, such as information on the weather, on sporting events, or cultural activities, which engage the attention irrelevantly from their very volume and persistence. Interference, indeed, may go so far as to take the form of deliberate jamming of the communications network by a strong meaningless signal. Or it may result within the system from the choice of information to be passed on to the decision-makers by the selectors who first receive the communication. And it may be distorted by overload, as already mentioned, the problem of which is that fear of it inhibits the selectors from exercising their function, and leads them to take the easy path of taking a random selection from the total volume of message-flow, and attempting to deal with it as if it were a representative one.

Communication between decision-makers, unlike that between one of them and a suppliant outside the élite, is specially inhibited by overload, since its effect is doubled. The member of the public only needs the opportunity to communicate, to be able to put his case in full at the drop of a hat. The decision-maker has to reply on the assumption that his brief comments will be fully expanded into their intended meaning. Personal rivalries and policy clashes make sure that this can never be achieved, though the presence of a common background of socialisation makes it more likely than otherwise, again a point in favour of the *status quo*.

Much of the process of internal communication is concealed by governments until no longer of great current interest to scholars. The importance of output communication is thus disproportionate to us, as the sector of the communications net most easily accessible to the investigator as political scientist. Most of the political scientist's impressions of government come from initial study of output communications, and though they can be enhanced by acquaintance with decision-making at first hand, lose objectivity from too close identification with government. In comparative politics identification of this kind is particularly unfortunate since it distorts comparison as well as appreciation.

Tracing communications back to their source is the essence of the problem. The complexity of the system stands in the way, and often causes the investigator to remain absorbed by them almost to the exclusion of the inputs associated with them. But it is the only way in which decision-makers can be identified as such, other than by reputational criteria, that is, by hearsay and common report.

Output communication is certainly designed to be presented as an attractive picture of government and an effective motivation of desired results in the societal environment. Assuming decision by individual or conference, it has its origin as a complex of ideas capable of being presented with full accuracy in a face-to-face statement, allowing for the correction of inadvertent errors. Where attractiveness of presentation is important, this precision is usually the objective striven for. In times of crisis, therefore, the head of government may choose to approximate to it as far as possible in reaching directly to the mass of the society, and make a personal television appearance.

Otherwise, this method loses impact from over exposure, and the absence of concentration on urgent events which leads misguided television owners sometimes to turn their sets off. The three most favoured methods normally used are well exemplified by those used when information leaves the office of the United States president. This occurs in one of three ways: through written messages, through a member of the staff, or through a visitor (including the presidential press conference, if not televised). The type of message varies with the status of the person handling it, and to the extent to which they are being used as a conscious vehicle of presidential policy, or as an unconscious agent in the transmission of a predetermined signal to third parties. Nor are they in any case purely passive agents: each wishes to show that he has presidential support either for his status pretensions, or for a policy of which he is a known initiator.

Each of these three types of message may have two different effects. They may be effective directly, in that the means chosen for their transmission ensures their delivery to a desired individual or group with a calculated emphasis and association of political pressures. Or they may be effective indirectly, through their actuation of servomechanisms in the system's administrative machinery. By servomechanisms I mean local government structures which are formally independent, but respond to central instruction. This type of action is most important because without it the operation by decision-makers of a modern administrative machine would be quite impossible. Its own articulation, its internal routing of messages is therefore of fundamental importance in assessing its effects, for the way in which it affects the outside world is more often indirect than direct. With the records of the machine before him, the investigator can analyse its characteristic pattern. This varies according to the direction, the volume and the content of the communication flow, and specifically in the ways set out here. Without such records, he must still rely on raw statistical indicators amplified by impressionistic judgements on their real interpretation.

The crunch comes at the most important part, discovering what (if anything) the messages are actually about. This involves understanding the code in which they are written.

As already indicated, it is in the nature of communication that messages are transmitted in code; it is not just an accident of time or place: and codes are not cyphers, that is to say, they are not meant to be secret, so there is no fundamental reason why a trained observer cannot learn them.

The first step obviously is to learn the language. For a student of comparative politics learning languages can become a major task in itself, for the language reflects the society which uses it; indeed it shapes society, a flexible language such as English taking on new concepts to the point of meaninglessness, while an exact language such as French implies a closer correspondence of ideas in the mind of speaker and hearer. The shaping effect of language is felt at those points at which ideas are taken for granted. Students of politics have long been locked into an earnest debate as to whether Marx expected the state to be *transcended* or *abolished*; the German word which he used *(aufheben)* inconveniently meaning both, and indeed also lifted, picked up, arrested, kept or preserved.[16]

Then, beyond the dictionary definition of words, societies employ general codes of social communication, in which words such as 'crown' or 'flag' carry wide-ranging overtones of political responsibility, and phrases such as the 'common law' in England, or 'the Fourth of July' in the United States, are heavy with meaning which the individual words of which they are composed totally lack.[17] Understanding of the general code of each society is, therefore, the understanding of the nature of political education.

Beyond these in each society lie restricted codes, applicable only within certain sectors of that society.[18] Communication within these sectors is conducted for most purposes in terms of the restricted code. The classic instance is the code employed by the armed forces, characterised by a small vocabulary in which each word has a very precise meaning, and hence, by two advantages, that ensure the general use of such a code by the soldiers of any country. One is that each order given to a soldier means one thing and nothing else. Under conditions of severe stress – under fire or danger from mines or aerial attack – the soldier given a command will respond instinctively without having to make a conscious and potentially fatal choice. The other advantage is that the limitations of the code deliberately leave him no room for concepts not covered by it, such as fear or flight (the latter being termed a tactical retreat). Indeed the deficiencies of the code are such that the soldier tends to supply his own two or three all-purpose words to fill the gaps.

Restricted codes are most important for this quality of exclusion, characteristic of all forms of professionalism, and nowhere more so than in government. They can indeed be implanted generally by education in political matters, so that the subject is bound to an official ideology, and is less receptive to destabilising stimuli. This can in turn be used to strengthen distinctions of status, or to impart values suggesting certain types of social patterning rather than others.

This is strikingly important in communications within and between Communist systems. For the USSR a phrase such as 'proletarian internationalism' means 'limited sovereignty for other Communist states', while for the Chinese 'Hold High the Banner of Marxism-Leninism' means 'oppose Maoism'.[19] But it is also found in other political systems. In Britain under Harold Wilson, for example, the phrase 'the Social Contract' was used to refer to the control of wages by government without the formal passage of legislation, but had the additional political benefits (other than deliberate vagueness) of suggesting agreement and social value.[20]

The use of a special restricted code within the administration combines all these qualities. It depends on its capacity and precision to carry large volumes of meaning in a short space, and ensure accurate response on the part of its servomechanisms. A circular from the Department of the Environment on building standards will be complied with by local authorities in a similar fashion, but with the necessary adjustments for regional variations of soil, climate, and so on. But when the same communication falls into the hands of a person who does not know the restricted code, his misinterpretation of it may lead to confusion.

By extension, tortuous and jargon-filled codes may be employed deliberately to restrict the circulation of information to administrative circles, while continuing to permit, apparently, full participation in the processes of government. They form, therefore, one of the many means by which participation is actively restricted. The use of simple language, coupled with the availability of good civics classes in school or adult education, has just the reverse effect.

Beyond this, though not intentionally, the use of restrictive codes can handicap feedback processes. Here the problem is that the code used within the system is not able to carry the range of meanings used by the plain language of those outside it whose opinions are being canvassed. Often this can occur because a wide range of views are reduced to a single formula. Since a great deal of uninformed hostility to government arises from just this feeling of not being understood, it is not surprising that codes play a major role at particularly crucial moments such as the consolidation period of revolutions.

The first task of a post-revolutionary government is to explain to the outside world in what ways it proposes to amend or annul the existing restricted code of government. Without this understanding, it cannot successfully explain how its policies differ from those of its predecessor, and it may not be able to do so at all except by adding large sections to the usual vocabulary. It is for this reason that on the occasion of the major revolutions a characteristic feature of consolidation has been the sending out of delegates or commissions to the provinces to act as the receptors for central messages until new receptors have had time to be established.

For example the interpretation of liberty as a single concept throughout the American colonies, and the establishment of unified action to secure it, was crucially dependent on the establishment of the Corresponding Societies linked to the Continental Congress, and to the common experience of congressmen themselves. The Declaration of Independence which ensued *assumes* general acceptance of the principle of liberty. Similarly the French Convention sent delegates on mission to provincial centres to establish a uniform application of revolutionary 'justice' and the administrative re-organisation of the country on new areas headed by new officials removed as far as possible from the traditional routine of the *ancien régime*.

An alternative technique in modern revolutions has been the retention of the old vocabulary given a long-term semantic modification towards the acceptance of the new *status quo*. Only when the new order had been accepted on empirical grounds, did, for example, the Castro regime in Cuba introduce by degrees a new code eliminating the pre-revolutionary aspects of the old. Such a process is normally more obvious a feature of peaceful governmental change, the long-term evolution of society through technological innovation and biological replacement. This should be distinguished from the use of catch-phrases to conceal absence of thought.[21]

This then is the last point to be made here about the process of communication, that insufficient attention has been given to the use of semantics in political discourse. The science of semantics, it is not too much to say, is in its infancy as far as the understanding of political concepts is concerned, but without its aid we cannot hope to make cross-national comparisons involving socialisation or ideology which have any complete validity, and hence any cross-national comparisons of a total culture. Even as between Great Britain and the United States the structure and implications of the English language vary greatly. So much we know. But how it varies, and where it varies, and what implications the variations have for political communication, is a problem for semantics.

In the late 1950s psychologists interested in semantics devoted much effort to the precise location of concepts in what, with Osgood, Suci and Tannenbaum, we term the 'semantic space'.[22] Questionnaires submitted to volunteer subjects called upon them to assess the position of words and phrases in terms of pairs of opposed qualities. Some extremely interesting results emerged. It even became possible, using related techniques, to build on identifications of concepts in two or more areas or regions – as in one study between the United States and Mexico – and compare their values in terms of a single attribute such as 'respect', maintaining semantic correspondence between the concepts used to assess variations resulting from purely societal differences.[23]

Lastly, it has been possible to make content analyses of speeches or statements by leading politicians, and to assess from elimination of ancilliary matter and purely functional expressions the presence or absence of qualities such as 'hostility' or 'aggressiveness'.[24] So far these techniques have mainly focused on ascertaining what politicians are actually saying – no small task in itself – though some writers claim to be able to construct a 'cognitive map' of the decision-makers' perceptions and values. Given a sound semantic foundation, however, we may expect great expansion in the use of all these techniques over the next few years. The result for the study of comparative politics, and for political science in general, will be wholly beneficial.

5 The Struggle for Power Resources

The characteristic feature of modern political systems has been the emergence of the *assembly* as the prime instrument of mass mobilisation. As we shall see later, the systems generated by this development are now undergoing further modification by the attempts of governments to substitute for the assembly forms of representation, such as by a party or the military, more easily directed in the perennial task of mobilising the population in support of its government, and in the performance of tasks which many of its members do not really want to perform. But the irruption of the assembly into the political structure of France in 1789 has had such wide consequences that it still forms the basic point of departure for all later developments. This is because its claim to power, based on its representation of the people, was within a brief period transformed into that type of unfettered assembly rule which received its fullest expression between 1792 and 1794, and which, as we have already noted, Verney terms 'Convention Theory' government.[1]

All modern states derive their basic political structures from a period of violent disruption and reconstitution. Such a period of disruption may either take the form of international war or of revolution. The phenomenon of revolution I propose to deal with in more detail in chapter 11. Here I am using it to refer to political and social changes accompanied by violence such as we associate particularly with England, the United States, France and Russia,[2] and in modern times with countries as diverse as Mexico, Turkey, China, Egypt,[3] Iran and Nicaragua. In all of these instances an important feature of these changes has been the attempt to claim power by people claiming to act directly on behalf of the masses, and in the majority of cases this claim has momentarily led to direct rule by a convention, a special type of assembly claiming complete control over every aspect of political and social life.

Historically, assemblies are of course much older, and anthropology suggests they must be as old as, if not older than, the monopoly of power in the hands of a representative of a lineage, as we have seen. Medieval European monarchs built up their power against the nobles by a deliberate alliance with the assemblies which represented not only the nobles, but the lesser lords in the country-side and the centres of wealth in the towns.[4] Between approxi-mately 1200 and 1400, assemblies were to attain a peak of power they were not to attain again for centuries. By the *Fueros* of Jaca the King of Aragon was made to swear, on ascending the throne, to rule justly, and in their oath his assembled subjects made it clear on what terms their allegiance was given in return. 'We who are worth as much as you and can do more than you', they said, 'elect you king for as long as you guard our rights and liberties . . . if not, not.'[5] Reference to Aragon in the debates on the United States Constitu-tion in 1787 indicates that its case was known to at least one of the delegates there.[6]

Between 1400 and 1550 rulers were able to reduce the power of the medieval assemblies by a process of divide-and-rule, in parti-cular by forging a direct alliance against the great nobles with the rising power of the towns. In the second phase between 1567 and 1660, assemblies were instrumental in deposing kings, and even executing them, but after 1660 there was again a swing back towards despotic monarchy in Europe,[7] with parallels in places as widely dispersed as Turkey, Iran, Russia and Japan. Ultimately, however, these, like all other despotic systems, faced the same crisis of power resources that had earlier led to the English Civil War and the secessions of the Netherlands and the United States, and which led to the French Revolution itself.

Before 1789 it had been widely believed that the only alternative to despotic monarchy was the self-rule of all – that is to say, anarchy. This position, associated with the name of the English philosopher Thomas Hobbes, turned out to be mistaken. But the rejection of the absolutist claims of monarchy did result in equally absolutist claims being made for the assembly representing the people. In the event, the result was the ascendancy of neither, but a new form of govern-ment embodying both, and in twentieth-century revolutions, as in Mexico or Cuba, the struggle has been not to establish an assembly, but to give real power to the interests already embodied in it, even if this has meant the suspension of the assembly, or its substantial modification in the search for better representation of popular will. In the course of this it has become apparent that the idea of the absolute power of the assembly is by no means dead.

The basic principle of an assembly is that its members are equal. In Convention Theory government all power is vested in the assembly, and all other centres of authority are destroyed, neutralised, or subordinated. The chairman of the assembly is its servant not its master, and the execution of its policies is entrusted to committees created for that purpose. The celebrated Committee for Public Safety itself was re-elected monthly throughout the entire period of the Terror and of its existence. In England parliament did not delegate even the ceremonial function of receiving ambassadors who were brought before the entire House to be formally introduced. Remnants of these and similar practices are still embodied in the formal Constitutions of states such as the USSR, China and Cuba. In practice, there and elsewhere, the system has been substantially modified in certain well-defined ways.

A second characteristic of Convention Theory government is a unifying political culture which seeks to make equal that which is not already equal. The consequence, therefore, is a conflict between centre and periphery, and more particularly, a conflict between two principles – the principle of *representation*, which favours having a big assembly so that representatives are as close to their constituency as possible, and the principle of *efficiency*, which favours small groups for taking day-to-day decisions. In practical terms this means that under the pressure of business the assembly sits for longer and longer hours, and in the end many of the representatives are tempted to hand the burden of work over to someone else. And popular pressure for them to do so may by then be very great, particularly where, as in the French case, the political system is threatened by attack and a speedy response is called for.

If an assembly is to survive for a long time as an effective and working instrument it must develop a system of committees. Such a development is most strikingly shown by the operation of the United States Congress, where the creation of a separate executive has created a *presidential* system. Where, on the other hand, one of the committees has come to assume the executive power while remaining within the assembly, as in Britain, the result is a *parliamentary* system. Both represent compromises by which a government, limited in its powers of decision, is in return guaranteed the right to extract a sufficient quantity of power resources from the society it governs. There are important differences, however, in the terms of the two compromises.

In Britain, as we have seen, the parliamentary system was not embodied in a single written Constitution. Ironically, therefore, the prototype parliamentary system for most of the rest of the world is the Belgian Constitution of 1831. Present-day examples of working parliamentary systems include not only Britain and Belgium, but also Australia, Canada, India, Israel, Malaysia, the Netherlands, Sri Lanka, West Germany and Japan. There is an independent origin for the parliamentary systems of the Nordic countries in Sweden in the eighteenth century.[8]

In a parliamentary system the functions of rule-application, nominally derived from a head of state, are in practice vested in a committee of the assembly, consisting of ministers appointed by the head of state, but responsible to the assembly for their political actions. In countries such as Britain or the Netherlands, where the head of state is an hereditary monarch, her functions are ceremonial only. In a state with an elected head, such as Iceland, Ireland or Italy, the president (as he is rather confusingly called), may have rather more power, though once elected he or she is expected to stand above the political struggle. And in most states, exceptions being Japan and Sweden, the head of state has to sign documents giving effect to laws, and retains in this, and the choice of a first or prime minister, reserve powers which may be activated by some unexpected crisis, but which otherwise remain latent.

The executive committee, or ministry, must normally consist of elected members of the assembly, though this is not the case in the Netherlands, Luxemburg and Norway. It is the assembly, too, which normally elects the head of state, where this office is not vested in an hereditary monarch. Five countries that are exceptions are Austria, Finland, France, Iceland and Ireland, whose presidents are directly elected by the people. In short, all power has to be exercised through parliament, the collective entity formed by the head of state, the ministry and the assembly. The fact that all power decisions pass through parliament has been confused in the past with the idea that power rests in it, or even, more misleadingly still, in the assembly itself. But like any other organisation its effective power is limited, sometimes dramatically so, by the constraints of time and space. Hence the powers of the ministry, which is only indirectly responsible to the electorate, may well not be effectively checked by the assembly either.

The other favoured compromise is the presidential system. This differs fundamentally from the parliamentary system. The prototype is the 1787 Constitution of the United States.[9] As a model it has been followed by a large number of countries, but at rather widely separated points in time. First, at the beginning of the nineteenth century, the system was adopted by Mexico, Central and Spanish South America, and part of Haiti; Brazil, originally a monarchy, coming into line in 1889.[10] Liberia, a colony for freed American slaves, had followed suit in 1847. After that there was a long gap, until the rising power of the United States created Hawaii (1892) and Cuba (1901); the Philippines, under American tutelage, from 1898 onwards, became independent in 1946. It was only from then onwards that the presidential system came to sweep the rest of the Third World, beginning with the Middle East and North Africa, and spreading throughout sub-Saharan Africa in the dissolution of the British and French colonial empires after 1960. But there can be considerable doubt whether many of these systems are true presidential systems in the original sense.

In the prototype presidential system the assembly remains separate and distinct from the executive. Rule-making remains the function of the assembly; rule-application is entrusted to one person, the president, elected directly for a limited term, who appoints officials to assist him, which though they are also commonly called a cabinet, are not a committee of the assembly, and are not politically responsible to it. And in the United States the potential conflict of function between president and legislature is met by a variety of devices, but most distinctively by the creation of an independent system of rule-adjudication with power to rule on the constitutionality of specific actions of either of the other two branches of government.

Since there is no focus of power, this system is dynamically unstable, and its invariable tendency has been for the president to destroy the compromise by assuming, often with the aid of force, control over all functions of government. To be a true presidential state, therefore, three conditions have all to be observed.

First, the president must be elected directly by the people according to agreed rules generally regarded as fair. He must not be an hereditary ruler, be self-appointed, come to power by a military *coup*, or be nominated by the chiefs of military regime.

Secondly, he must be elected for a definite term. There is a subtle but definite difference between being elected for a series of definite terms and being in power indefinitely, but in practice one tends to lead to the other. Consequently constitutional provisions limiting presidential terms are normal, though they are often abused, if necessary by the systematic rewriting of constitutional provisions, as with the Somozas in Nicaragua. Assumption of the presidential office for life invites the corollary that the shorter the life, the shorter the term. In practice, of the seven presidents of Haiti who have been elected for 'life', only Dr François Duvalier actually died in office; his predecessors were deposed. One of the ways in which he safeguarded himself was to hold municipal elections in 1961; at the top of each ballot paper was his name, and after the votes were counted Haitians were told that they had unwittingly given him an overwhelming vote of confidence.[11]

Thirdly, the delicate balance between president and the assembly must be maintained within certain limits. The president must not be able to dissolve or suspend the powers of the assembly during its fixed term of office. In practice this is often done, as in Uruguay in 1973, by the leaders of military or military-backed regimes, making use, in most if not all cases, of emergency powers, which I shall discuss further later.[12]

To make the balance easier to attain, furthermore, the president should be elected at the same time as the assembly. Even where the elections are held simultaneously, as in the United States, different political parties may be chosen to represent the people in each of the branches of government. In the United States between 1969 and 1977 a Republican president confronted a Democratic Congress, and since 1981 a Republican president has again had to accept a Democratic majority in the House of Representatives. But in Chile after 1963 the timing of the respective terms was such that political conflict between the branches was actually made worse, though the Christian Democratic majority in congress in 1970 properly accepted the verdict of the popular vote and ratified the election of President Salvador Allende, he was unable in turn to achieve a popular majority for his proposals for radical reform.[13]

Though there must, if government is to function at all, be a close relationship between the two areas of competence, summed up in the American phrase 'checks and balances', they must be reciprocal and there must be limits on the president's ability to influence the assembly. This is not as easy as it seems. The executive president is both head of state and head of government; he owns no superior, and he can – and does – convert the ceremonial duties of his role as the one into political power for the other. Speaking on behalf of his government, particularly in foreign policy or in times of national crisis or disaster, making use of the resources of the media, and in particular being seen visibly associated with concrete evidence of achievement in the form of new roads, airports, dams or military installations, all can be used to generate or to strengthen existing support. And, as Montesquieu observed: 'It is an invariable experience that every man who has power is led to abuse it; he goes on until he finds limits.'[14]

The president, unlike the head of government in a parliamentary system, is not limited in his power to recruit and to appoint heads of departments by the need to draw them from the ranks of the assembly. Ratification of his choice, therefore, may be little more than a formality. Once appointed the heads of department are his subordinates, his secretaries, and they are politically responsible to no one else.[15] If the president's power to choose them is limited to an extent by the need to obtain congressional approval, the power to dismiss them is not, and there is a limit to how long any assembly, however powerful, can go on blocking presidential nominees. A prime minister can also reshuffle his Cabinet, but since he has to choose among his colleagues, who have each a separate and distinct electoral base, his power to do so is very much more limited.

If, on the other hand, secretaries are given the power to sit and vote in the assembly they become to an extent responsible to it, and the result is a mixed system which is neither presidential nor truly parliamentary. Peru, before 1968 and after 1980, is an example which has had a long history. A more recent, and in other respects anomalous example, is France.[16] In both, the tendency is to make the president the focus of power, whereas in the true presidential system there is no focus of power.

In the Weberian sense, the parliamentary and presidential systems as I have here described them, therefore, are 'ideal types'. Even in its homeland, in the age of the 'Imperial Presidency' and in particular under President Richard M. Nixon, there were noticeable deviations from the strict constitutional assumptions of the presidential system. The parliamentary system does not depend on such a rigid set of criteria, and, as the case of the United Kingdom shows, it can evolve within a relatively short period of time. But there must be limits to this process. Heads of republics in parliamentary systems such as France have been given more power. Monarchs, as in Sweden, have been rendered virtually powerless.[17] Yet such is the complexity of modern political systems that we cannot deduce from these facts alone either that the French President or the Swedish *Riksdag* has become all-powerful. The visible Constitutional structures are only a partial guide to the real structure of power and decision-making.

This can be even more clearly seen in the case of India, where an old dimension of organisation – federal government – has been assimilated to the structure of a parliamentary system. The Indian Constitution of 1949 modifies the traditional assumptions of federalism considerably, the basic one of which is that both federal and state governments will have clear and distinct areas of authority by providing for the federal government to impose 'President's Rule' on a state which was regarded (by the federal government!) as being unable to govern itself responsibly. Direct rule from the centre, carried beyond a certain point, would destroy federalism and create a unitary state, though the point at which this might happen could be difficult to determine with certainty. But it is quite compatible with the overall sovereignty implicit in the concept of the parliamentary system, and it required an actual *coup* by Mrs Gandhi to change the form of government radically.[18]

The key concept on which we base our assessment of these and similar changes is, in short, the concept of *participation*.

Almost all states nowadays consider that they are either democratic or aspiring to democracy. That is to say, their rulers believe that under their form of government, as far as human fallibility allows, the ultimate decisions are either taken by the people at large, or will be, as soon as they can be taught how to do it. Unhappily, there are two basic strands of thought as to what is meant by democracy. The fact that these differences involve differences of technique rather than belief makes them of as much interest to the student of comparative politics as to political philosophers, and indeed they reflect the observations of those who first formulated them of the political systems of their own day.

Both views are concerned with the process of choice by which the people select their representatives and that by which people or representatives reach decisions on specific issues. The older view, represented in ancient times by Roman practice, and in modern theory by the writings of Rousseau, see both as aspects of what Rousseau termed the general will.[19] The general will of the people is not just the will of the majority, nor even of all individual people, it is a coherent expression of the feeling of the society as a whole. It is therefore possible to say that the general will cannot be understood and interpreted by a series of individual choices, but that anyone who can perceive what the general will is can point it out and advocate its support to his fellows. This was the view of Robespierre and the Jacobins, and it is one congenial to individuals or groups under the 'mixed' constitutions of most modern societies.

The more modern view, represented by Locke and Mill among theorists, is that all government is a process of compromise, and that the general will – if it exists – cannot be arrived at except by approximation. This approximation can be arrived at by accepting the decision of the majority in all processes of choice involving large numbers, but in the self-restraint also of that majority in tolerating the views of the minority.[20] Thus a series of shifting coalitions becomes possible on individual issues. Recent American writers, such as Kornhauser, have increasingly emphasised the importance of keeping the process of choice essentially one of bargaining in a 'free market' of ideas.[21]

As already pointed out, the belief of the Communists in the absence of antagonistic conflict within their states and the role of the Party as vanguard of the proletariat necessarily implies their adherence to the general concept of the general will. A similar justification has been used by the rulers of various authoritarian systems to justify their actions as being guided by a superior form of legitimacy. Writers on these aspects of government have therefore propounded a number of schemes of ideological classification which takes these facts into account. Some have chosen to focus on the location of power in the system, others on the degree to which theory is reflected in a valid attempt to replace counting heads by a system for reaching a consensus of views. Thus Talmon distinguishes between 'representative' and 'totalitarian' democracy in his study of the conflict of the emergent ideas in the French revolutionary period,[22] while Almond and Coleman distinguish in Asia and Africa between 'Western' systems based on the acceptance of majority decision, and 'non-Western' systems in which attempts are made to include criteria of value on the process of decision, and to promote the solidarity of turbulent states by making decisions only when they command universal assent.[23] Both terminologies, however, are highly unsatisfactory, and 'competitive' and 'non-competitive' are better.

Whatever the terminology employed, the fact is that structures of similar names perform different functions in each type of system. Thus political parties, which for some 'competitive' systems are largely concerned with articulating and aggregating interests, are for the 'non-competitive' systems primarily a means of mobilising support. 'Non-competitive' systems, abhorring overt conflict, do not allow for the open operation of pressure groups, and predetermine the result of elections by various devices designed to monopolise political power for those favoured by the regime. But these facts are not the product of the differences in terminology; the terminology has been selected to reflect just those differences. To make specific areas of operational difference clear, we must concentrate on the concept of participation.

Participation may be either qualitative or quantitative. A football match involves twenty-two players, a polo match eight. That is a quantitative difference. But a football match may also involve the participation of a handful of spectators, if amateur, or of thousands, if professional, but the differences may have little impact on the performance of the players compared with the quantitative difference in the teams themselves if a member of one is sent off the field. And participation can be further restricted or enhanced, other than by simple, clean-cut numerical criteria. Thus the fact that a goal-keeper's function is to remain within a defined area of the field is counter-balanced by allowing him increased freedom to handle the ball, while the fact that other players have greater freedom on the field is limited by the fact that the goal is only of a certain size, and so on.

In politics the most important differences between modern states are the number of levels on which, and channels through which, participation can take place. There are many possibilities of participation in European states short of taking part in government itself, the actual decision-making process. There are the possibilities of, first of all, interest in politics; secondly, voting; thirdly, political organisation – taking part in some kind of mechanism designed to influence the political process, taking up party membership; possible candidature for the assembly, and actual choice to be a member of the government itself. These are all *levels* of participation involving greater involvement in the system and a greater say in what goes on. But at each level, except at the top, there are a number of alternative *channels* through which participation can be effective, and include elections or referenda, interest groups, political parties and local government organs. The same is true in, for example, China, but there the channels include the wall poster, the Red Guards, and the revolutionary committees that were features of the Cultural Revolution. And when we come to compare one country with another, we find that what varies is not simply participation, but what is considered to be political. In other words, political participation varies between one country and another with the definition of what is properly the concern of politics and what the proper way of being political is.

It is for this reason that one has to make a functional separation between one aspect of government and another, rather than a purely institutional one, because what is defined as being one thing in one country may be defined as being something quite different in another.

To take the obvious case, people participate in elections in almost all countries. But the degree of individual participation in the voting process varies from country to country, depending on what the actual likely outcome of the vote is – that is, the degree to which it is connected to the rest of the political process.

What we are immediately concerned with is the highest echelon and the choice of government itself. Why should there arise this urge for total involvement that we call Convention Theory? Why was there this period in various countries in which rule by total participation in the workings of an assembly was considered as most desirable as a form of government?

First, until the eighteenth century at least, as we have seen, this was seen as being the only logical alternative to rule by one man.[24] Rule by one man existed already under monarchy; if you wanted to have rule by an assembly, then the whole assembly had to do the ruling. Then, when this was tried in England in 1649, France in 1793 and other countries at other times, in fact, the converse also happened – total participation by the assembly led to the return of one-man rule, and the only major example of convention rule (that of the United States) which did not lead to one-man rule, did in fact lead to that compromise which we call the presidential system. These factors are therefore not independent of one another; they must be related. The reason for this seems clearly to lie in the size of the United States, and the fact that it developed not only a system of separation of powers, which did not work, for example, in France in 1791 – the 1791 Constitution they never even used – but also a federal system with power divided between the states and federal government.

Yet this idea of total participation is by no means dead. We still see it cropping up daily in talk of democracy in trade unions and universities and, in fact, if anything it is at present undergoing something of a revival in British and American government. We therefore ought to be aware of what some of the survivals that we have mean.

First of all, we have traces of it in the conduct of the assembly. Television viewers in Britain will all have seen that part of the opening of Parliament when Black Rod goes up to the door of the Chamber of the Commons. It is smartly slammed in his face and he has to knock on it. This is a relic; though no more than a relic, perhaps, of the theory that you must not interrupt the conduct of the assembly even if you are the head of state. (The fact is that the MP inside the House of Commons, who happens to be speaking at the time, is nowadays immediately told to sit down because he is out of order.)

However, the conduct of the assembly has a very real meaning in countries in which the conduct of that assembly has been more controversial. Even in the United States a major civil war has been fought within the last 150 years and this has a considerable effect on American attitudes towards the way in which things work. The United States Congress, considered on a broader scale, is characterised above all by the equality of its members. The facts show this in that they all have an equal right to speak; time in debate is allocated equally between the parties; committee places are drawn by party caucus, and this, in turn, has displaced a system in which such choices were made rigidly by seniority of service. The control of the right to dissolve parliament has not been given up because under the congressional system the calendar regulates the right to dissolve. Lastly, and most significantly, the one power which Congress has always been reluctant to yield – which the British parliament has not retained – is the right to rule the city in which it happens to meet. Almost all working presidential systems seem to be coupled with a notion of congressional control over the capital in which it meets. There may, alternatively, be different capitals for different branches of government, as in Ecuador and South Africa. Where this control has been swept away, or replaced by purely executive control, the conduct of the assembly is very seldom, in fact, free.

The second thing is that although at national level the pressures of politics do not always allow for the degree of direct participation that one might perhaps hope for, in many states the conduct of local government is subject to noticeably less rigour and control. It is still possible for many societies, for example Yugoslavia, India, Tanzania and Brazil, to permit decisions at the local level to be made by the general gathering of citizens or by a locally elected assembly, subject to some kind of overall control from the centre, but with only a very generalised degree of control.

In a British local authority there is an assembly in which, again, everybody is equal; again, the control of business is in its own hands, and it controls its own place of meeting. This is a relic of an old freedom which can operate at local level because there is a check in the over-riding national interest. The total reconstruction of local government in Britain in 1973 shows just how tenuous that freedom is.

As we shall see later, the concept of total participation also is embedded in the characteristic political structure of communist states and a handful of other socialist states too, in a special way which varies significantly from the structure of liberal democratic, presidential or parliamentary states. Both the parliamentary system and the presidential system as compromises are, moreover, subject to certain types of mutations, and these types of mutation are most inclined to happen when governments fail to resist the pretensions of small groups within the state to assert authority over the majority. There are other circumstances, but these are the ones in which most differentiation in states has occurred.

Parliamentary systems fail or mutate when the collective responsibility of the executive collapses. The problem with an executive that sits in parliament and is continuously responsible to parliament is that whether for psychological, social, or political reasons, it finds it difficult to withstand the pretensions of the assembly, which are, after all, embodied in the constitution of the state, unless it can count on the collective loyalty of its members. This is possibly the only good argument against coalition government, namely that if people rush from Cabinet meetings to give press conferences saying they think their colleagues are swine, in a very short space of time the system ceases to work, because everyone is getting so cross with one another. It is necessary, therefore, if the very close and intimate interrelationship of the executive and the assembly is to continue, for the executive to remain collective. If one man becomes paramount, then the hostility of the assembly and of others becomes focused upon that one man.

The other possibility is monopoly, and this has been a feature of those governments that have inherited the parliamentary system from a colonial country. States with parliamentary systems such as France and Britain that had colonies early in the nineteenth century have tended to implant parliamentarianism in them, and very successfully so. One need only look at the Bahamas, Canada, Australia and New Zealand for example. In these kinds of state there has been relatively little tendency to move away from it.

But a great many of the French and British colonies were acquired with great haste near the end of the last century, and the social systems, structures and decision-making processes of those states were subordinated without actually being removed. In other words, there is continuity between pre-colonial and post-colonial times, because the intervening period of colonial organisation has been relatively short. Furthermore, in protectorates such as Malaysia or Morocco, by definition, the existing social structure was left largely untouched and rule was indirect, leaving the existing decision-making mechanism substantially intact.[25] The tendency in many, but not all of these states has been away from parliamentarism, because it has been felt uncongenial in view of the colonial associations it holds. The very natural, if perhaps misplaced, desire to get back to the state of affairs as it was before colonisation began, coupled with the habit of accepting authoritarian decisions engendered by the very nature of colonial rule, make the parliamentary system with its compromises temporarily unattractive. Faced with the burdens of development, the new executive is inclined to envy the apparent freedom of action of the presidential system and to urge its adoption, as in numerous examples, Ghana and Nigeria, Zaire, Guinea, Ivory Coast, Angola and Mozambique included.[26]

This is a reasonable, predictable and understandable development. It was to be expected that a new compromise would have to be reached in new states. What is improbable is that the presidential compromise, as at present understood, is going to last for a very long time. It necessarily involves the overt conflict of interests in public, and that seems, on the face of it, very unlikely beyond the next ten or twenty years.

The parliamentary system comes to an end when one of three things happens. First of all, when the head of state assumes power, as in Germany under Hitler in 1933, or France under Pétain in

1940,[27] and the ability of parliament to function is suspended. This may be, as in Germany with the Enabling Act, with the formal approval of parliament itself. And here intimidation is obviously possible and was actually used, as it was in a different way with Mussolini's March on Rome in 1922. It is fairly easy to get a unanimous vote in favour of one man assuming all powers when there are squads of soldiers standing immediately outside the door with fixed bayonets, as rulers have discovered on many occasions. Even in England, Richard II (1377-99) held meetings of parliament with an armed bodyguard of archers at his back and he was, therefore, highly successful in his dealings with the parliaments, unlike some later rulers.[28] And, as in Czechoslovakia in 1948, the threat may be provided by foreign troops. Secondly, there is the possibility of the total suspension of the assembly. Rulers can simply physically close the doors of parliament; barricade them out; refuse to let the assembly meet – which may then, of course, go off and take an oath in a tennis court as the French did in 1789. The fact that they do this kind of thing, however, can be taken as a warning that political pressures against the executive are rather greater than it thought they were.

The third possibility – a much more sophisticated one – is where an extra-parliamentary mechanism controls the choice of the assembly. In other words, where there are not wholly 'free' elections (whatever that may mean) in the sense that anyone can be elected to the assembly, but where there is a deliberate system of control of the choice of the assembly,[29] and this system of control is controlled by the executive. It is true, to some extent, that all choices for the assembly are always controlled by something. The very existence of political parties in their role of interest aggregation mechanisms in most societies means that there is a degree of control of choice of the assembly. The only remedy against this is to invent more and varied political parties. But the control of the process of choice by the executive necessarily reduces the possibility of the parliamentary system of compromise functioning until it disappears altogether. Examples here might be the Falange in Spain after 1939 on the one hand,[30] Czechoslovakia with its National Front, the GDR with the SED, Bulgaria with the Fatherland Front, and Poland with the United Workers Party, combining the PDR and the PPS.

Presidential systems, on the other hand, collapse when collective responsibility of the assembly weakens. In the clash between a single presidency and a multiple congress, if the congress fails to function as an efficient counter-balancing unit, then, necessarily, the system fails to work properly. And it ceases to work when one of three things happen.

First of all the system may evolve into what we can call 'Democratic Caesarism', in which the state continues to be ruled by a president, and regular elections may even be held, but the system is wholly dominated by the executive power, through the abdication of power by the legislature, either voluntarily or involuntarily. So the democratic Caesar is the ruler of the presidential state, and the system is characterised by 'omnipotent executive power and a sub-servient legislature'.[31] The reason is usually that the congress lacks a real basis of dynamic conflict, because it simply doesn't have enough political clout, as Americans say, to counter-balance the force of the presidency. The presidency can deliver all the possible goods, and as long as it can continue to deliver them there is no role for congress; congress merely signs blank cheques in advance by approving the presidential budget, and endorses them afterwards by approving the expenditure. A good test of this is the regular, unopposed passage of supplementary estimates for expenditure already incurred.

This is often coupled with, or relates to, the possibility of the military taking over political power, as in Chile or Brazil. When the army takes over, clearly the presidential state does not really exist any more because the executive is not elected.

The third possibility is again that some kind of extra-assembly organ controls the choice, either of the assembly or the presidency, or both, as in Haiti under the late President Duvalier with his personal armed force, the Tontons Macoutes. The special limiting factor therefore is the army, but there are other possible forces limiting choice, the most important of which is the Party *apparat*.

An *apparat* is a complex concept, and the term itself derives from party organisation in eastern Europe. Basically, what it amounts to is that in certain one-party states a political mechanism exists for the professed purpose of changing society. It is, thus, the exact opposite of a structure such as the army, whose task it is to preserve the *status quo*.

Ghiṭa Ionescu defines the *apparat* as a network of power which controls the formal structure of power. In Communist states this network consists essentially of the Communist Party and its appendages, with the interesting consequence that an individual's status is determined not by his formal position in the state, but by his standing in the Party. But Ionescu draws his net wider to take in in non-Communist states 'any centralistic organisation which in an oppositionless state holds, in proportion to its share of responsibility in the running of the state, a smaller or larger part of the power of the state'.[32] And effectively this means a centralistic organisation which uses part of the coercive power of the state to control the rest.

Why does this happen? Simply because of the contradiction in Communist theory between the theory of democracy and the commitment to change. In such circumstances there will be, may be, are likely to be, or have been, a substantial number of people who did not like the idea of too much change. But Milovan Djilas argues, and others would support his argument, that the rise of the *apparat* is in fact the result of the petrifaction of the party, which today is composed of a 'new class' of officials who exercise their collective power to impede, and perhaps even reverse, the possibility of movement towards a more egalitarian state.

Whichever way we look at it, therefore, we cannot wholly overlook the formal structures of Communist states.[33] The Soviet Union, Poland, Hungary, Romania, Bulgaria and Outer Mongolia have Convention Theory-style governments, at least on paper. In theory they have a system of government based on soviets or some similar form of committee. In it, there is a pyramid structure of responsibility, running from the bottom to the top of the society, in which each level elects delegates to the next highest level, but the supreme control is vested in the vast assembly, in theory fully representative of the entire nation. The executive is, again in theory, only a committee of that assembly, and there is not even a formally designated head of state, only a chairman of the executive committee.

We can see the influence of Convention Theory very strongly in the Soviet Constitution of 1936. Under it the Soviet Union did not have a designated head of government – Stalin was only chairman of a committee, as was Mao Tse-tung in China. It is by no means the same thing to be a chairman as a president. A president has, or may have, executive power of his own; a chairman, notionally, only acts as a voice for the committee which he heads. It is hardly surprising that Leonid Brezhnev has preferred not to remain just a chairman,[34] as chairman of the Praesidium of the Supreme Soviet, though strictly speaking he is not yet a president.

Secondly, a very characteristic feature of the Soviet system which has been retained is the collective responsibility of everyone, at any given level, for whatever others around them may be thinking or doing.[35] Everybody is responsible for the deviation of a single individual; collective responsibility does not stop at the executive as against the legislature, or the legislature as against the executive, as in the parliamentary or true presidential systems. Collective responsibility runs throughout the society and involves collective responsibility of every group for every member of it. This again is no new phenomenon; it was no less characteristic of Spain in the time of the Inquisition or Geneva under the rule of the Saints, but it is no less coercive in its effect on the individual, since its corollary is that no deviation can be countenanced without endangering the logic of the entire structure.

What is new about it is, thirdly, the fact that the basis of control of the state is vested in a single party, and that this party claims to have a special and unique ability to decide what is in the best interests of the community as a whole. This special knowledge is not an original idea; what is original is the fact that it is regarded as being vested in a political party, and not in a religious priesthood. Political parties were, of course, well established features of politics in Europe when in 1902 Lenin first enunciated in *What is to be done?* his view of the political party in its special role as a vehicle of continued agitation for revolutionary change.[36] It is from this role, and from the fact of his seizure of power in the name of the party in 1917, from which derives the characteristic notion of the party as a permanent directing feature of government, carrying out a specific plan for change. This role, moreover, is specifically written into the Soviet Constitution of 1977.[37]

This leads, fourthly, to that distinguishing feature of Communist systems which makes us accept 1917 as a second turning-point in political development, comparable only with 1789 and the emergence of the assembly. This is the assumption by the state of complete responsibility for economic matters. As it states in the 4th Article of the 1936 Constitution of the USSR:

The economic foundation of the USSR is the socialist system of economy and the socialist ownership of the instruments and means of production, firmly established as a result of the liquidation of the capitalist system of economy, the abolition of private ownership of the instruments and means of production, and the elimination of the exploitation of man by man.

Aspirational as this inevitably is, it should be read in conjunction with Article 11:

The economic life of the USSR is determined and directed by the state national economic plan, with the aim of increasing the public wealth, of steadily raising the material and cultural standards of the working people, of consolidating the independence of the USSR and strengthening its defensive capacity.[38]

Since the control of the state is vested in the party, it follows that though the USSR has chosen to set up political forms with a strongly Convention Theory tinge, there is no reason why the same form of governmental control should not be combined with any other system of government generally accepted as democratic. This is, in fact, what has happened. What is interesting is that the control of one party was not expressly stated anywhere in the 1936 Soviet Constitution; it was merely assumed to follow from the claim made in Article 126 that the party is the sole organisation representing the working people there.[39]

Czechoslovakia and East Germany still continue to have formal parliamentary governments. In fact the German Democratic Republic adopted in 1949 a Constitution surprisingly similar to the old Weimar Constitution; the same one that one is often told was so inefficient that stable government could not be maintained in pre-war Germany, and therefore Hitler came to power. It works well enough if all political groupings are abolished except one. At the top, moreover, after an experiment with 'collective leadership' in the early 1950s, power and the title of head of state have been combined in one man long before this idea had been accepted in the Soviet Union itself.[40]

Then there is the really curious example of Yugoslavia. Yugoslavia is a 'presidential' state with an executive nominated by the assembly. It is also a federal state in a sense, registering the old divisions between Serbs, Croats and Slovenes. But it is a state also in which there is a very high degree of workers' democracy, and in which the characteristic structure of intensive participation in committees exists underneath the existence of the presidential state. Its formal head is not one man, but an Executive Council, originally created to help the executive function, and to prepare for the transition when Tito died, when it suceeded to the executive power. In other words, the two are combined together: socialism and the formal structure of the presidential state, democracy in formal structure also of the pyramid committees, so that Yugoslavia's compromise is unlike that of any other country, and unique to Yugoslavia.[41]

The People's Republic of China was originally constituted on the Soviet model after the Communist seizure of power in 1949. In the 1960s it passed through the spectacular period of the Great Proletarian Cultural Revolution, when Chairman Mao attempted to renew the state by direct participation and self-criticism. During this period the formal institutions of government were not only disused but actually in disfavour, with the sole exception of the People's Liberation Army which came to hold much of the effective power.[42] Since this period a slow return towards constitutional order has been made culminating in the writing of the 1975 State Constitution. Even this retained many of the revolutionary committees of the 1960s, a large number of which were eventually abolished and the authority of the Communist Party restored at the meeting of the fifth National People's Congress in February 1978.[43] Despite this, the structure of Chinese government resembles the 1936 Soviet version rather than the 1977 one, except that the central organ is the Executive Committee of the *Politburo*, the body of which Chairman Mao was chairman.

Cuba, on the other hand, remained quite different from other Communist states until 1975, when, under pressure from the Soviet Union, it established a series of formal state structures culminating in a National People's Power Assembly chosen by regular elections, which had, in common with the 1940 Constitution, been in suspense since 1959.[44] During this very long period Cuba resembled what in any other state in Latin America would be called 'democratic Caesarism' in that Fidel Castro, then nominally only prime minister, effectively controlled the government of his relatively small country by direct communication – radio and television. Even the formal structure of the Communist Party, though older than the state structure, came into existence relatively late to conform with the doctrine of Marxism-Leninism that a true proletarian revolution could only be led by one.[45] Here, too, the military influence has been growing until, with nine military members of the small Cabinet, Cuba began to embark on a series of overseas ventures in Africa which have interesting implications for the future role of smaller states.

The fact is that the formal structure of all states embodies the real feelings of their governments towards the participation of others, in that the most common reason that they do not work the way they are apparently supposed to do, is that they have been carefully designed not to do so. Some variation, fortunately, occurs as the art of designing political institutions is as yet by no means perfect, and so governments cannot always stop their people having an effective say. Modern states, therefore, can be divided into two categories according as the notion of participation is itself divided, and as they exist to do at least two things – satisfy demands and generate supports – which are not compatible with one another – they all depend on some sort of compromise.

All governments seek to be efficient, rich and successful. This in turn means external obligations such as maintaining a surplus on their balance of payments on overseas trade, and keeping their currency strong against the US dollar (unless, of course, they already have dollars). And for internal reasons they want, as visible signs of their success, such things as new motorways, airlines, shipping fleets, oil wells and public buildings. All of these things cost money and inconvenience people, so there is a direct conflict latent with what people would vote for if they were actually asked –

who, for example, might be yachtsmen, railway users, householders or gardeners. Since it is impossible to build a motorway with a kink in it to avoid someone's cabbage patch, or to allow people to eat Swiss chocolate if it unsettles the balance of trade, governments tell their citizens that their sacrifice is necessary for the good of the nation at large. What this means, in plainer terms, is the maintenance of the government itself in its existing framework of political obligation, by promises to benefit those who support them at some unstated time in the future.

6 How Demands are Presented

Demands upon the political system originate in the minds of individual citizens, often in a quite unformed state. They may well not be immediately recognised as political, and whether they are seen to be or not will depend on the nature of the society concerned. If he wishes to, the citizen may in most societies express his demands as an individual by speaking or writing to someone recognised as his representative in some level of government. This is as true in the Soviet Union as it is in non-Communist countries.

However, except in a very local sense, the voice of one individual in a modern society will normally carry little weight unless the demands he articulates are those of a member of the decision-making body – what Easton calls 'withinputs' or 'intraputs'. If he is not himself a decision-maker, it is most likely that his views will attract attention first in conjuction with others who share a common interest.

INTEREST GROUPS

It is now recognised that interest groups – patterns of people sharing a common interest – exist in all societies, though usually in a latent rather than an active state, waiting to be activated by a relevant issue. In a sense they cover the entire field of political interest articulation other than that of the individual, for the family can be regarded as an interest group, and many of them aggregate interests also into a common action programme. But the interest group differs from the political party (which we shall consider later) by not seeking political power for itself; it seeks merely, when it acts at all, to influence decisions taken by others.

For the purpose of comparative politics, the most useful system of classification of interest groups is that of Almond,[1] who divides interest groups into four categories.

First comes the *non-associational* which is, for the most part, latent. People do not join non-associational groups; they are born into them. They include family and kin groups, castes, classes, religious sects and ethnic groups. Membership of such groups is, at least at the beginning of their politically interested life, a given in their environment. They are defined as non-associational, therefore, indicating that they have not joined together in the specific way, they just happen to be a member of this common bond of interest.

Secondly, there is the *institutional* interest group. This includes all groupings to which one belongs by virtue of economic necessity – the need to earn one's living. They include bodies like the armed forces, police, civil servants, teachers, professional groupings generally, and other occupational groups. This does not mean strictly speaking the AMA or BMA for example as an organisation, but rather doctors as an institutional interest grouping, bound together by their common profession. In practice, at least in the United States and Britain, the two are not distinguishable. The AMA or BMA expresses the views of doctors whether the doctors like it or not, since all doctors have to belong to it. So at the institutional level we move from the more usually latent level of interest grouping to the more overt participatory level.

This is even more marked in the associational interest group. Nobody is born a member of an associational interest group, he or she opts to join one. Straddling the boundary-line between institutional and associational groups are the trade unions. It is necessary for many purposes in many countries to belong to a trade union in order to earn one's living, but in Britain they are, at least, still considered to be in some sense, voluntary bodies, as in the United States. They are therefore regarded, for most purposes, as being an associational interest group. The associational category also includes most of the various forms of pressure groups. Bodies that might be included under this heading include those which are designed to defend interests on the one hand, and those that are designed to promote interests on the other. The National Farmers Union, the American NAACP, the French Wine Growers Association, all these fall under the associational heading.

Lastly, Almond describes a category which he calls *anomic* interest groups. Anomic refers to a state of alienation from the normal processes of society, and this is indeed implicit in Almond's use of the word anomic.[2] However, Almond does not define his use of the word anomic in this sense, which is extremely confusing. Anomic bodies, to Almond, are those groupings of temporary existence which express interests for a limited period of time and have no formal organisation. He defines them as 'spontaneous irruptions from the society into the polity'.[3] Riots, demonstrations, strikes, walk-outs, and sit-ins form anomic interest groupings to Almond.

Now the interesting problem that arises straightaway is that anomic interest groupings, considered as politically active entities, in fact are not distinct from non-associational, institutional and associational groups. Some are only actions performed by established groups and the rest can be regarded as a different type of associational group – a temporary one – which happens to have only a very limited existence in duration. There are some that are institutional, and there are some that are non-associational as well, so that it might, for some purposes, be more convenient to think of anomic interest groupings as a completely separate category of political action, one in which violence becomes rather more important than discussion.[4] This point will be elaborated in chapter 11.

Almond implies, I think correctly, that no society lacks interest groups, and that for the purposes of comparative politics what is interesting is not whether or not there are interest groups – because there are going to be interest groups, if only latent, in any given society selected for study – but the preponderance of one type rather than another. However, there is an implicit suggestion in Almond that the sophistication of the society is measured by the extent to which it manages to separate off political processes from the general social world. In other words the more complex the society, the more advanced it will be. And thus, for example, India is characterised as having 'poor boundary maintenance between the polity and the society'. That is to say that the kind of social organisations which exist within Indian society also perform political purposes, and Almond considers this to be a sign of inadequate differentiation and therefore not sufficiently 'modern'.[5] In fact there is here an implicit 'traditional-to-modern continuum' of development which owes its origins to a view of political development as being something directly comparable to economic development, that can be measured in one unit, and recorded in accumulation of greater wealth, greater resources, and so forth and so on. The sophistication of the society can therefore be measured specifically in a shift from non-associational or institutional interest groupings towards institutional and associational interest groupings. As a society becomes more efficient so one will get the development of interest groups which form the basis for their hopeful views of pluralism. The non-associational survivals, such as the religious base of Northern Ireland politics for example, struck Almond and Coleman as being archaic, which is certainly correct, but does not explain why one gets this curious obsession with religion, of all things, in the more developed and industrialised end of Ireland. This suggests that political and economic development are certainly not following parallel courses.

There is, in any case, a very vocal school of opponents of this view (the Kornhauser school) who say that the more associational interest grouping occurs, the more it downgrades individual action, and the less weight, therefore, the individual has within society.[6] Although this thesis cannot be wholly sustained from a conventional perspective, of course, its testing, its examination, is undoubtedly one of the tasks of present-day comparative politics. No doubt our information on this so far is in many respects inadequate.

All these groupings are only significant in so far as they can be related to the political process. There has, in short, to be some kind of linkage. This linkage can be supplied by many sorts of organisation. But the almost universally recognised mechanism for the articulation of interests, for the communication of articulate interests to the aggregative process, and indeed for the partial or general aggregation of interests, is the political party.

POLITICAL PARTIES

Today it is generally felt that there are two main types of political party, but there are various terminologies. Communists distinguish between 'bourgeois' and 'proletarian' political parties. However, this does not appear to accord with any well defined differences in the origins of their members. American and European writers often distinguish, in another terminology, 'western' political parties which compete with other political parties, and so-called 'non-western' political parties that do not compete with other political parties.[7] Both perform the function of interest articulation as well as to a greater or lesser extent that of interest aggregation. But the fact is that it is the differences within these that we are most concerned with, and this requires us to seek a much more rigorous ground of classification than mere geographical location. In any case there are cases in which it would be positively misleading to do so – in Japan, for example[8] – so I shall term them 'competitive' and 'non-competitive' parties, as I have indicated above.

In the life of any community, at some stage, there emerges a cause of dispute or faction. The reasons are obvious enough and they have recurred again and again in the history of new nations from the American Revolution down to our own times. For almost

every practical task, and that includes *a fortiori* the task of government, there are a multitude of possible ways of doing it. And
faction, therefore, is almost inevitable in political discussion. It is
not wholly inevitable. It is possible for everyone to agree, at least
for a time, on most things. But, generally speaking, the possibilities
of disagreement increase rapidly in direct proportion to the number
of people actually engaged in the political process. By the time there
are as many people as there are in a modern industrial state the
possibilities of disagreement are not only practically infinite, they
are almost constantly exercised, which is even more important.

Competitive political parties came into existence in the late eighteenth and early nineteenth centuries in a number of European
countries, and spread rapidly, coming to be recognised not only as
existing but as having a right to exist.[9] By contrast twentieth-century
political parties have in general been created from scratch, with the
assumptions of competitiveness already established. It is interesting
to note that in the periods when political parties were still forming,
in Sweden with the Hats and Caps, or in Britain with the Whigs and
Tories, in each case the parties' name was derived from disparaging
epithets attached to them by their opponents. For example, Tory
means 'an Irish robber' and Whig 'someone who drives a horse to
look for corn' – presumably someone else's![10]

So 'competitive' political parties in Europe, and even in the
United States though there for a much shorter period, were shaped
by the slow yielding of acceptance, and a pattern of evolution which
gave them a particularly close relation to their society. Specifically,
they emerged before the old assumption that property was necessary to give one a stake in society had gone, and the age of the mass
political party had not even dawned, and so were specifically shaped
by the expansion of the franchise. In other words they came into
existence as relatively small groupings with an interest aggregation
role to play, and they expanded outwards from this into mass
organisations over a set of stages which gave them a particular kind
of rather detailed historical relationship to their societies. Twentieth-century political parties have been created as mass organisations all in one go, and this gives these parties a very much more
diffuse and less separable relationship to the interests. It means that
whereas, on the one hand, the competitive political party in its
traditional guise is much more intimately related to the interests
that it is supposed to be aggregating and therefore a better interest
aggregator on the whole, conversely, it is, or course, also much
more under the domination of those interests.

The expansion of the franchise as it happens is now almost a null
question in Europe, now that it covers all adults of sound mind over

the age of eighteen. Interestingly enough, the European countries have in fact been rather late in this. In Latin America, for a good many years, it has been possible for a married man to vote at the age of eighteen, though an unmarried man, not being a responsible member of society, could not vote until he was twenty-one. A woman there, of course, could not vote until she was twenty-five in extreme cases even thirty.[11] And no one who was illiterate could vote at all. All these formal vestiges of discrimination are now, however, very rapidly disappearing, and, with the anomalous exceptions of Switzerland and Leichenstein, universal adult suffrage is practically speaking accepted, even though it is not always implemented.

Secondly, parties are limited by their articulation, as Duverger somewhat awkwardly calls it.[12] They follow the configuration of the country in which they operate – physical, economic and demographic. They are shaped, above all, by its political structure, and in particular by the nature of the electoral system as a system of choice. Whether the most tangible prizes are to be won locally or nationally – or, in a few federal states, regionally – determines the nature of the contest for which they gear themselves.

Thirdly, the party may be limited in its possibilities on either of these counts by the nature of its ideology. Ideology is a term which has caused much argument in political science. Marx used it to refer to a system of ideas held by his political opponents, which prevented them from seeing the logically compelling nature of the real truths of politics. Gradually it lost these critical connotations as it came to be used as a handy term for distinguishing between different systems of ideas.

As a result, the proponents of ideologies still tend to regard the term as impolite when applied to their own system of beliefs, which, in general, they prefer to term philosophies. No such imputation is here intended. I use the term simply to refer to the fact that political parties thrive on ideas – within reason, and only so long as they remain or can be represented to be logically consistent with one another and with the traditional clientele of the party and their interests. Ideology thus limits the positions which a party can adopt in any given situation.

Largely for ideological reasons, no satisfactory classification of ideologies has ever been achieved, and it is highly unlikely that one will be. There is one we are all familiar with – the division of political parties into left-and right-wing parties, arising from the semicircular seating plan of the French Assembly. The symbolism of the left as the seat of true progressive thinking, assiduously propagated in Europe in the inter-war period, dies hard, even in an age when there are parties to the left of the Communists, and only two decades ago the Gaullists in France strove hard to avoid being seated on the right because of the unfavourable image it held even for them. But on the other hand the attempt to use other axes of classification for political parties is fraught with difficulties. Some stem from the indefinite nature of the enterprise since, in the nature of the case, ideologies cannot be weighed and measured scientifically. Others stem from the uncertain agreement between observers, as we have seen. But most stem from the determination of the participants themselves not to be labelled, so that a term such as populist, for example, which is very useful in studying political parties in Latin America, is bitterly resented by members of populist parties themselves.

Fourthly, when we turn to structure, we are on firmer ground. There are basically two structural types – direct and indirect.[13]

Direct parties are those mass parties in which there are direct channels of communication from bottom to top. They can be based on either of two kinds of unit – the branch and the caucus. The caucus is a small group of people who meet for a common political purpose. In Britain the origins of Liberal and Conservative political organisation stem from such groups, both at the centre and at the periphery, which, with the expansion of the franchise, found that they had a common cause to work for. Organisation at the local level was necessary because parties at the centre were dependent on it for their survival.

The branch is much more common today – political parties are formed in new states as centralist organisations which try to set up branches (like the Abbey National Building Society in English High Streets, or HFC in every American Main Street), so that they can tap sources of interest articulation and, more importantly, finance. This for them means primarily support rather than demands, although they will then receive the demands from these various areas and it will deal with them accordingly. The distinction between the caucus and the branch is quite noticeable; the caucus has some kind of independent possibilities of survival. Caucuses can regroup themselves around another party grouping, for example, as in Northern Ireland where the Unionist Party every so often breaks up, selects a new leader who invents a new Unionist Party, writes a new Constitution, and so on, yet all the same people all seem to be taking part in the same game all the time.

The branch of the Labour Party in Britain which attempted to do the same kind of thing would be disowned, and a rival organisation would be set up in its place which would have the official cachet of being approved by Transport House.[14]

Direct organisation relates the individual in his membership of the caucus or branch directly to the political party in the sense of being a group of rulers of the country potential or actual, or potential or real. A constituent can write directly to his MP. In the direct political party there is some kind of implied direct membership; the individual has a direct relationship to those people who are engaged in the political process of decision-making.

The indirect political party, of course, also depends on the branch, but the branch is then related to it through a degree of hierarchial structure. A natural tendency, perhaps, in very large countries is to create a pyramid structure of relationships from one level to another. You might think, of course, this must be a sign of tremendous technical sophistication. In fact, in a primitive society such as Tonga, there is a very elaborately hierarchically structured political process which depends entirely on the giving of presents of food at each level. The grower presents food to his local headman according to a certain ritual; some of it is put in the back of a Land Rover and rushed off to the next level of hierarchical integration, the local governor of the district, and there presented to him. Then a tenth of that is presented to central government, and so it goes on. The whole structure is very complex, in fact, even in what to our untutored eyes would appear to be a 'primitive' society. Indirect structure is not, therefore, a sign of modernisation, it is just a sign of good organisation; and good (or bad!) organisation people are quite capable of attaining at any stage of their economic development.

But the branch is not the only possible form of organisation. It is also possible to organise the political party on a cell basis. This is particularly useful where the central government dislikes rival political parties and therefore the rival must be clandestine. The other possibility is to organise it like an army, where everyone is subject to central control but there are a number of junior officers or NCOs whose duty it is to carry out central orders. This is the so-called militia-structured political party, and the fascist movement of the 1930s was of this type. The idea of organising a political party on a kind of quasi-military basis is very attractive to people of certain political persuasions, and it is also very effective for limited purposes. As Duverger points out, these two forms tend to occur together.[15]

The fifth criterion which we can use to distinguish political parties is the criterion of membership. Is it a cadre political party or a mass political party? Does it intend to have a mass membership? Is membership open to all, or is it limited to those cadres who have passed through a process of training and initiation? The existence of such tests is certainly not a sophisticated, modern idea: they are, it seems, one of the most primitive social rituals marking the stage of transition to full adult citizenship rights.

The existence of tests of membership – other than the formal paying of dues – has significant implications for the nature of the political party. It cannot therefore be an associational body open to all, but must be more narrowly defined in terms of non-associational or institutional membership. Thus candidates for membership for the CPSU (Communist Party of the Soviet Union) must be nominated, fulfil certain conditions, and be accepted; currently only some 5 per cent of the Soviet population are members.[16]

Ferdinand Tönnies, whose distinction between community *(Gemeinschaft)* and company *(Gesellschaft)* is fundamentally the same as that between non-associational and institutional groups, proposed a third type of organisation distinct from either, namely the order *(Bund)*, which caters for all the needs of its members. Ironically, in view of its particular association with Fascist parties in the historic past, this category is perhaps best represented today among competitive political parties by the Mapai of Israel.

Lastly, political parties differ by the criterion of recruitment – namely, how are their leaders chosen?

If, despite Sartori, 'personalist' parties are regarded as parties, then in some cases the leader chooses the party, and not the other way round. Hitler held party card no.7 in the NSDAP (National Socialist Workers Party) – but who could possibly have suceeded him as Führer? There could never have been, and could not be in logic, a Führer training-school. Even a man who rises to unusual eminence in an established party, such as Roosevelt, Stalin or Churchill, takes care not to provide for the succession of a man who could challenge him while he still holds power; and of their three successors, only Truman, a man with an independent fount of power in the American political system, managed to survive long, and he had the extra advantage of constitutional arrangements designed to maximise his strength.

It is, of course, the hallmark of a well institutionalised party that it does not matter whether it has a good leader or not, the system survives despite him. Some leaders, such as Truman himself, or Attlee in the United Kingdom, seem to lack charisma, yet they grow in office and develop their own personalities in their years of power. But not all politicians do grow in office: some even shrink. In a stable party with a strong organisational base continuity will be maintained until public support returns.

The question here is, do the leaders of political parties in a given country become leaders because they start their own parties? If so we can expect to see a very large number of parties of very short life with little or no institutional continuity, and we may well feel, with Sartori, that such bodies do not really deserve the name of party at all.[17] Many have actually taken the name of their leaders for their designation, but others which have adopted a more ideological designation, such as the Justicialist Party of Perón in Argentina, have scarcely survived the deaths of their founders before they begin once more to be resolved into the factions which, properly speaking, they are.[18]

Parties, in the true sense of the word therefore, are distinguished by permanence of structure, a deliberate attempt to win membership, and orderly procedures for recruitment of leaders at higher levels. Parties grew up in Western Europe in the nineteenth century, and to this day there, and in other parts of the world where similar views prevail, the ideal form of politics is seen as involving universal mass participation in universal militant parties free to operate in a highly aware population. General participation in universal militant parties is, in fact, to the people who live in these areas, the distinguishing feature of democracy, and the parties they have, therefore, are direct in structure, mass in membership, with institutionalised recruitment patterns, and non-ideological in their appeal for votes.

The interesting thing is that despite this ideal, in a number of 'western' states there are single-party systems to which no effective opposition is manifest, but where there do not appear to be any very good reasons why such an opposition might not develop. We do not, of course, assume that all single-party states enjoy the support of all the people who live in them; we are referring here only to those in which opposition parties enjoy some freedom to organise in a sufficiently aware population.[19]

The example of the Congress Party in India seems to illustrate both the reasons for this situation, and the limitations on it. There the party of Nehru enjoyed its initial hegemony as the combined effect of its leadership of the struggle for Indian independence coupled with the presence of Pakistan as a target for organisational and individual hostility. Nehru himself strengthened this position through the international good will and attention India obtained as the result of advocating, on behalf of smaller and less influential countries, a theory of their place in the world which they found congenial. But basically the supremacy of the Congress Party was maintained as the result of its success in monopolising patronage and being able to 'deliver' on its political promises.

The importance of these rewards was such that, regardless of the intentions of the national leaders, local political activists had no reason whatsoever to see the monopoly challenged. As Turkey found previously, and Mexico is finding today, in these circumstances it is extremely difficult to develop a second competing party so long as a single ruling party controls national political life and with it the national economy. Effectively, the only real possibility of such rivalry developing will come from competition within the ruling party, which is most likely to occur as the result of changes within the social order precipitated by a crisis.

If the crisis arises outside the community, however, the effect may be very different – to unite rather than to divide the political community. And in countries where the inhabitants perceive a constant external threat the compulsion to form or to maintain a single party is overwhelming. For ideological reasons, namely the belief that the bourgeois world will stop at nothing to destroy them, Communist states experience this compulsion. In the case of the Soviet Union it rests to some extent on a real historical foundation, the invasion of Russia by the allies in 1919, and the experience of German attack in the Great Patriotic War (1941-5). But in other European Communist states it rests more on the fear that without the Soviet Union their regime cannot survive. What I am suggesting, in fact, is that the nature and structure of the party system in these one-party states cannot be explained by internal factors alone, but must be sought in the wider context of world politics.

Is there then a similar explanation for two-party and multi-party systems? As regards two-party states, it seems significant that they grew up in the period before the control of the economy became an accepted part of the burdens of government. This being the case, the government of the day did not enjoy the ability to use these constraints to cut off opposition. It is the very sophistication of modern governmental control over banking, imports and economic production that enables it to discriminate against its political opponents in a way so subtle that the necessary resources for opposition are hard to accumulate unless a base for them can be found on foreign territory. Two-party systems, also, seem to be associated most effectively with regional strongholds or bases as in Britain, the United States or Colombia, and most often rooted in a conflict between centre and periphery as in Australia, or between two co-equal regional centres with pretensions to national leadership, as with the Liberals and Conservatives in Nicaragua. In such regional strongholds, economic resources and political strength go hand in hand.

Finally, therefore, it is for ideological reasons, centring on their desire for control of the entire economic system, that the non-competitive, one-party states are created.[20] They believe that their formula is the sole one for future success. They are future-directed in that they believe that their role is to modify society in a very specific way. Hence the party as a vehicle for what people want must give way to an instrument for compelling people to accept what they are supposed to need.

All political parties, whatever the nature of their system, operate in a process of ultimate choice, which either directs their decisions or enforces them. Fundamental to this process of choice is the electoral system, which, as we shall see, is capable of considerable elaboration, but may equally be very simple indeed. It is at this point of choice that the party changes from a body intended to present demands, into one which is designed to mobilise support. This is done by permitting the public at large a carefully graded share of participation in the formal process of choosing representatives, provided that that share is compatible with the continued maintenance of the governmental system. If that is not possible, as we shall see later, other parts of the system come into play and the elections are nullified or re-run under conditions which will give the right answer.

As Sartori warns us, no country has yet passed from a one-party to a multi-party system, or vice versa, without a fundamental discontinuity in its political process, namely, the use of force.[21]

7 How Support is Shown

Elections are extremely interesting, above all to those who take part in them. Certainly there is nothing like practical experience in taking part in elections to show the possibilities they offer for enjoyment and otherwise. On the other hand, many people who do take part in elections become so keen on them that they come to believe that they are what politics is all about, but that is not true, as is easily shown by the fact that many political systems have little or no place for them.

Elections are a process of choice. But they are not necessarily a choice between alternatives, and, if they are, they are seldom if ever a simple process of choice. Most electoral systems, in fact, are required to enable the electorate to do at least two rather different things at the same time. One is to choose candidates, the other is to register the approval of certain policies.[1] Now it is not wholly possible to register approval or disapproval of any specific policy by the choice of candidate, because candidates do not necessarily agree with one another on specific policies even where they regard themselves as being of the same party or holding very similar views. There are, moreover, numerous policies to be accounted for, many of which may seem relevant neither to an individual candidate, nor to the electors in the area in which he is standing. All elections, therefore, involve some compromise between things as they ought to be and things as they are.

The nature and importance of elections within any given society depends in the first instance on the concept of agreement, or consensus as it is often termed, in that society. The unanimity theory holds that society must express Rousseau's *volonté générale* or general will – the true wish of all the inhabitants.[2] This will particularly be the case where elections are seen as the ratification of policies, since agreement on policies naturally involves the reaching of a common view by all concerned. If agreement on policies is not essential, and the most important thing is to choose men to carry them out, then the majority theory will serve. It will be sufficient to count heads and give the decision to those who have the greater numbers. Indeed, to them may well be delegated the task of doing all those day-to-day things that the rest of society does not wish to be concerned with. This involves a degree of sophistication, so that we shall find it best to begin with unanimity systems.

UNANIMITY SYSTEMS

Unanimity systems claim our attention first for three reasons. First of all, they are the ideal of political philosophers; secondly, they appear to have come first in historical time, and to have formed the basis upon which all other systems of choice have been erected; and thirdly, they remain the daily principle of everyday choice in small communities everywhere, even where more complex systems have been developed for making choices of representatives or policies on regional or national level.

Examples are all around us. Many forms of committee, from church organisations to university senates, will go to enormous lengths to avoid the divisive consequences of taking a vote, and will deliberate at enormous length in the hope that a general agreement will be reached. Often there will be an expression, usually by the chairman, of what the Quakers call 'the sense of the meeting'; that is to say, the policy which no one person has actually advocated but which combines the salient features of all those principal policies which have been advocated. Similar behaviour has been noticed in many other societies, from the Soviet Politburo to the Indian *panchayats* or the *cofradias* or fraternities of Central American villages. Wherever it occurs, it is another example of the belief that reasonable men, discussing a range of policies, ought to be able to arrive at a just and fitting solution which is not necessarily likely to result from the mere counting of heads.

Indeed it is possible, as Duncan Black has shown, to prove mathematically that in many kinds of issue the mere counting of heads will not produce the answer that most people want. It can, and often does, produce the solution that is wanted by almost nobody.[3] This mathematical demonstration, moreover, is quite independent of the fact that the rationality of group decisions, however small the group, is limited by their human nature. Discussion can be terminated by irrelevant factors long before the point of rational agreement is reached; such factors include the fatigue of the participants, their desire to get up and move around, to have a cup of tea, to go home and have dinner, or the fact that the bar opened ten minutes earlier. And with larger groups the problems are considerably worse, and no one can pretend that if you get, say, a hundred people sitting in a hot, overcrowded room after several hours of discussion they really reach the most rational possible conclusion, unless it is to postpone the whole debate to a later and more suitable time.

At this point, too, come into play the many tricks by which individuals seek to steer the course of the decision in the direction they favour. These tricks, particularly those open to committee chairmen, are indeed as lovingly described in that fundamental work *Microcosmographia Academica*, which remains of perennial importance to all students of committee behaviour everywhere, and not just in universities.[4] And no doubt it was the observation of them, a generation before Cornforth, by Charles L Dodgson (Lewis Carroll) which set that mathematician and logician to devise a system of choice by which policies could be selected by small groups on the basis of a mathematical procedure. This system, a modification of what he termed the 'Method of Marks', involved each member listing the policy options before him, including that of not doing anything; if a vote on the agreed list failed to produce a majority for any single proposal, then each issue would be voted on in turn against every other, and if this produced a cyclical majority (A beat B, B beat C, C beat A) there should be no decision, this evidently being the favoured option. Significantly enough, on the most important occasion on which this method is known to have been used, the Fellows of Christ Church agreed to combine two proposed policies, rather than to accept any one of them.[5]

Obviously this is not something you can do when you have to choose candidates, rather than policies. You cannot combine two or more candidates, though it is only fair to say that you can choose a candidate who is not on the original list by way of compromise (a 'dark horse'). How then, otherwise, do you choose candidates who command the unanimous consent of the electors?

Before answering this question, we must ask another. How relevant is the question of choice? If you believe, as the Athenians did, that all citizens are equally well fitted to hold any office of state, then you might as well do as they did, and choose your candidates by lot.[6] Arguably this is the most democratic way, and certainly it is the only way which is at least as fair as holding a vote. If the House of Lords is ever to be reformed in the United Kingdom, it would be an excellent idea to replace it with a Chamber selected by lot, by electronic means, from all adult citizens, to serve for a year at a time. Such a Chamber could be a really effective check on the House of Commons, which would in itself probably be a very good thing. No doubt its members would not have the specialist knowledge of a professional body of representatives, but they would not share their prejudices, and in any case election is not a good way of choosing people with specialist knowledge, as those Greeks discovered who tried to choose their military commanders that way. It may or may not be a good idea to have a large number of lawyers in parliament, since parliament's job is to make laws, but if it is, then a better way of ensuring that members had the necessary legal knowledge would be to set them a competitive examination.

If, secondly, the question of choice is irrelevant because the office is powerless, then the methods by which it is filled become quite meaningless. Heredity, for example, has in the past been an essentially random process, and it may do as well for selecting formal offices of state as any other. The Greeks retained it, curiously enough, to a late stage in the selection of priests, when secular offices had long since been made the subject of popular choice. But notwithstanding the aspirations of the short-lived Central African Empire, or of brief dynastic succession in republics like Nicaragua, heredity is not normally adopted as a constitutional device today.

On the other hand, when the principle of democracy is applied too literally to an election the results are curious. For if everyone is equally worthy, then there is no need to make a choice, and the electors may find themselves confronted with a single slate of candidates which they have only to ratify. This is the case, notably, in the Soviet Union, where the elector can either drop an unmarked ballot paper into the box, thus voting automatically for the single name on it, or he can enter a polling booth and cross the name off. Consequently, to avoid the imputation of disloyalty it is 'not done' to vote in secret, unless you are a very high party dignitary, so the right to cross names off is a dead letter, at least as far as elections to the Supreme Soviets of the Union Republics and of the USSR itself are concerned.

If the right is exercised at city or province level, then it is ineffective.

At elections to village, settlement or district soviets, however, the right is exercised and a limited number of candidates do fail to get majorities: in June 1973 eighty candidates were rejected in this way. A second election is then held with a fresh official candidate, nominated, as before, by a section of the CPSU or of a recognised social organisation, such as a trade union, factory or farmers' collective, *Komsomol* or cultural society, often one recognised as having the right to nominate to that seat. Candidates, even for the Supreme Soviet of the USSR, do not have to be members of the CPSU. In the 1970-4 Supreme Soviet, for example, 421 of the 1517

Deputies (27.8 per cent) were non-party members.

In Poland the *Sejm* contains officially a coalition of parties, and elections are held by the list system. Only one list is nominated for the seats to be filled, giving rise to the possibility of crossing off some names rather than others. As early as 1958 this facility was used, though not to any great extent, and certainly not to the extent that any one candidate was actually deposed. It has been suggested, netherless, that the ruling party is keenly alert to any evidence from the electors that a particular candidate does not enjoy the popularity of his fellows, and may take care to see that he is given a less prominent task to do in the future, thus preserving the principle of unanimity, but at least taking note of the electorate's views.[7]

There are other parts of the world in which the fact that only one candidate is presented for election is not regarded by many people, and particularly perhaps not by Russians or Poles, as a sign of unanimity. The single candidate election (*candidato unico*) or plebiscite has been a feature of Latin American systems since the early years of the last century, even before Louis Napoleon seized power in France in 1851 and ratified his *coup d'état* by a plebiscite that year; and confirmed his self-appointment as Emperor in 1852 by a second plebiscite.[8] Sometimes the candidate himself does not allow anyone else to stand, but perhaps more frequently no one else seriously thinks there is much point in trying, or opposition parties fail to agree on a candidate, as in Mexico in 1976. The point is that here we are not talking of meaningless offices, nor are we, in general, talking of legislatures where seats may be keenly contested in the very states where the president holds absolute power, as in Brazil since 1968. We are here talking of presidential elections, where one man, however elected or chosen, will in the end represent an entire nation with all its cross-currents of opinion. Clearly, it is an impossible task. We can scarcely be surprised therefore that it is seldom well performed.

PLURALITY SYSTEMS

Next to the principle of unanimity in order of age comes the idea of a plurality, as it is termed in the United States, or, as it is known in Britain, a simple majority. In the United States a majority means one more than 50 per cent of all the votes cast, and so the American terminology offers less possibility of confusion and is worth retaining on that account.

The first attempts to reach a mathematical approximation to the views of the people in a given area were certainly not devised by political scientists, and they were not devised by people of much mathematical skill, so the concept of a plurality, being the simplest, was easily adopted. The fact is that it did not really matter that such a simple method was used until political parties came to be accepted features of the political landscape, it was just when they were – towards the end of the eighteenth century – that the French Encyclopaedists, and in particular the scholar and mathematician Condorcet, began first to study possible alternatives which gave less peculiar results.[9]

The only plurality system still used is the single member, single ballot system (*scrutin unique à un tour*) used in the United Kingdom, the United States, Canada, New Zealand and South Africa. Under it the country is divided into geographical constituencies each of which will return one Member. On the appointed day the electors vote for one candidate by marking a cross on a ballot paper; the candidate who has a plurality of the votes, even if he lacks a majority, is declared elected. If a tie occurs, as it frequently has done at English municipal elections, and recounts fail to disclose an error of counting, the tie is broken by the drawing of lots.

Table 3   Caithness and Sutherland, 1945-70

	1945	1950	1951	1955	1959	1964	1966	1970
Con.	5564	6969	9814	10453	–	4662	4662	5334
Lab.	5558	5767	6799	5364	6438	6619	8308	8768
Lib.	5503	6700	3299	2674	–	7894	8244	6063
Ind.Con.	–	–	–	–	12163	2795	–	–
SNP	–	–	–	–	–	–	–	3690
Maj.	6	269	3015	5089	5725	1275	64	2705
Result	Con. (gain)	Con.	Con.	Con.	Ind.	Lib. (gain)	Lab. (gain)	Lab.

The system, then, is exceptionally simple, but it does have disadvantages. Locally these are well illustrated by the example of the constituency of Caithness and Sutherland in Scotland in 1945, where only some sixty votes separated the winner of the three candidates from the bottom of the poll, which was where the sitting Member ended up. (Table 3).[10] The subsequent history of the constituency, the boundaries of which have since remained unaltered, shows an even more remarkable sequence of anomalies, as will be seen. Nationally the system merely generalises such anomalies, so that in the general election in Britain in February 1974 the Conservatives obtained the most votes, but the Labour Party got the most seats, so that it was they who formed the new government despite the fact that in a three-party election the overwhelming majority of the electorate had voted against them.[11]

In fact in the United Kingdom since 1945 at no election has the winning party obtained an overall majority of the votes cast, and in the American presidential elections of 1960, 1968 and 1976 the same problem occurred.[12] And it should not be forgotten that it was by the same phenomenon that in South Africa in 1948 the Nationalists obtained 51.6 per cent of the seats, with only 40 per cent of the votes cast, and, having once obtained power, proceeded to change the entire structure of government and society so that they could not be deprived of power by any legal, or even illegal, means.[13]

Lastly, the use of the single member, single ballot system results in what A.J. Milnor calls (I think accurately) 'the blatant punishment of parties of limited appeal and the reward of pragmatic competitors'.[14] In the United Kingdom this means that the Liberal Party can get, as it did in February 1974, 6 million votes for only a handful of seats, while Nationalist parties, hitherto even more unfairly treated, were suddenly given a quite disproportionate importance in the balance of seats in Parliament.[15] Of course, the very existence of the Liberal Party proves that it does not eliminate all variety of opinion; it would hardly have been acceptable for so long if it did. Nor did it prevent the rise of the Labour Party as a third party at the beginning of the twentieth century. What it did do was to accelerate its arrival as the second party, just as it did with the Republicans in the United States between 1854 and 1860. Since then no third party has gained more than ephemeral success in the United States. On the other hand, in each country, the comment has long been fairly made that the two parties left contesting for supreme power have increasingly come, as they strive to capture the 'middle ground', to resemble one another, though this has recently been reversed in both cases with consequences that have yet to be seen.

Hence, under this system the big rewards are allocated as the result of the capture of a rather small group of so-called 'floating voters' whose votes in a rather small number of constituencies – about eighty (12.5 per cent) in the United Kingdom – determine the outcome.[16] And if there is a really serious criticism of the system it is not so much that minorities have very little say, but that the vast majority have very little either, as their massive votes, piled up in so-called safe seats for one or another party, contribute very little to the result, and so can virtually be taken for granted by the party managers in determining party policy and strategy. In other words, though nationally the balance in both Britain and the United States may come out about right, it is the result of good luck, not good management.

Now the problem with good luck is that it is always liable to run out when you need it most. And when you need it is not when you are composing a legislature, such as the British House of Commons or the American Congress, but when you are choosing a government. Under the parliamentary system this is done indirectly by the choice of individual members of parliament of the majority party or parties, and they have to live with the result, which makes them appropriately cautious. It is not surprising, therefore, that when people have sought to impose some check on the choice of an executive president (or governor of a state, or mayor of a city), they have usually chosen to have the selection of the people ratified by the legislature. This, it should be emphasised, does not make the plurality system a majority one, but in theory it should make the president more generally acceptable.

In practice, however, it merely introduces new complications. Thus in 1970 in Chile, Salvador Allende, candidate of the Popular Unity (UP) coalition, secured 35 per cent of the popular vote between three candidates and so a narrow plurality. Congress had therefore to ratify the election, but the majority of his opponents, being committed to the principle of popular choice, felt impelled to accept the plurality as the expression of the popular will.[17] Instead, however, of accepting the limitations of his position, Allende then proceeded to carry out a very far-reaching programme of social change, culminating in the formation of large-scale armed movements forcibly seizing and redistributing land without any form of legal sanction, and ultimately the army stepped in, deposed Allende, seized power, and having once seized it refused to give it up, leaving Chile with a totally unconstitutional regime.

MAJORITY SYSTEMS

Leaving aside the question of the numerous other factors that contributed to this unhappy result, what could the Chileans have done to their Constitution which might have helped to ensure a presidential majority? They could have adopted a majority system of choice, as indeed their neighbours the Argentines had done on the other side of the Andes, where they had a second ballot, or 'run off' election as it is known in the American states, between the leading contestants. A number of countries, especially France under the Fifth Republic (1958-), use the same system in the choice of their legislatures.

As applied to presidential systems, the second ballot merely means that the top two candidates have to fight it out at a second round, thus ensuring that one must have a majority of the votes cast. This certainly does not guarantee that there will be no argument, and the history of Argentina since 1955 demonstrates that even the best constitutional arrangements are useless if key people are determined to disregard them. But given goodwill it is a simple and effective device.

In France, elections to the National Assembly are conducted on the same system (*scrutin unique à deux tours*).[18] The country is divided into 491 constituencies, each returning one Deputy. Two ballots are held on successive Sundays. On the first ballot only those candidates who achieve a majority of the votes cast in the constituency are elected, provided also that they are the choice of at least 25 per cent of the registered electors. In the remaining constituencies all candidates who have achieved in the first ballot at least 12½ per cent of the votes enter the second ballot, in which a simple plurality suffices to elect. In 1978 on the first ballot only sixty-eight of the 491 seats were filled.[19]

Though this is a proper majority system it still has its faults. As applied to a single constituency, it gives a reasonably fair result; but applied to the country as a whole, in France, the result is by no means proportional. In 1978 the parties of the left, for example, obtained 49 per cent of the votes on the second ballot but still received only 40 per cent of the seats (182). This is because the population size of the constituencies varies very considerably, and this variation in size leads in France, as in Britain, to the piling up of useless majorities in many seats which happen not to return members which support the government.[20] The same phenomenon used also to be true of the United States, but as the result of a Supreme Court decision there the 1960s saw a thorough reapportionment of the congressional districts and other electoral districts in the search for more exact proportionality,[21] a move which has so far been postponed in the United Kingdom where the advantage of the present system to the Conservative Party is of the order of 3 per cent.

A second type of majority system involves holding the second ballot not afterwards, but before the main election. This is the system, invented in the United States, of the 'primary election'. Electors who register as members of one or another political party may take part in an official ballot to select the candidates of that party in their area or district. Where there is not more than one party likely, in normal circumstances, to win, and that means in about two-thirds of the United States, this system will not guarantee a majority, but it will at least ensure there is some kind of election. This situation, from the region with which it is most often associated, is often termed 'the southern primary', and in states such as Florida, where a large number of party factions might otherwise result in the election of a candidate with very little popular support, a second primary election is required if a majority is not achieved on the first round.[22]

The third type of majority system is the most logical of the three, since there is no second ballot at all, the process of forming a majority being combined in one. This is the alternative vote, as used in Australia for elections to the Federal House of Representatives. Here the country is divided into single member constituencies as before, but the voters, instead of making a single mark on their ballot paper, number their candidates in order of preference. If no one candidate secures a majority on first preferences, the second preferences of the bottom candidate are added to them, and so on until a majority is achieved.

Unhappily, even the alternative vote does not seem to work very well. Between 1900 and 1951 some 77 per cent of successful candidates achieved a majority without it, and in only a handful of cases, it seems, would the result have been different under the single member, single ballot system.[23] The figures alone, on the other hand, say nothing of the situations from which they arose, and it is probable that the system, which is widely used in non-governmental organisations with small memberships, does much in these circumstances to avoid embarrassment. It is open to the same objections as the systems earlier discussed that nationally it does little or nothing to produce a result which is proportional overall.

PROPORTIONAL SYSTEMS

Before truly proportional electoral systems became generally known, there were a number of attempts to improve older systems. A few of these semi-proportional systems are still used. The *limited vote*, by which the elector has fewer votes than there are seats to be filled, was used for a few constituencies in Britain between 1867 and 1885, and ensures at least some representation of minorities. It is still used in Gibraltar. The extreme form of this system, the *single non-transferable vote* in a multi-member constituency, has been used in Japan in election to the Diet since 1900. And another variant, the *cumulative vote*, where the elector has as many votes as seats but can give any or all of them to any candidate, was used in Cape Colony from 1850 to 1909, and after 1870 in school board elections in the United Kingdom. In the United States it is still used in Illinois.[24]

Each of these systems in different ways lessens to some extent the importance of party membership to the candidate. It is, accordingly, ironic that the first truly proportional systems to be devised, and those still most widely used, are the list systems, which have exactly the opposite effect.

Under the list system (*scrutin de liste*) the country is divided into multi-member constituencies, which may be simply the existing provincial or regional boundaries. The elector casts a vote not for an individual candidate, but for the party list of his choice. The votes are then counted and seats allocated to each party in proportion to their respective totals. In the simplest form of the system the candidates are chosen in the order simply in which their names appear on the list, and under this system, used for example in France in 1945 and 1946, great power is given to the parties and within them to the local general secretaries, whose names tend to appear at the top of the lists.

There are two ways of making the allocation. The simpler is also the earlier: the largest remainder system (*le plus fort reste*). Here the number of votes cast is divided by the number of seats to be filled to give a quota. Seats are then allocated to parties for each complete quota they have received, and the one not allocated by this method goes to the party with the largest remainder – hence the name. Unhappily this system, which favours small parties and for just this reason was retained in Paris in the 1951 and 1956 elections, is also open to manipulation by any large party that has the ingenuity or courage to divide itself into two or more parts. It has therefore been superseded by the d'Hondt system, or system of the largest average (*la plus forte moyenne*).[25]

Under this system the seats are distributed between the parties in such a way that each party has as near as possible the same average number of votes per seat. The arithmetic is quite simple if on the face of it the reasoning behind it is inscrutable. The totals cast for each party are set out in order of magnitude, and below them the results of successive divisions by 2, 3, 4, etc., of each of the larger values to the last value *before* that achieved by the smallest party. The figures thus produced are then arranged in rank order, and that one corresponding to the number of seats to be filled, the 'electoral quotient', is used in the same fashion as the quota in the largest remainder system to determine the allocation of seats. Any remainders are then disregarded.[26]

This system favours large rather than small parties, and again for this reason was used in France in 1951 and 1956 for all constituencies outside Paris. But it was not intended to have its usual effect, which in this case would have been the over-representation of the extremes of the Communists on the left, as well as the Gaullist RPF on the right.

It was therefore used only with the ingenious addition of the *apparentement*, a provision that any party *or coalition* obtaining a majority of the votes in a *département* would receive all the seats of that *département*. This blatantly unproportional feature of an otherwise apparently proportional system did not work perfectly, but it worked well enough in 1951 for the centre parties to get 60 per cent of the seats in the Assembly for only 51 per cent of the votes, and for the Communists to get only 16 per cent of the seats for 24.8 per cent of the votes.[27]

Other modifications of the d'Hondt system have generally been made in the direction of greater choice by the elector of individual representatives. The most spectacular case in which this has not been done is Israel, where the whole country forms one vast constituency, the optimal condition for proportionality, but at the cost of the isolation of the elector from his representative, made evident by the fact that over half the members of the Knesset live in Tel Aviv.[28] The unmodified system is also used in Turkey. It has been modified to enable choice of one candidate in Belgium, the Netherlands and Denmark; of more than one candidate within one list in Italy, Norway, Sweden and Greece; and of candidates from more than one list in Finland, Luxemburg and Switzerland (National Council). In recent years its use has spread to other parts of the world too, notably to Argentina, Guatemala and Guyana.

A very different proportional system was devised by the Allies for West Germany, and has been retained every since. In 1977 a modified form of it was proposed governmentally for adoption in Mexico, where since 1963 the basic single member, single ballot system had been modified by the addition of extra members to increase opposition representation. It is correctly described as a mixed system.

In West Germany, the country is divided into 248 single member constituencies. There are also 248 seats allocated by region (*Land*) to the political parties to make the overall balance of parties in the Bundestag proportional. Hence the voter has two votes, one for a candidate and one for a party.

Counting begins by totalling all second (party) votes on a national basis. Then all parties that have achieved at least 5 per cent of the national vote, or three elected seats, are allocated a total number of seats in proportion to their national vote. These seats are then divided by *Länder*. Meanwhile, as will already be evident, the first (candidate) votes will have been counted by constituency and the results declared. The number of directly elected seats achieved by each party in each *Land* is then deducted from their proportional total, and the balance made up from the party list of that *Land*. In the rather rare eventuality that it has won *more* directly elected seats in any given *Land* than its national share would give it, it is allowed to keep them, and the overall number of seats in the Bundestag is increased by that number (*überhangsmandaten*). A by-product of the system is that, as is usual with list systems, there are no by-elections; in the event of a vacancy occurring, the next name is selected from the regional list.[29]

The West German system is of course the product of a compromise between the three rather different electoral traditions of the allies, and was designed to avoid the multi-partism of the pre-war Weimar Republic (1919-33), which had used the unmodified d'Hondt system. As Lakeman points out, the same number of parties had in fact existed under the single member, second ballot system used before 1918, and the causes for their number lay in the nature and complexity of German society and not in the electoral system;[30] and Duverger confirms that, though proportional systems tend to preserve a multi-party system, they do not appear to act very strongly to create one.[31]

If, however, the West German system was based on a misconception, it succeeded excellently. The number of parties represented dropped sharply during the 1950s to leave the country with a stable 'two-and-a-half' party system giving a strong government regardless of which party or combination of parties was in power. And, despite this, the results, considered nationally, have been strikingly proportional, while to date the ability of the parties to manipulate the lists has been used with reasonable restraint.[32]

Under the third and most proportional system, however, party influence is reduced to a minimum, for the simple reason that it is the only system which enables the individual elector to choose between individual candidates regardless of party which still gives an accurate overall balance of party representation. This is the system known in the United Kingdom as the single transferable vote (STV), and in the United States and Australia as the Hare System, after Thomas Hare who invented it in 1857, two years after it had been devised independently by C.C.G. Andrae in Denmark. It is used in Australia for the Federal Senate, for the Upper House in New South Wales and the Lower in Tasmania, in Ireland for both Houses, in Malta, and for the South African Senate. In the country where it was invented it was used from 1917 to 1949 for the election of university representatives, and is considered the best system for the Northern Irish and the Scots, but not so far for the English or Welsh, or at least not for those who have not had a university education.[33]

It is not necessary to have a university education to understand STV, however, and one need not be more than literate to use it. All the elector has to do is to mark on his ballot paper an order of preference (1,2,3,4, etc.) for the listed candidates, and drop his paper into a box. Such arithmetical problems as then arise are handled entirely by the returning officer, who undeniably has to enjoy the confidence of the contestants.

Under STV the country (or area) concerned is divided into multi-member constituencies which should, for best results, each return five or more representatives. (In Ireland a very large proportion of the constituencies return only three members of the Dáil, the balance of which is in consequence somewhat distorted. The reason, the desire to keep constituencies as small as possible in a predominantly rural country, points to the only disadvantage of STV. It is very well adapted to a heavily urbanised area, like England.)

In each constituency counting begins by ascertaining the total number of votes cast. This determines the quota, which in this case is called the Droop Quota, after H.R. Droop who proposed it in 1869. The Droop Quota is the minimum number of votes a candidate must have to be certain of being elected and is expressed by the simple formula:[34]

$$\text{quota} = \frac{\text{votes}}{\text{seats}+1} + 1$$

While the quota is being determined, the first preference votes (1's) for each candidate are being added up, and any candidate who has achieved the quota or more is declared elected.

If he has got *more* votes than the quota, however, his surplus votes are 'wasted', and it is one of the basic principles of STV that no one's votes can be wasted. The second count, therefore, involves the distribution of any surpluses from the first in order of magnitude if there is more than one. Now, obviously, the surplus votes are not just taken off the top of the pile, that would be ridiculous. What happens is that all the fortunate candidate's ballot papers are counted a second time, this time by the second preferences (2's), and a bundle placed on the existing piles of the other candidates. But not all of them, only the proportion of each corresponding to the size of the surplus, is credited to the account of the candidate receiving the votes. Any candidate who has now received the quota is elected, but if the seats are still not full the count proceeds.

The next step is to eliminate the bottom candidate. None of his votes has yet had a chance to do any good, so they are all redistributed to the second preferences. If he has received any second preferences from the transferred surplus, they are transferred on to the next preference candidate marked on them, if any, but only at the reduced value at which he received them. That is to say, the bundle he received is sorted, but the smaller packages made up from it are again credited only at the reduced value to the account of the remaining candidates.

If at the conclusion of this second count there remain any further seats to be filled the process will be repeated until the final result is achieved, which occurs either when the necessary number of candidates has reached the quota, or when the number of candidates left in the running is equal to the number of remaining seats, or when one seat alone remains to be filled, and one candidate has a majority over all the other candidates left in the race, whichever is the sooner.

Of course it is quite a valid criticism of STV that even if its mathematics is not particularly obscure, the fact that it does involve the element of trust makes it unsuitable for general use. As we have now seen, there is much truth in the view that for any given desired result, an electoral system can be devised. And in consequence, proportional systems, paradoxically, occur in two quite different situations; one, where this condition of general trust manifestly exists, as in the countries of Europe, and one, where the condition manifestly does not, as in Latin America, where one is forced to the regrettable conclusion that it does not matter anyway, since the vote is free in inverse proportion to the importance of the result. Electoral systems are determined by governments and not governments by electoral systems. It is therefore to governments that we now return.

ELECTION RIGGING

If a government feels that, for the sake of its national and international reputation, it must hold elections, but wishes to guarantee that it does not lose power as a result, it may arrange for elections to be rigged. Undoubtedly election rigging is a widespread practice in ostensibly 'democratic' countries with allegedly 'free' elections, and governments in those countries are frequently charged with it in the speeches of their political opponents. Unfortunately, rigging is also found locally in elections in countries where the government does not exercise any direct control of them, so individual cases are often very difficult to judge. The reason is quite simple. Although a government may be quite confident that a free election will return it to power, or accept an arrangement by which its tenure of power is shared from time to time with its political opposition, local officials with their political careers at stake may not take the possibility of personal defeat so calmly. Hence, unless central control is strong, paradoxically elections may be marred by a greater or lesser degree of interference in the freedom of choice.

The weakest point in any electoral system is the candidate. If candidates are unwilling or afraid to present themselves for election then no free choice can take place.

In all countries, candidates for election have to fulfil certain basic legal requirements. They must be citizens of the country, of full age and of sound mind, and not have a criminal record. Frivolous candidates are discouraged by a formal process of nomination by established individuals or groups, and, in addition, in the United Kingdom by the requirement that the candidate must deposit £150, which is only returned to him if he secures more than 12½ per cent of the votes cast.

Candidature may be discouraged simply by social pressures. A would-be candidate may discover that his position at work is threatened either by his colleagues or by his employers. If he is a professional man or self-employed he may find that his livelihood is threatened by the refusal of others to supply him, to work with him, or to consult him. Where membership of a trade organisation or of a trade union is obligatory in order to work in a particular occupation, fear of having this membership withdrawn may be more than enough to discourage political activism.

Then it is possible to construe the basic criteria of fitness more or less strictly, applying a legal prohibition to candidature. In the USSR political opponents of the regime have been certified as mentally ill, and detained as such; in Brazil and Uruguay they have been deprived of their political rights, but allowed to retain their liberty; while in South Africa restrictions can be and are placed on their freedom of movement, speech and assembly by the Minister of Justice.

In many countries, people are imprisoned for their political views, sometimes, as in Cuba and Paraguay, for very long periods of years, sometimes, as in Argentina, Chile or Iran, in response to specific challenges, though it is impossible to draw a hard and fast line between these. The political nature of the imprisonment, too, is

normally disguised by presenting charges of involvement in conspiracy; charges which, by the nature of the secrecy surrounding
state security, are usually very difficult to refute altogether.

In extreme cases, political figures who presented a threat have
been murdered. The instigators of the death of Jorge Eliecer Gaitán
in Colombia in 1948 are still unknown, but the belief that it was
politically inspired was sufficient to touch off a major civil war,[35] as
has happened more recently and on a smaller scale with the murder
of the opposition newspaper editor, Pedro Joaquín Chamorro, in
Nicaragua in 1978.[36] In the latter case, there was widespread belief
that the government was directly involved, and it was overthrown
the following year. Similarly, in Guatemala in 1966 the assassination of Mario Méndez Montenegro, the principal opposition presidential candidate, backfired when his brother stepped into his place
and was swept into office on a tide of public and international
sympathy which neither the government nor the army could resist.[37]

Restraint on candidature is imposed less dramatically but more
effectively by institutional means, by restraining the freedom and
scope of action of political parties, which in many countries serve as
the sole legal vehicle for nomination. Parties may be dissolved
altogether, as in Chile or in Peru after 1968. Only official parties
may be recognised as having legal status, as in Brazil or Egypt. Or
'extremist' political parties may be singled out for special treatment,
as with the banning of the German Communist Party in West
Germany, where the rise of Fascist parties has been similarly
guarded against.

Even where candidature or political organisation are both officially free, the electoral process itself may be subject to several
kinds of manipulation.

In Britain voting in public, normal down to 1884, displayed
evident abuses in the form of intimidation of electors, which led to
its abolition. But there are two ways in which the same effect can be
achieved by different means. In the USSR and other Communist
countries, as we have seen, it is simply socially 'not done' to make
use of the secret voting facilities which are available. To do so is to
suggest you have something to hide and to attract unfavourable
attention. This is the exact opposite of the system in the United
States, where to use the voting machine the voter has first to pull a
handle which ensures that curtains are drawn tightly round him,
ensuring complete privacy.

Alternatively, facilities may be provided that are not in fact secret
although they profess to be so. An ingenious example was the
French referendum in Algeria in 1958 on the adoption of the Constitution of the Fifth Republic. For the convenience of the largely

illiterate population, the authorities had thoughtfully provided them with two voting slips: one white which said 'Oui', and one purple which said 'Non'. It was, of course, the aim of the exercise to secure the largest possible number of votes that said 'Oui', and the colour purple for the 'Non' slips was deliberately chosen because it was regarded as being unlucky. However this was not all. When Moslem voters, clad in long flowing robes with no pockets in them, went into the booths to vote and went to fold up their slips and put them into the box, they discovered that no repository had been provided for the slip they did not use. They could either drop it on the floor, in full view of the soldier stationed outside, or they could walk out holding it in full view.

In the same election other artistic touches included the careful distribution of polling stations so as to keep them well away from centres of opposition – one was even stationed on an island in the middle of a river, where the only boat was operated by the army. Where all else failed, the army supplied the necessary number of voting papers to make up the balance. 'Ballot stuffing' is perhaps the most common, and almost certainly the tidiest way, of rigging elections, but it has to be carefully done. In the Bolivian elections of 1978 votes cast were found to exceed the number of live electors by an astonishing amount. Even in the United States, where the control of elections is in the hands of the state governments and local interests, maladministration still occurs and may indeed have important consequences. In the presidential election of 1960, the very narrow margin in favour of President Kennedy could be accounted for by rather dubious totals from Cook County, Illinois, and from Texas, both areas notorious for electoral malpractice, characterised by long counts in which earlier returns are reversed by a sudden disclosure of late totals from the more remote areas.

To sum up, therefore, the problem of securing a genuinely free electoral choice is not an easy one. Fortunately, even where there is extensive local or national interference in the outcome of elections, they continue to be of great political significance as evidence of the real balance of political power within the society.

8 Inside the Black Box

At the centre of government, where the ultimate decisions are taken and inputs converted into outputs, we seek to identify the decision-makers. It is here, inside what has been playfully termed the 'black box', that the popular imagination places unimaginable mysteries. It does so, moreover, despite the many memoirs by leading politicians and statesmen, which tend on the whole to show that the business of government is very much like any other managerial job, the main difference being the scope of the decisions taken.

The fact is that people in all countries look to their political leaders for something called leadership. They do this whether or not they have chosen them to do the job, and the surest sign of the legitimacy they attach to their leaders is the ease with which they accept their right to lead, even if they do not agree with what they are doing. Generally, however, they set some distance between themselves and their leaders, indicating that they belong to a distinct political group. Such groups, forming a relatively small part of a society as a whole, are often termed élites – a term invented by the Italian sociologist Vilfredo Pareto.[1] Traditionally, the ability to lead, and hence the right to membership of a ruling élite, has been attributed to the outstanding qualities of the individual or individuals concerned. Weber, as we have already seen, regarded this kind of claim to political authority, which he termed, 'charismatic' authority, as being the earliest or original form of authority, seeing it being 'routinised' in modern societies into the alternative form of 'legal-rational' authority.

LEADERSHIP

Quite a lot of work on leadership has been done in laboratory conditions by psychologists. They work with small groups, but this in itself presents the student of politics with no problem, because most councils, cabinets, committees, boards and the like, are rather small. True, we cannot study these groups under clinical conditions, and in the absence of the responsibilities they have we can only simulate them to some extent. What we can and should do, however, is to use the information we do have to deduce the way in which such groups should behave, checking our deductions against the information about their actual behaviour which subsequently becomes public.

Our deductions are much more likely to be accurate if we remember that psychologists now regard *individual* personality as only one of the three factors of leadership.[2] The other factors are the nature of the *group* and the *situation* with which it is confronted. The leader plays a crucial role in maintaining what is termed group *syntality*, that is to say, keeping the group together and in good heart to perform the task in hand. And in open-ended experiments with small groups, usually of soldiers or student volunteers, where leadership is not necessarily predetermined, it appears that there are four main ways in which leaders may emerge.[3]

The 'problem-solving' leader is the person who knows how to deal with the problem in hand, and shows the others how to do so. The 'salient' leader assumes leadership in all situations by a combination of the inadequacy of the others or the adequacy of the leader himself. The 'sociometric' leader is the one whom the others say they would choose to lead them if they were given a chance to do so. But in practice he may well not be the same person as the one who comes in the fourth type, the elected leader, the man who is actually chosen. He may not be the same person as the person who is most popular, and indeed, as we have seen from our consideration of electoral systems, there are structural reasons why he will often not be.

These then are the four types of leadership that have been identified in small group situations. Clearly, these findings must in some way be relevant to the problem of leadership in politics, and we must reckon that when we are comparing aspects of leadership between different countries, we shall find it useful to use these categories. First, however, we must find some general principle which explains how the differences between leaders can be expected to vary.

We find this in the psychologists' overall conclusion that, in any given situation, it is easier to suit the task to the leader, than to find a leader to undertake the task. It is the understanding – or misunderstanding – of this principle that determines the development of structures of government, for the two problems cannot in fact be separated from one another. A particular leader long in office alters the job to suit his approach to it; the initial response of his successors is usually, but not always, to try to continue with his methods, in which in any case they have a vested interest, but when they find that they cannot effectively work within the same structures they set to work to alter them. This is why, generally, rapid periods of institutional change follow long periods of stable succession. The prediction of such periods of rapid change, and determining whether or not they are likely to follow a given course, is one of the fundamental questions of political science.

We have already seen how although in primitive societies the form of monarch was not universally adopted, nevertheless it was widely used, and historically lies behind the formation of most modern states. Monarchy, replicating the primitive structure of the extended family, was in small societies where the monarch was approachable and so to a considerable extent accountable, effective because efficient.

As states grew, the monarch was no longer able to oversee all the business of government. Simply ordering individuals to carry out tasks *ad hoc* without any long-term responsibility for them lightened the load only slightly. The remedy was delegation. The most frequent form seems to have been the delegation of all the tasks of government by an hereditary leader to a single figure, the vizier responsible for all the tasks of government, but this form positively encourages the palace *coup*, and though durable under a succession of weak rulers was speedily restricted by strong ones. Delegation of the powers of government to those territorial magnates who wanted it, on a geographical basis, similarly proved to have its weakness, in this case the danger that the state would be split up altogether, as nearly happened in the case of late medieval Burgundy, from its relationship with the French monarchy. In each case the danger to centralised control was the alienation of the balance of military power. Once lost, it could seldom be recovered, and then only by good fortune coupled, perhaps, with external aid.

The solution was found by developing the structures, not of the family itself, but of the household in the wider sense. The separation of functions already familiar from the organisation of large bodies of servants in a great house, was modified to make use of its distinctive feature, the division of responsibilities among a large number of people by the subject, and not the geographical area, of their responsibility. Out of this developed, ultimately, the concept both of a ministry, or body of men responsible for taking delegated decisions, and of a staff organisation for implementing them, which in turn was to provide the foundations of our modern civil services or, as they are now commonly termed, bureaucracies.

Leadership has first to be related to this staff and what it is like, this body of people who implement decisions. And this involves, secondly, the question of whether or not political power actually is monopolised by a relatively small group of people. For if it is not, deductions drawn from our experience of small groups may well not be applicable. Thirdly, leadership involves constant and subtle communication with the led, and so is inseparable from the 'style' of the society in question.

BUREAUCRACY

The permanent staff of government are known as civil servants, or, less happily, as bureaucrats, and the state of affairs in which they take the principal decisions of government as bureaucracy. Bureaucracy is used even more loosely to designate decisions which the speaker regards as unsatisfactory, and this in turn reflects the fact that most ordinary citizens do not really understand just how complex the network of governmental decision-making really is. Hence, if they do not get what they want from it they attack 'bureaucracy', in the same way that if their television set does not work they give it a good thump.

This is unfortunate, because one of the major characteristics of the modern state is the fact that it possesses a permanent bureaucratic structure. In fact the word itself was coined in the eighteenth century by Vincent de Gournay to designate a new and modern type of state, one in which power itself had passed into the hands of salaried officials.[4] In fact, historically, he was wrong; bureaucratic systems had been devised independently in several of the historical bureaucratic states, for example, Egypt and the Byzantine Empire; while the Chinese, who developed in pyramid administration the foundation for a remarkably stable social as well as administrative structure, were in due course, through the Northcote-Trevelyan reforms, to influence the formalisation of bureaucracy in the British Empire.[5]

But de Gournay lived at a time when in Europe there was much concern about an individual's right of recourse against the state. There were, then, three possibilities. In the *Rechtstaat* a clearly formulated system of administrative law set out precisely what the citizen's rights were, and provided a remedy through special administrative courts. (This is the position today in France and other countries of the *Code Napoléon*.) In the *Justizstaat* there was no separate system of law or courts, but the citizen had recourse through the ordinary courts to the remedies afforded by common law. (This is the case today in Britain, the United States, Ireland and the Commonwealth countries.) In the *Polizeistaat* the state assumed the right to 'police' every citizen for the common good, and there was no recourse; the general power, found also in other states, is still known rather misleadingly as the 'police power' in the United States.[6]

The bureaucratic state differed from all three types. There, though the formal recourse through law existed in theory, in practice it was denied by the secrecy attached to the bureaucratic process. This is a complaint which has had new life in the twentieth century. What then is bureaucracy, and why has it spread so widely?

Weber, analysing the characteristics of bureaucracy, found ten aspects that he considered of particular importance, in defining the position of the bureaucratic staff in its purest form.[7]

1   They are personally free and subject to authority only with respect to their impersonal official obligations.

2   They are organised in a clearly defined hierarchy of offices.

3   Each office has a clearly defined sphere of competence in the legal sense.

4   The office is filled by a free contractual relationship. Thus, in principle, there is free selection.

5   Candidates are selected on the basis of technical qualifications. In the most rational case, this is tested by examination or guaranteed by diplomas certifying technical training, or both. They are *appointed*, not elected.

6   They are remunerated by fixed salaries in money, for the most part with a right to pensions . . . primarily graded according to rank.

7   The office is treated as the sole, or at least the primary, occupation of the incumbent.

8   It constitutes a career. There is a system of 'promotion' according to seniority or to achievement, or both. Promotion is dependent on the judgement of superiors.

9   The official works entirely separated from ownership of the means of administration and without appropriation of his position.

10   He is subject to strict and systematic discipline and control in the conduct of his office.

Three themes run through these distinguishing characteristics. The first is the importance of strict *legal* criteria delimiting the sphere within which the official operates, which in turn depends on a strong accepted concept of legality. Second, is the clear separation of the private from the public aspect of the official's life; he is fully *accountable* to his superiors, but only for the job he is paid to do, and he is not accountable in any way to the general public. Third, is the way in which *rational* criteria determine both the nature of the job and his fitness to perform it. As an 'ideal type' the picture of the legal, rational and accountable bureaucrat is obviously attractive to those who wish to see such principles operate in government. It therefore appealed both to governments, as in Europe, and to their citizens, as in the United States, as a systematic solution to the problem of reconciling their divergent interests more closely. Its continued extension in the twentieth century is the clearest proof that this reconciliation has been seen as a success, even if it is at the same time attended by steady criticism.

To understand why bureaucracy was so successful we must first recall another aspect of the system that preceded it. The basic unit of this system was not the individual official, but the council. A council consisted of a group of men each of whom was an expert on one aspect of affairs of state, but collectively they were not specialists. Yet they had to discuss and resolve all matters brought before them, regardless of subject. The process was thus tedious, time-wasting and highly inefficient. A viceroy of New Spain in the eighteenth century is said to have said of the Council of the Indies at Seville: 'If death came from Spain we should all be immortal.'[8] Conciliar government has been retained at the highest level, the Cabinet, in the British parliamentary system, but there too its inefficiencies have had noticeable effects: the Privy Council gave way to the Great Cabinet, the Great Cabinet to the Cabinet proper, and in time of war the Cabinet to an Inner Cabinet, a War Cabinet, or a system of 'overlords'.[9] Ironically, it is bureaucracy that has enabled the Cabinet as such to survive at all, since it provides the individual ministers with the capacity to do their jobs, and keeps the lesser decisions off their desks.[10]

Bureaucracy is criticised for another obvious success, the increase in government employment that it brings with it. In Britain, no significant reduction in the size of the bureaucracy has been achieved by the cuts imposed by the Thatcher government; the latest version of a theme taken up in C. Northcote Parkinson's *Parkinson's Law*.[11]

Thirdly, in one respect, it is more equitable; it operates, as Weber noted, by implementing common instructions impersonally without regard to the power or position of the individual.[12] If efficiently maintained,[13] this can be an admirable feature, and it is certainly much preferable to any older system where the will of the prince is law. In modern times, however, it has increasingly been found necessary to mitigate the apparently harsh effects of impersonal decision-making by strengthening the process of appeal against administrative decisions. Britain, France[14] and West Germany have each found very different solutions to this problem, but the fact that so much has been done in each country since 1950 indicates the felt need for change. A major problem is that administrative tribunals themselves tend to be suspect as part of the bureaucratic structure,[15] and the Scandinavian countries were the first to appoint in the office of ombudsman an independent authority outside the administrative structure with the power to quash or vary administrative decisions.[16]

The problems of administration in many developing countries are different again, when the system has been seen as being imposed from above, by the colonial rulers. Bureaucracy there is seen as having been invented not for the sake of the local inhabitants (although their interests have not necessarily been infringed), but for the sake of the colonising power, and civil servants in post at independence may well have been regarded as collaborationists.

Riggs' classification of bureaucratic systems was designed to reflect this developmental perspective,[17] using an analogy drawn from optics, namely the passage of light through a prism. Traditionally, in the conciliar state, decision-making was 'fused', the decisions in different areas being incorporated in the same body in the way that white light contains all the colours. In a modern government, on the other hand, the areas of competence of government is split into functional areas, each the responsibility of a different government department. Decision-making, therefore, is 'refracted', as white light leaving the prism is refracted into different colours.

However, most developing countries (and even, for some strange reason, Scotland and Wales) have mixed institutions in which functions are incompletely separated. This prismatic model, Riggs suggests, is characterised by what he terms the *Sala* system of administration; namely an over-centralised system in which every decision has to be taken several times over, and people still hanker after the multi-functional model. They speak to a friend of a friend, they write to the President of the Republic, or they take his private secretary to lunch, trying to find a single point at which all decisions that interest them can be decided.

There are three consequences: decision-making becomes, or remains, over-centralised, every decision is taken several levels higher up than is really necessary, and the top level in particular is both over-worked and over-powerful; there is serious waste in public spending because money gets spent two or three times over also; and thirdly, no one knows exactly how much is being spent, and in such an atmosphere administrative and political corruption flourishes.[18] Many of the military *coups* that have deposed governments in recent years have had as one of their two or three principal avowed aims the ending of corruption. The bitter irony is that within months the new military regimes are usually at least as corrupt.

DECISION-MAKING

When we have identified the leaders and their staff, however, we have done no more than lay the essential foundation for assessing how they actually make decisions. It is easy to assume that those taking the decisions are rational persons freely operating in conditions of full information and unlimited time. Yet as we have already seen, such is not the case. It was dissatisfaction with the obvious weaknesses of what he terms the '*Rational Actor' model* of decision-making, particularly in foreign affairs, that led Graham Allison critically to compare it with two rival models of the decision-making process, using the Cuban missile crisis of 1962 as the subject of analysis.[19]

The 'Rational Actor' model assumes the rationality of the decision-making process as a whole: it will have clearly formulated goals, and make decisions so as to maximise its objectives in attaining those goals. In doing so it chooses among a range of rational alternative policies so that, by examining the action taken, the observer can deduce the reasons that led to the adoption of that policy option. Such a model is inherently satisfying on logical grounds, but it leaves much unexplained. The two alternative models which Allison offers, however, seek not only to explain what the first model does not, but to do so in a way which is itself coherent and meaningful.

The *Organisational Process model* sees government as a constellation of organisations grouped in parallel and in hierarchy, each with different tasks and different procedures.[20] There is no one set of goals, but, for each level of disaggregation, the goals are the maintenance of the organisation itself in terms of budget, manpower, job satisfaction and esteem. All problems therefore are 'factored', different parts of the problem being handled by different organisations in terms of their perceived goals. Such is the volume of routine work, moreover, that each organisation develops *routines*, or standard operating procedures, by which the majority of its work is handled. The 'answer' to a new problem, therefore, involves, not a complete *search* through all possible policy alternatives, but what has been termed *satisficing*, the acceptance of the first routine that comes to hand that will handle the task in terms of the organisation's perceived goals at that moment. Such routines, and even more the complex *programs* of routines of large, complex organisations, are inflexible and unlikely ever to be wholly appropriate to any specific task. Moreover there is a general tendency to avoid uncertainty about the future by constructing responses to likely *scenarios* which are thought particularly likely to happen, though such long-term plans are likely to be ignored thereafter in the construction of lesser plans and routines used also for day-to-day action. Change therefore proceeds *incrementally*, and major changes in policy within the organisation can only proceed from deliberate intervention from a higher level aimed in such a way as to prevent the attempts to circumvent or forestall it by standard operating procedures.

Such processes, however, are no less characteristic of the highest level of decision-making than of its subordinate organisations, and there, in Cabinet or Politburo, where disagreements from time to time come into the open, we are aware that policy outcomes are themselves the product of the competing individuals of which the organisation as a whole is composed. Allison therefore offers us what he terms a *Governmental Politics model*,[21] but on which others have preferred to call a Bureaucratic Politics model, though its usefulness is not limited to examination of the workings of the bureaucracy.

The Governmental Politics model sees individuals as players in a game, whose output is the sum total of all their decisions. The player's power to influence decisions depends on his job; his possession of that job in turn determines how he will look at every issue ('Where you stand depends on where you sit[22]). The game proceeds along action channels structured by *rules* and *deadlines* that have to be met, by a process of *bargaining* in which action on one issue is traded off against action or inaction on another, and this bargaining is vertical as well as horizontal in its implications, as between those who have much power ('Chiefs') and those who have little ('Indians'). Since the noise level is high and time short, decisions taken to meet deadlines tend to be based on the minimum of evidence and defended much more strongly than a rational examination might suggest desirable, and decisions are both mis-perceived by the participants and mis-communicated to others. But because of the importance of hierarchy to each individual, gains may be maximised by *reticence* such that major objections are not voiced despite being seen or felt.

Though this model comes closest to the position adopted in the organisation of this book, it is, as will be seen, not in any way an exclusive *explanation* of the way in which government works. The fact is that the Governmental Politics game is 'played' by members of hierarchically structured organisations, who as part of their working beliefs about the game *as a whole* hold that their actions, in some not wholly clear way, contribute to the 'national interest' and must therefore be 'rational' in overall terms. Moreover Allison, in outlining the Governmental Politics model, deliberately excludes customary terms, like 'actor' and 'role', which relate to the theatre,[23] and yet which clearly have a meaning in terms of a fourth, as yet undefined model. This model, which I shall term the *Dramatic Actor model*,[24] could be described as follows.

Again the basic unit of analysis is the individual, whose job, however, is to play 'roles' more or less completely determined, but where an inadequate script, too small a cast, and other factors, require him to *ad lib* much of the time. This he does by repeating fragments and chunks of well remembered plays, strung together according to the limits of his ability, with ideas drawn from the world of life and letters, his memory and his ingenuity. The criterion of success is the esteem in which he feels his *performance* is held by fellow actors, critics and the public. If in a *leading role* he will seek rave reviews for his individual projection of the part; if merely one of the supporting players, he seeks what he sees as the success of the company as a whole, and may be content to accept his salary and develop esteem in other spheres. Decisions are the stuff of the performance, but it is not what they are but how they are 'put over' that matters. Once he is assigned a part, or volunteers for one, his actions, moreover, must fit the society's dramatic conventions.

Hero, Villain or Fool, he must *act the part* he has taken on, [25] and any inconsistencies must not be such as to outrage the conventions, though they may be accepted if they occur 'off-stage' or can be seen as contributing in some ingenious way to the development of the 'plot', in a way that the audience is prepared to appreciate. When all else fails, in military or political defeat, *The Show Must Go On*, until new players enter from the wings to carry on, though the performance goes to pieces in the face of a storm of abuse and the dissatisfaction of the supporting cast.

It is obviously much easier to sustain a high level of performance if the cast are only seen at times and places of their own choosing, and in scenes carefully contrived to maximise dramatic quality. Democratic societies require their actors to be 'on-stage' almost continuously, but the effect of this attention is limited by the public attention-span such that it is often difficult to be sure who exactly is 'on-stage' at any one moment, and even more difficult to be sure who is really a *leading* actor. In politics, the 'cast' of possible actors is often referred to as an élite.

ELITES

Outside the ranks of the political leadership and the bureaucracy we can identify in most – if not all – societies a number of people who, together with the political leaders and the senior bureaucrats, monopolise a disproportionate share of political power. In so far as this forms a self-conscious group of men and women aware of their special position we term it an *élite*.[26] It is a term, however, which defies easy handling in the comparative context because of its indefinability. Although we all know what an élite is when we see it, we seem to have a great deal of difficulty deciding what exactly an élite is not.

Pareto's original concept of an élite as a group conscious of its own existence was straightforward enough. But relatively few people have read Pareto, and for most English-speaking readers the concept has been fundamentally transformed by C. Wright Mills in his book *The Power Elite*. The 'power élite' for Mills is not an élite in the older sense, in that the members of the power élite – if there is such an entity – do not necessarily know each other, and indeed they may not be sure that each other exist;[27] they are people in business, the armed forces, or government who will act together in a certain kind of way without having common links between them, or indeed without really knowing that they are acting together.[28] The power élite seems much too diffuse to be useful in a comparative context, and for that reason is best abandoned.

What then of the élite proper? This is probably best considered as a phenomenon, not of societies as Pareto originally envisaged it, but of organisations, as Michels suggested in the context of political parties, and the political decision-makers do form such an organisation. As such they can be identified, labelled and studied. When this is done, some trends are immediately obvious. In the small group of key decision-makers women are scarce; minors are excluded altogether. And not all males of adult age can take part, because they lack some or all of the necessary qualifications.

So much is obvious enough. What is not so obvious is the astonishing number of these qualifications, and the extent to which the possession of a sufficient number is restricted to a very few. So much is this the case that even in the most 'democratic' state the access to political power is broadened, if at all, not by widening the circle of eligibles, but by limiting the time that they can stay in positions of power, which may be done by formal as well as informal limitations on the duration of office.

When all the necessary exclusions have been made, we are left with a small group of about a hundred people who appear to be the most influential people in the society. But by this method we really prejudge our results. By saying that the country is run by an élite we accept that these people really run it, and that we know who these people are, and we may well not be right on either count.

Where there is agreement that élites exist, we can identify two distinct but overlapping types. Traditional élites are rigid, and the distinctions by which they select themselves are absolute. If to be a member of the élite it is necessary to be male, it is no use being female, and it is no use complaining about it either.

But how relevant is this today? In the UK there is no formal barrier against any citizen becoming a member of parliament, and in due course becoming prime minister. But in practically all presidential states there is a constitutional requirement that the president must be a natural born citizen of the republic. So Dr Henry Kissinger, President Nixon's Secretary of State, could not become President of the United States under its Constitution, because he was born in Germany, and so was a German subject when he was born.[29]

As this rather special case shows, it is not necessary to be able, even in the United States, to become president in order to be a member of the political élite. But to be a member of a political élite does *not* imply equal possibilities of access to all levels of it, and Nixon could appoint Kissinger Secretary of State without any danger to his own political position, since he could not become, by that fact, a rival candidate. Had he not been fortunate to live when he did, the same problem might have befallen Alexander Hamilton, who made the mistake of being born in the West Indies.[30]

In some other countries the restrictions on access to the highest office are even more constraining. In Mexico, the president must not only be a natural born citizen, but the son of natural born citizens.[31] A similar restriction would have excluded Woodrow Wilson from becoming President of the United States.

Transitional élites are relatively flexible. These are groups which use acquired characteristics in their strategies of 'social closure' – excluding the non-élite. Such a characteristic *par excellence* is education. In both Britain and France, though in very different ways, the nature of the educational process is crucial to access to the higher reaches of political power. Religion is another characteristic which may be acquired; so too, historically, is race, for there is no biological basis for racial discrimination, and the interpretation of what constitutes a 'race' has varied historically so much that its role as a strategy of 'social closure' is shown very clearly. Other, perhaps even less definable criteria are often lumped together into a generalised notion of 'social class', based loosely on income, wealth or occupation. Again, there is no way of assuredly separating individuals into distinct groups by such criteria, partly because there is not meant to be. Lastly, occupation itself may serve as a criterion on its own, as in the case of the military profession. Flexibility here is limited to an extent depending on the degree of skill involved, and you would not, for example, have stood a chance of being a leading Spartan had you not been good at the arts of war, whatever the arts of war may be.

Two points about these criteria are of particular importance. Many of them are interrelated, or may be interrelated, such that deficiency on one account may be made up for by proficiency on another. All of them tend in practice to be related to wealth, itself a measure of power resources. Wealth, status and political power can be traded off against one another, and inherited wealth, in particular, implies early advantages in education and training which predispose an individual to leadership. And, historically, two types or aspects of training have been of particular importance. As Pareto himself noted, there are two types of leaders – 'lions' and 'foxes'.

The 'lions' are the military forces today. At one time, perhaps, they actually were the strongest members of society, though skill must always have been very important too. But the introduction of firearms has been a great leveller in this respect. The 'foxes' are the intellectuals. Not all the intellectuals, certainly; intellectual ability in itself is no qualification for political power, and indeed may be a serious disadvantage if it does not fit in with what others believe. In east European states the convention is, following the Soviet example, to term them the 'intelligentsia', and to regard them as a distinct stratum (not class) in socialist society. The Chinese used to call them, rather more accurately, the *literati* – those able to read. If 'intellectuals' were not so firmly fixed in social science usage the older term would undoubtedly be preferable, since the most serious delusion afflicting intellectuals in politics in all ages is the belief that intelligence entitles them to hold and control political power. Since writers on the political system are themselves intellectuals they tend to share and propagate this belief. But the mere ability to read and write is quite enough – as witness Pancho Villa in Mexico (1915), who needed only to be able to sign his name to be able to issue all the money his armies needed.

The views of political thinkers on élites can be categorised according to three criteria: whether they believe that they are inevitable or not; whether they believe they are desirable or not; and whether they think they are part of them themselves or not. Among those who considered they were inevitable were Pareto, who invented the word, and Michels, the sociologist who demonstrated that they were a feature of all types of organisations and not just of government.[32] It was Pareto who regarded the ultimate determinant of political change as being the possibility of the 'circulation of élites', that is to say, the replacement of a spent élite by a new one.[33] But as we have already seen, this tells us little that we do not know already, particularly since the replacement of members of an élite will happen anyway through the ineluctable processes of mortality. And it is perhaps more rewarding to regard, as Michels does, élites as being in a perpetual state of competition, and to try to identify their characteristics more precisely.

The sort of questions we may ask ourselves, and should do before accepting the assumption of a ruling élite uncritically, are these: Is there really just one ruling élite, or do different élites control different organs of government? does the army, for example, come under the same sort of control as civilian organisations? are there different answers for different regions? what do we mean by *ruling* élite? how many of our so-called élite actually rule, and how often can they expect to get their own way? These are difficult questions to which we may expect to get different answers from our own observations and from asking others in the society what they think, and we may well agree with Geraint Parry that some combination of the two methods alone can give any satisfactory answer for it is doubtful if the word élite will ever be anything more than a vague collective noun for the government of the day and its friends.[34]

CLASS

The problems of study encountered in applying the theories of élites, however, are as nothing compared with those of class analysis. By class, we refer, with Marx, to a group of people with a common relationship to the factors of production, that is to say to a large group of people with a relationship to political power determined by their economic position.[35] Marx saw the concentration of economic power in the hands of a few as leading ultimately to the impoverishment of the majority of the economically productive, leading to violent conflict and the displacement of class by class. Since this process is supposed by most if not all of his many adherents to be the dominant political fact of our time, obviously the empirical study of comparative politics should be able to ascertain exactly where and how far this process has advanced. In practice, however, it cannot. Again there are several reasons.

To begin with, Marx himself defined class in a variable manner, saying that though there were three classes that mattered, only two of them would come into confrontation, and a fourth stratum, that of the intelligentsia (namely the politically aware section of the *literati*) would throw their lot in with the ultimately dominant proletariat. This last point has led to considerable uncertainty as to whether those movements led by the intelligentsia that claim to be acting in the name of the proletariat are actually repesentative of them or not.

Secondly his definition, though widely accepted by intellectuals, superseded an earlier popular definition of class as being what we would now more accurately term *status*.[36] By status we mean a perception of relative social standing, which may of course be due to hereditary factors or education, and so largely independent of economic factors. So when we ask people what class they consider themselves to be, in practice they answer in terms of status. Again we may attempt to combine empirical observation with questioning, but the standing of what we determine is even less certain than is the case with the idea of an élite owing to the much larger social groupings involved.

Lastly, there are still very few examples of successful movements achieving power by the route Marx predicted – some would say none. So the ability to predict political consequence from class origins has in this sense not been validated. Indeed, unhappily for these predictions, ruling élites, if such there are, now generally include in their process of political socialisation some instruction in Marxist theory, and in consequence their members have come to realise that there are a number of ways in which they can help to prevent themselves from being overthrown.

9 Maintaining the System

Once in power, the major task of any government is to stay in power. Formally, this is done through the administrative apparatus, seeking to satisfy demands made upon it, and through the law and the courts, regulating disputes and averting the development of potential trouble in the social system. Behind the authority of these agencies lies the sanction of force, the ability to use which is more or less prominently displayed according to the nature of the state, but includes as a matter of course a substantial army, an extensive police system, and some kind of paramilitary reserve or militia that can be called upon in emergencies.

The maintenance of a stable government is the fundamental assurance of the political control of a ruling élite. Losing control of government means at the least that their power will be severely curtailed, at most that it will be lost for good. But maintenance of a government is only part of political control since it can only operate effectively if the system of relationships around it is maintained also. For this reason the need of a political system to maintain itself is usually referred to as 'system maintenance'.

System maintenance as a phrase, however, conjures up a misleading picture of a rigid, static framework, preserved from decay, but not needing or capable of adaptation to meet new needs and circumstances. We have already seen that the ruling élite is imprecise and vague simply because it is in a necessary state of constant change. The same is equally true of governments themselves. Certainly there may be few if any differences, as far as most citizens are concerned, between one government and the next, for the administrative structure around it changes more slowly than it does. But on the other hand no government, even a dictatorship, remains the same for very many years at a time. In the case of a very long lasting regime, such as that of Franco in Spain, the mere combination of ageing in office with the blockage of promotion for younger elements, may postpone but is not in itself sufficient to prevent change in the system overall, even during the ruler's lifetime.

The maintenance of governments is ensured by a judicious combination of rewards and punishments. Rewards for members and would-be members of the élite, and no less significantly for potentially useful people who might otherwise be political opponents, include promotion, co-option, patronage, pensions and honours. Punishments include demotion, dismissal, fines, imprisonment, banishment and even execution. There is a significant difference between the two. Rewards are wholly within the control of the government, provided always that they can extract the necessary power resources from the population to pay them. Punishments, however, can only be freely used where their impact is wholly political, for the fear of citizens of the arbitrary use of power by a government is such that the use of the more extreme forms of punishment, without clear legal sanction, will destabilise the entire system.

Making war on another state is a reward to some and a useful opportunity to punish others without fear of retribution. It is therefore useful for the coercion of reluctant supporters, as is the threat of it, as Hitler seems to have understood very well.

REWARDS

Maintenance of a government depends in the first instance on rewarding those within it who form, as Machiavelli pointed out, the most dangerous rival claimants to political power.[1]

Anticipation is the key to reward. The reward that one gets is seldom as good as the reward one thinks one is going to get, as every child has speedily found. Hence a well organised, stable political system places great emphasis on an elaborate system of ranks, and promotion within it. This is not as easy as it sounds, as the higher offices are necessarily fewer in number than the lower ones, and fewest where they become most desirable. Perhaps the most efficient such structure, and certainly the longest lived, was that of the mandarinate in the Chinese Empire. All modern civil services are organised on much the same lines, with fixed rules of retirement and rotation in office (as with ambassadorships) to ensure the constant expectation of vacancies to be filled.

In the United States from the time of President Andrew Jackson (1829-37) onwards civil service positions were filled with political appointees on the 'spoils system', and today the highest positions in the various departments continue to be filled by political appointees. This calls our attention to the value of a career structure in political office, which is very conspicuous in the United States, where experience in a lower elective office is almost indispensable to be taken seriously as a candidate for a higher one. At first sight, this would seem to be quite independent of the wishes or needs of the government. But in practice the administration may be conferring a period of appointive office on someone, to make him a possible candidate for a much higher post.[2] In Mexico rotation in elective office is guaranteed by a complete prohibition on re-election. Consequently, candidate office-holders alternate spells of elective and appointive office in a pattern in which service in the ruling party forms the main criterion in political advancement.[3]

In the Soviet Union both formal governmental offices and posts in the party hierarchy are elaborately graded, allowing at the top level journalists to play the fascinating game of assessing the relative standing of members of the Praesidium by the places in which they stand on Lenin's tomb on May Day, and the order in which they are listed on the occasion of state visits.[4] The corresponding process of assessment in Washington, London or Paris could only be a matter of rumour and gossip, though these might well anticipate important changes in the composition of a future government.

When a vacancy occurs in an appointive office, that vacancy has to be filled. Apart from promotion, this is also an opportunity for co-option – the bringing in of new members of the political élite into formal governmental positions.

Co-option may be used to maintain an existing regime in power as far as possible unchanged despite the inevitable processes of ageing and mortality. An extreme example is Taiwan, where the government has since 1949 continued to operate on the assumption that it is the legal government of something called the Republic of China. Since no by-elections can be held on the mainland, for obvious reasons, vacancies in its parliament have been filled by co-option.[5] And one of the major disadvantages of co-option is that any government left to its own devices tends to appoint safe, dull and uninteresting people who will not form a threat to their political control. This process is unlikely to be challenged as long as the senior leaders remain capable of discharging their duties, since there are few people who will take the risk of offending them. Those within government have got used to them and refuse to believe that they will ever go. Those outside console themselves with the thought that they cannot last for ever, even though a feature of politics since 1945 has been the number of men who have been able to retain political power to an age far beyond that which would be permitted in most other occupations – men like Franco in Spain, Salazar in Portugal,[6] De Gaulle in France,[7] Tito in Yugoslavia,[8] Mao in China[9] and Brezhnev in the Soviet Union.

Co-option may, on the other hand, be used much more subtly to bring in young and active members of society who, from their political connections, charisma or ability, might otherwise come to form dangerous political opponents. Their talents, harnessed to the service of the government, can then be of positive value in ensuring that adaptability and correct political judgement are maintained. The example of Mexico has already been mentioned. France is another, where the institution of the *cabinet*, or small group of personal advisers surrounding a ministerial hopeful, makes an institution of the process of gaining experience in the inner circles of government before launching out on one's own.[10] In the United States each presidential hopeful carries along with him a team of advisers, which, as with the men from Georgia surrounding President Carter, will, if required, follow him to Washington as the key figures in setting up a new administration. Some of these 'President's men' have thus begun an independent political career, notably Clark Clifford, who began his career in the White House under Franklin Roosevelt.[11] But Roosevelt is an excellent example of a president who appointed political opponents, valuing the conflict of ideas and advice that they brought him, while other presidents have thus disarmed important sections of political opposition, as did President Nixon when he appointed Governor Connally, a Democrat from Texas, to his Cabinet.

Patronage is a loose word which covers not only appointment to jobs of office-seekers, but also appointments on their behalf which act to strengthen their political position or to reward their family, friends or supporters. In Latin American countries it is accepted that political office brings with it the duty, as well as the opportunity, to use patronage on behalf of one's family. This is, then, distinct from, though often found in connection with, the illegal making of personal gain out of one's office. Well placed personal connections also ease the task of government, particularly in the case of sensitive offices, as with President Somoza of Nicaragua who placed his half-brother in command of the National Guard on which he relied for his ultimate support.[12] In Cuba, Raúl Castro is a Lieutenant General, Second Secretary of the Communist Party and Minister for the Revolutionary Armed Forces.[13]

Pensions and retainers ease the task of getting rid of members of the government who otherwise would impede necessary or desired changes by softening the financial shock of retirement or dismissal. For the sake of appearances they may be combined with some kind of office which though honorific is more or less a sinecure, but many are content with the honour rather than the reward.

Honours are the most insubstantial and the most versatile of all forms of reward. In Britain an elaborate system of badges of distinction, conferring the right to use certain titles or letters after one's name, serves to recognise by enhanced status the long service of many people who have worked for many years in the routine tasks of government, or who by their efforts have achieved distinction in fields of endeavour which the government wishes particularly to commend. It is a system which uses practically no financial resources beyond the slight cost of the badges and ribbons conferred, and for elaboration it probably has no parallel. But though it derives from the system of real rewards conferred by medieval monarchs, it is not by any means confined to monarchies, even if the King of Spain can still confer the Order of the Golden Fleece which is the senior of all European honours. In France the *Légion d'Honneur*, in numerous gradations, has been democratised in a fashion appropriate to a republic, but is no less valued for being widely conferred. In the United States, President Kennedy instituted the presidential Medal of Honor. Peru has the Order of the Golden Condor, Mexico the Order of the Aztec Eagle, and Guatemala the Order of the Quetzal, in five categories. In the Soviet Union and the east European countries honours and medals abound, one of the more unusual of which was the title of Hero of Soviet Motherhood instituted in 1944 for women who had had five or more children. One certainly deserves something for having five or more children.[14]

Such honours, which involve an advancement in status without necessarily a change of class or rank, are only the formal aspect of a much more widespread phenomenon. In the court of Louis XIV, as in other European courts of the day, physical proximity to the king served to grade the status in political terms of members of the society, and every action of the monarch was invested with political significance.[15] Eating in public, for example, ceased to be a method of ingesting food and became a demonstration of power, with the inconvenient result that royalty seldom enjoyed a hot meal. Invitations to formal banquets remain to this day symbols of status in most societies, while in presidential states generally the opportunity to gain the ear of the president, even for only a brief moment, marks out political standing as much as it ever did in the old monarchies of decadent Europe.

In the Soviet Union the leaders avoid contact with the people so that the make and size of their official cars becomes the chief sign of their status to the outside world. But although the official car is equally a sign of status in the United States, candidates for office are required to undergo the gruelling initiation of a campaign in the course of which they are expected to shake as many hands as possible. Even the most superficial contact, as Edward, Prince of Wales discovered on the course of his Australian tour in 1921, can leave your hand so bruised that it can become entirely unusable, and he caused concern at home by having to shake hands with the left hand; something which, as we have seen earlier, is completely contrary to the symbolic meaning of a handshake as a sign of friendly intent.[16] Hence honours, whatever they are, have to be maintained at a manageable level. They have not got to involve too much wear and tear on the system – or the hands.

PUNISHMENTS

Down to the time of President Kennedy (1961), the American Eagle, which appears on the Great Seal of the United States holding an olive branch in one claw and a sheaf of arrows in the other, used to face towards the arrows. The President, feeling that this suggested aggressive intentions inappropriate to the modern world, had the eagle reversed to face the olive branch – and the Vietnam War followed.[17]

Obviously, there is no direct connection between these two events, but the story does symbolise the great importance attached in all ages to a government's ability to punish transgressors, in this case from outside. The ability to punish people who break the internal laws of a government is symbolised in the House of Representatives by two great reliefs, one on either side of the Speaker's chair, of the ancient Roman symbol of authority, the *fasces*, a bunch of sticks bound round an axe. Symbolically the rods are for beating people and the axe for cutting their heads off.

In modern governments the sanctions for internal opposition within the élite are seldom as drastic as this, and the power to punish is, in its more severe manifestation, reserved for criminals. But the government does still use sanctions to retain control of the political process.

The most useful punishment for prominent figures, where available, is dismissal. In Britain in 1962 the Prime Minister, Harold Macmillan, dismissed seven members of his Cabinet in what came to be known as 'The Night of the Long Knives'. One of the men dismissed, the Foreign Secretary, Selwyn Lloyd, went simply because he seemed to be unpopular.[18] In the United States, President Nixon dismissed his Acting Attorney-General when he refused to carry out orders he believed to be illegal.[19] In the Soviet Union, as we will see later, Marshal Zhukov was dismissed from the Politburo when it was feared he might be becoming too powerful. There is a great deal of power to sack in most political systems.

Demotion, either real or symbolic, may be less severe in its consequences, but it is no less real. It can either take the physical form of transfer to a less significant office, or the symbolic one of exclusion from the centres of power and decision-making. No specific action is needed to qualify for such treatment, the failure to support sufficiently vocally or consistently the power of the decision-makers may in itself qualify for sanctions, though the possession of a strong independent power-base or other useful qualities may protect to some extent.

Exclusion from prospective rewards may in itself be sufficient punishment. This is particularly the case where the ruling élite is rigid in its criteria for admission and can control access, as with the *Broederbond* in South Africa. Failure to be admitted to the 'club' of the powerful is not subject to appeal. But the position in society of a political opponent may be made absolutely untenable by being subject to mass denunciation and abuse, as was the case in China during the Cultural Revolution.[20]

The treatment of suspected opponents in Communist states is particularly disagreeable since the individuals subjected to such treatment, or, worse, to physical detention or molestation, have to secure permission from the state to leave the country, and such permission is often denied, evidently in the belief that a desire to leave the country will be a bad advertisement for the country they leave behind; the Berlin Wall stands as a memorial to the fact that, prosperous as life may be in East Germany, politically it has been so restrictive that thousands have been willing to risk death to escape from it. The Soviet Union has shown signs in recent years of realising that banishment may have its uses, as in the case of Alexander Solzhenitsyn, in calming opinion abroad while removing the danger at home.

And at the other end of the scale of tolerance, the practice of voluntary or forced exile as a treatment for political opponents is so much part of the Latin American tradition that it has given rise to important initiatives to recognise the right of political asylum in international law. Many Latin American politicians spend a noticeable proportion of their lives in exile: men such as Víctor Raúl Haya de la Torre, President of APRA, in Peru, who during one dictatorship spent six years in the Colombian embassy in Lima,[21] or Hugo Banzer in Bolivia, retired from direct involvement in politics by diplomatic exile as Bolivian ambassador to Argentina.[22] The importance of political exiles in other parts of the world, however, is no less, as the exile of ex-President Milton Obote of Uganda in Tanzania, of ex-King Norodom Sihanouk of Cambodia in China, and of the Ayatollah Khomeini of Iran in France bears witness.

When we turn to the arrest, detention and execution of political figures, we enter an area in which the government cannot necessarily act wholly arbitrarily, though it may do so, as we shall see later, under emergency powers. Arrests in themselves may have no custodial intent, but merely be used to break up foci of political activity. Since, though, they are often used as an opportunity to beat up or torture captives regarded as opponents of the regime, their mere possibility acts as a deterrent to political opposition. Detention of political opponents for longer periods is in any case so commonplace that it was a feature of resistance to decolonisation by Britain in places as far apart as India, Kenya and Cyprus. Detention differs from imprisonment in being an arbitrary act of administration rather than a judicial procedure, but the conditions and consequences need not be any different. Execution of political opponents, other than in a time of overt civil war, is seldom practised openly by governments for fear of international repercussions, though the governments of, for example, Chile, Uruguay and Guatemala are reported in the recent past to have connived at it, either at the hands of the armed services or, as in the last case, at the hands of an armed secret society linked closely to political interests similar to that which existed in Serbia before the First World War ('The Black Hand').[23]

LAW

When sanctions of reward and punishment are applied not to political control of members of the government and of the élite, but to the social control of the society at large, the economy of force dictates that the principal agency of the government will be the law and the structures particularly associated with it.

Because of the technical nature of the subject, knowledge of the law in most societies is the especial property of a guild of men and women who regulate admission to their profession collectively through examinations or similar means. Even in the Soviet Union lawyers are self-employed persons,[24] and where their guilds are well-established and strong, as in the United States, France or Britain, they can attain a high degree of autonomy within the political system.

Since it is from the ranks of those people that those who have to judge cases are drawn, we can expect a high degree of conservatism in legal systems, and in fact they appear particularly resistant to change, retaining their formal structures even in times of revolution or civil war, unless, as in the case of some of the Communist countries, they are then superseded by 'People's Courts' in which lay people sit as assessors of guilt or innocence.

There are, otherwise, two different forms of legal systems: those that depend, in the fashion of France, Italy or Spain, on the application of a codified law, and those which seek to interpret an uncodified law resting primarily on tradition. The latter system, often called rather misleadingly the Anglo-Saxon system, was once universal, for, as we have already seen, the belief in a system of law seems in most early societies to have come before the development of a distinct structure to interpret it. We associate it principally with the United States and with the Commonwealth countries, though traditional law is also found in many other parts of the world, notably in the Arab countries and Egypt, where the world's oldest university was founded in order to teach it.[25]

With the French Revolution was introduced the idea that the law ought to be the common property of all citizens, and capable of being understood by them. Hence it should be codified, and the 'Code Napoléon', completed in 1806, stands as a monument to the success of this ideal, having been adopted as the basis of the legal system of many other countries in Europe (Belgium, Holland, Spain), in the former French Empire and in Latin America. The Spanish case is particulary interesting, since the Laws of the Indies, first codified in 1682, pre-dated the Code Napoléon by more than a century, and were probably no more difficult to understand.[26]

Code law restricts the role of the judges in interpretation, but leaves them a wide range of powers in the conduct of cases, where the institution of the examining magistrate, who scrutinises every aspect of a case and hears witnesses before the case is formally tried, is particularly noteworthy. Anglo-Saxon common law, on the other hand, leaves the judges free to interpret according only to the precedents set by higher courts, but restricts their power in court by the institution for serious offences of a jury, whose task it is to decide simply on the question of guilt or innocence. Though judges in both systems are in general appointed from within the legal profession by a specially constituted committee or committees of the executive, lower judges in the United States are elected at popular elections, though officially on a non-partisan basis, giving them quite a different sort of popular authority for their actions.

In all cases, however, the formal operation of the judiciary represents only part of the structures associated with rule-adjudication. Decisions of government, such as appeals, the hearings and decisions of tribunals, and the arbitration of industrial disputes (where such are permitted), all involve the adjudication of rules and are normally performed by political or bureaucratic structures, into which the specialised personnel of the law need not venture. The operation of the police force or some similar structure is essential to bring certain classes of case before the courts. Those cases are those in which the government has decided as a matter of public policy that the general good, as it sees it, can only be secured by centralised enforcement of the law. Other cases, involving only the dispute between two persons or legal entities as to their respective rights, will be brought before the courts anyway, though the extent to which this is freely done – itself an indicator to the extent to which the authority of the government is accepted – depends also on the financial cost of justice and the amount of time it takes.

In France appeals against administrative decisions are handled by special courts under a separate code of administrative law, thus clearly distinguishing the public from private responsibility in the matter. In the Anglo-Saxon system, such recourse is through the normal courts. In closed societies, such as the east European states, such recourse is extremely difficult to obtain by any means, attempts to pursue one's rights being met with more or less forcible reprisals, in the belief that any criticism of government constitutes a threat to national security. In fact historical experience demonstrates that long-term survival of a regime and its élite is more securely established by guaranteeing cheap and speedy recourse to the victims of minor injustices, such as seem inseparable from the functioning of bureaucracies as from all human institutions. It is not for nothing that, in monarchies, the prerogative of mercy was seen as the distinguishing mark of a just ruler.

STATE OF EMERGENCY

The ultimate defence of a political ruler is to return to the pre-Constitutional order and to proclaim a state of emergency. This is quite a simple everyday concept. In any country, from time to time, war or natural disaster creates a situation which, in the interests of the citizens, requires that a government acts without normal legal restraints. The ability to proclaim a national emergency is so much part of the normal functioning of government that it was used in Britain, for example, five times between 1970 and 1974.[27]

Its role as a response to war, or threat of war, internal or external, is better reflected perhaps in the Spanish term *estado de sitio* ('state of siege'), suggesting a condition in which a government is imminently under mortal threat from a hostile force.[28]

The ancient Romans had already faced this problem. In some period in their dim historic past they had overthrown their kings and had established a republican government. Therefore, they established a rather curious system by modern standards, a system in which all power was concentrated in two separate people, who checked each other. So when they were under serious military threat and needed to concentrate their power they instituted the emergency office of dictator.

The dictator was given supreme power in the state for a period of six months,[29] then at the end of that time he went back to being a private citizen.

I want to distinguish very clearly here the word 'dictator' from the word 'tyrant'. The word 'tyrant' was not originally a Greek word, but was adopted from the Lydian by the Greeks to refer to a kind of political boss, a man who made himself the sole ruler within a republican state.[30] It was originally, therefore, a value-free term which was attached by the Greeks to one-man rule.

But, after Solon's time (594 BC), it came to mean selfish rule, rule in one's own interest. A tyrannical government was a government by one man in his own selfish interest, or in that of his family, friends, relations, and so forth. So the word 'tyrant' became critical, and was adopted into Latin also as a term of abuse for a man who was an autocratic ruler and a bad ruler at that.

So there are two terms here: the idea of tyranny which has been considered bad since the time of the Greeks, and the idea of dictatorship which, until modern times, was still relatively value-free. The bad thing in Ancient Rome was to be a king, not a dictator: to be a dictator was perfectly respectable. It was the attempt of Julius Caesar (as people thought) to make himself a king, that led to the conspiracy of Brutus and Cassius and so to his assassination, not the fact that he held the Roman emergency office of dictator. So that when the idea of dictatorship as a form of government was revived at the time of the French Revolution it was in fact quite widely used. Dr José Rodríguez de Francia was elected Dictator of Paraguay in 1814, and Perpetual Dictator in 1816. Juan Manuel de Rosas was formally recognised as Dictator of the Argentine Confederation in 1835 by twelve provinces outside Buenos Aires.[31] When he started an organisation to kill off his political opponents, insisted on everyone wearing red cockades to show they were on his side, and had his picture exhibited in all the churches for public veneration, Argentines finally rose against him, but only after eighteen years, and with foreign help. Even Simón Bolívar, deservedly regarded as the hero of South American independence, was Dictator of Peru (1825-6) at the same time as he was President of Colombia, and received, incidentally, no salary for either post.[32]

Dictatorship, then, is a republican office which values the forms of legitimacy. It was originally considered to be respectable until so many people were not terribly good dictators they gradually made it disreputable, and, by the beginning of the twentieth century, the term had become rather pejorative.

Nevertheless, Western Europe had its age of dictators in the twentieth century, and not in the nineteenth; in our parents' time if not in our own. The idea of dictatorship as an emergency office at the time of the great depression when it was adopted in Germany, Austria, Hungary, Yugoslavia, Bulgaria, Greece, Italy, Spain and Portugal, was still not wholly dead. What has contaminated dictatorship since was the Mussolini fiasco and his behaviour in Abyssinia, and the way in which Hitler massacred the Jews and gypsies in the eastern European states; not the actual office of dictatorship. And it has had a great revival in the new states, where General Idi Amin of Uganda declared himself an admirer of Hitler.

So, to sum up, what is characteristic of a modern dictatorship?.

It is, first, something that values the forms of legitimacy, internally involving recognition by an élite group, particularly by opinion leaders – the elders of the state and the military. It may not actually dare to seek mass recognition by plebiscite, but it usually does. One of our early modern examples in Europe, Napoleon III, did just that – he started in 1851 the French custom of holding plebiscites.

Secondly, dictators always enjoyed the kind of legitimacy they won externally, and today they like to be recognised by other heads of state. Lacking initial internal support as they do, external recognition by peer states is very important to them, especially that of the older, constitutional states, and of the great powers.

Thirdly, the dictator does not recognise the rights of individual people. For instance, Napoleon I (one of our earliest dictators), regarded the people as being the vehicle of his political programme, as it were, for France. He created the French Empire in the style in which it ought to be created, and with it the *Ecole Polytechnique*, deliberately to obtain an élite to maintain the system.[33] That is why *polytechniciens* have been valued ever since by French governments, whether the government is actually a dictatorship, a monarchy or a republic. The idea of moulding the people to need is very much inherent in the idea of dictatorship – it is such an emergency office that all rights are given up to it, and those exercised in the name of the country as a whole.

Fourthly, it has always shown a tendency to create a new form of 'aristocracy', in the shape of the active military. Because it is a military emergency office, the military tends to become the élite, and generals and colonels hold regional political power, in the way that earls and barons did in the middle ages, operating within a military command structure, and becoming a new 'aristocracy', as in Brazil since the inauguration of the Republic (1889).

Lastly, dictatorship creates no regular form of succession. The very emergency character of the dictatorship is absolutely incompatible with the idea that dictators can have successors or can other than succeed themselves. No other person can replace the dictator in the sense in which the regular devices of elections, succession, and so forth can operate.

10 Force and Political Stability

We have already seen how the state can be defined as the entity holding the monopoly of force within a society. This monopoly presupposes that it has been obtained by the exercise of control over rival centres of force within the community. These centres may either be regulated or suppressed.

If they are regulated, then they are subject to specific restraints in a code of laws or etiquette, such as those governing the duel or feud in Corsica or Sicily. Beyond this point comes the development of the state in which, as in feudal times in England, the use of force is dispersed throughout many levels, but in each is subject to regulation by that immediately above, and the general arbitration of a code of behaviour recognising obligations to the community as a whole.

If the centres are completely suppressed, then they must be suppressed by the use of force. In either case, the regulation of suppression of force must provide for the existence of a regular corps of specialist users of force to defend the national territory. This performs a useful dual function. Though the socialisation of the regulated community involves members inhibiting their aggressive instincts with the aid of mechanisms of sublimation such as sporting contests, there are always some members who lack the ability to fall in line. Some can be usefully employed in the specialist corps.

Now although we have talked so far of the regulation or suppression of force in general terms, it is of course inevitable in human societies that there will also be some sort of unregulated or unsuppressed minimum. This minimum we can conveniently refer to as 'violence'. The definition of violence as the unregulated use of force is normal, though in popular usage force and violence may be – and often are – considered as interchangeable terms.

The process of control by the state begins with the socialisation process of youth. Foremost are the traditional values of the society embodied in stories, proverbs, legends and nursery rhymes. These may also represent specific norms of behaviour. Thus the story of Sir Walter Raleigh casting his cloak before Queen Elizabeth I inculcates the value of respect towards authority and femininity, and the social norm of keeping women from having to walk through puddles, from which was derived the specific rule that men walked on the outside of the pavement nearest the road.

It is interesting and significant how far the material for early socialisation differs even as between Britain and the United States. The basic social virtues are perhaps not so very different. But the political aspect is different. The frontiersman image of Davy Crockett or Daniel Boone is more alienated, less social, than the well-knit community of outlaws of Robin Hood, while against the diet of modern cowboy stories the American child seems to have relatively few patterns of civic (as opposed to legal or police) authority. This is associated with the very low esteem for the police in the American community, and the high emphasis on force as a means of settling disputes in the folk mythology of its members.

Political socialisation not only involves the inculcation of certain values, more or less unconsciously, but also the code by which aggressive behaviour is ritualised and sublimated. Here the cowboy game and the symbolic gun fight probably come into their own, filling a void that sporting contests alone can seldom have fulfilled, since, anyway, the days when Rugby football was first conceived as a substitute for roasting younger boys over the study fire.[1] The more elaborate the ritualisation, and the more the members of the society incorporated into it by undergoing a common system of education, the less likely force becomes in actual fact.

POLICE FORCES

There are a number of distinct ways in which states use forcible restraints on adults, the principal of these being directed in all cases towards those who break the formal laws of society. In assigning to these a number of levels at which force is applied, we may conveniently begin with that of the regular police force.

A police force exists to provide for the use of actual physical constraints by the state to enforce its norms on others, in the belief that society's survival as a community is at stake. The law recognises the differences between offences by assigning stated penalties, but the fact that a penalty is fixed at all means that all are in some degree acts hostile to the accepted order of society, and all are punished in some way, whether the crime is stealing a pile of old banknotes, or hitting an old lady over the head in a country post office, since the alternative is to allow the will of the anomic individual to prevail over that of society.

However a great deal depends on what the norms of the society are, and what the successive regimes that direct the state choose to make laws about. Laws for the maintenance of the society or the state are in a different category from laws for the maintenance of the regime. Though there is general agreement that there will always be some laws to ensure the maintenance of regimes, there is a vast difference in the perceived desirability of regimes, and how far regimes see themselves as being indispensable.

There are two broad types of police organisation in modern states, often termed the 'Anglo-Saxon' and the 'Continental'.[2]

The 'Anglo-Saxon' form derives from the experience of medieval England as formalised in the Statute of Winchester (1285) which made citizens collectively responsible for aiding the King's officers in enforcing the apprehension of criminals. At the time when other European countries were developing a regular police force, however, in the seventeenth century, England was reacting to the unpleasant experience of martial law as administered by Cromwell's major-generals. Consequently the introduction of a uniformed constabulary was delayed until the beginning of the nineteenth century, and, characteristically, was tried out first in Ireland (1787). Even after the formation of the Metropolitan Police for the capital in 1829, the rural areas of the counties had to wait nearly thirty years for the formation of a police force to be made compulsory (1856).

Characteristic of the 'Anglo-Saxon' police is that it is loose and decentralised in organisation; its members are limited in their powers, are normally uniformed and identifiable, and in Great Britain and the Republic of Ireland they are on routine patrols except with special permission armed only with truncheons. In England the Home Secretary is the police authority for the capital only; in the rest of the country his powers are those of an inspector rather than a commander. In the United States police are a state and not a federal responsibility, and the first creation of a federal investigation agency, the FBI, did not occur until 1924.

The 'Continental' form is derived from the experience of France above all European countries. There had been a police force in the capital, Paris, from time immemorial, but its powers began to increase dramatically at the end of the middle ages, and in 1667 the King's Lieutenant of Police 'ruled the city despotically and had jurisdiction over beggars, vagabonds and criminals'.[3] The equation of crime, disorder and dirt is highly suggestive. The police had the power of summary arrest and fining on the spot for infringements of the law, and the Crown retained the right to hold prisoners without trial indefinitely. The French revolutionary governments, however, though they began by breaking this system, soon recreated it, and put in charge of the new and extended police organisation a Minister of the Police 'responsible for the safety of persons and property, for the maintenance of public order and for the security of the state'.

Hence in France there emerged three principal forces: the prefecture of police responsible for the Seine, the National Gendarmerie, responsible outside the capital and major towns for the internal and external security of the state and so capable of being used as an auxiliary military force, and the Sureté Nationale, organised in urban areas under a Commissaire de Police working under the Mayor and Prefect of the Department. These were merged into the Police Nationale in 1968.[4] There is, in addition, a riot force, the Republican Security Companies (CRS), used in 1958 and 1968, and on many lesser occasions besides.

The 'Continental' system is heavily centralised, with responsibility for the whole in a minister. It operates not only in uniform but as a matter of course in plain clothes, its members having exceptional powers denied the ordinary citizen, including the power of imposing summary fines, and in addition being armed, sometimes heavily.

It should be added that the influence of the French form today derives primarily not from earlier times but from the unifying effect of the Napoleonic Wars, and the admiration for things French in other parts of the world, for example Latin America, in the nineteenth century. It was for this reason that the system was copied by the Russians, who, under Nicholas I, added the dreaded 'Third Section' or secret police. The term 'police' was so distasteful to the makers of the Russian Revolution, that Lenin and his colleagues (like the Irish) dropped it altogether, and replaced the police with a people's militia. After many vicissitudes the militia was placed under the Ministry of Internal Affairs (MVD) in 1946. Though decentralised somewhat in 1956 following the general move towards de-stalinisation, it retains the general characteristics of the 'Continental' type. An important difference, however, in the societies' respective attitudes to the police lies in the Soviet assumption of the common responsibility of all citizens to admonish or bring to justice any individual committing even a trivial crime.[5] In Cuba, the organisation of the militia on a block basis, coupled with the trial of offenders before people's courts staffed by lay assessors, reminds us of the revolutionary origins of both systems. From this responsibility, it is only a very short step to the political offence, since the essence of a political offence lies not in its visible damage to person or property, but to the invisible assumptions of the society in question.

STATE SECURITY AND THE SECRET POLICE

If the maintenance of the regime involves the continual use of regular police action to restrain a substantial sector of the population, the legislation maintaining it must be political, and the state can be described as in some degree a police state.[6] Restraints of this kind however are common in many countries against large groups who are defying the government of the day, such as strikers on railways or in docks, or students demonstrating against what they conceive to be the follies and iniquities of their elders. But in South Africa, for example, the use of police restraint has gone even beyond this point to involve the persistent regulation of the movement and communication of an unparalleled majority of the population. Pass laws, residence restraint, segregation, are all enforced by the same mechanisms as control parking or apprehend thieves. This use involves the conscious moulding of society by the creation of attitudes and behaviour alien to it.

This pressure is applied in the name of the security of the state, and disapproval of it has in the past frequently been attributed by spokesmen to the actions of foreign agencies. This is significant, since for this purpose almost all societies recognise a special category of police behaviour, but this forms only the second level of application in South Africa.

Special police organisations for state security exist in almost all states. Their duties are to restrain infiltration and espionage activities by foreign nationals who might, using these means, achieve the sort of result normally to be expected only from an overt hostile act of war, or which would enable such an attack to be launched with an effectiveness significantly greater than might otherwise be expected. As befits a complex nation with a traditional distrust of power, the United States divides this function between two main agencies, the FBI and CIA, and several minor ones.[7] In Britain the Special Branch of the police force is less open in its methods. In either case, unlike the KGB in the Soviet Union, the operation of these agencies is subject to the over-riding control of the state and is not primarily concerned with political affairs as such.

A secret police is something very different, an organisation that applies the same techniques to the civil population because it fears danger from them regardless of outside influences. The distinction between a secret police and a police force engaged in secret activities may, however, be purely conceptual.

In Europe, within living memory, almost all states have suffered from the attentions of a secret police. Its characteristic is that it is no longer merely a body ancillary to the rule-enforcement agencies – the public prosecutor, the courts, and so forth – but is a rule-enforcement agency, having its own volition as to the assignment of prosecution and punishment. It is directly responsible through its bureau chief to the head of government, regulates its own hierarchy, and is concerned with a wide range of activities in the day-to-day operation of the state which are not disclosed to other members of the community. Its ability to use forcible sanctions is thus limited only by the resources available, and the ingenuity of its members.

The secret police, therefore, is an output mechanism entirely divorced from the imput functions generated in the society as a whole. Not only, however, does it act to screen out pressures on the decision-makers, but it performs an even more difficult task in attempting to create the impression of spontaneous political support from the masses for a policy prefabricated by the élite. This particular form of output activity we may conveniently term *input control*. It therefore does not fit exactly within either the terminology of Easton or of that of Almond's developmental model of the extractive and regulative processes of government.[8] Easton as we have already noted makes provision for the concept of 'gatekeepers' limiting the degree to which pressures affect the decision-making process, but the context makes it clear he is primarily concerned with the orderly transaction of business as represented by forms, procedures, committees, etc.[9] Like him, Almond retains in his latest model the basic assumption that the original fount of power is located in the mass, and not in the élite.[10] While this may be true in fact in most cases, and in theory in all, it is not true in fact in all. Input control ensures that only favourable inputs, e.g. supports, are felt in the system as a whole, that is, among all citizens in their political roles.

The other important attribute of secret police, apart from the free use of forcible restraints, is the acquisition and monopoly of a centralised bank of data on members of the community, available for manipulation by the élite for political purposes – that is to say, their own maintenance. The nature of this information is not known to the individual from whom it has been secured. Gossip, misunderstanding, error therefore maintain a status in it equivalent to fact, and may be preferred to it as more exactly conforming to the needs of the state.

The maintenance and extension of this sort of information are greatly enhanced by quasi-military status, such as that enjoyed by the SS in Hitler's Germany (1933-45) or the NKVD in Stalin's Russia (1928-53), both of which maintained paramilitary units as political 'shock troops' for use in actual warfare. The NKVD's successor, the KGB, still maintains frontier troops among its responsibilities. In turn, these are to be distinguished from military intelligence organisations such as the German FSP or the Soviet GRU; military units on the regular establishment engaged in military intelligence duties. They are also different from the category of paramilitary forces other than secret police.[11]

PARAMILITARY FORCES

There is nothing particularly secret about the paramilitary police forces of Malaysia and Thailand. Nevertheless, they exercise very different political roles within the community, despite their common origin in the intention to maintain a force other than the military which could be engaged in counter-terrorist activities and the suppression of 'bandits'. That of Malaysia is a professional organisation, used openly in armed combat against insurgency during the Malayan Emergency (1948-59).[12] That of Thailand is a paramilitary police force similarly engaged and similarly equipped with sophisticated weapons, such as tanks and machine-guns, but which, because of the nature of the political process in that country, has come to form an important part of the capacity for power of more than one regime since 1946. It was the major strength of Luang Pibul, who dominated Thai politics for a generation, and was fully engaged in both the abortive *coup* of 1949 and the successful revolution of 1957.[13]

The paramilitary force can be used against a wide range of possible 'enemies of the government', and in certain circumstances very effectively. Equally it can form the active force of a militia-based revolutionary organisation, as did the SA for Hitler or the *fasci di combattimento* for Mussolini. The period of the Second Spanish Republic (1931-9) offers interesting examples of both formations. The severe problems of integrating the SA with the state machinery and the regular forces, exacerbated by the circumstances of the Röhm *putsch* of 1934, was not solved by the solution

of developing the SS as counterpoise. The consequences for the
unnecessary weakening of the system were particularly well exemplified by the rivalries of the Cicero affair.[14]

MILITARY FORCES

The last resort of government, in internal as well as external
matters, is the military, the 'ultimate argument of kings'. Their
employment within the community, however, is restricted by a
number of factors: their need to maintain combatant status in the
event of foreign attack, the disproportionate effect of their powerful weapons, and their size, not easily accommodated in the absence
of special barracks and cantonments in the appropriate regions of
the state. These attributes are capable of generating a considerable
amount of hostility, and give rise to important theoretical considerations which must be considered in the broader context of the
phenomenon known as militarism.

It should be noted in passing, however, that effective as the
military may be at dispersing demonstrations and strike-breaking,
by substituting for the strikers in the performance of distribution
functions, they are not at all effective against clandestine intrigue.
In protecting the personnel of government against a *coup d'état* or
assassination they are not only useless, but themselves dangerous as
a focus for disaffection.

The phenomenon of militarism is hence of great importance in
the understanding of politics over the greater part of the earth's
surface.

There are two types of militarism which must be carefully distinguished. There is 'military' militarism – militarism among the military personnel themselves, and 'civilian' militarism – militarism
among the civilian population. The terms we owe to Alfred Vagts.[15]

Military militarism is a caste pride, a pride in the glory, honour,
power and prestige of the military forces. This type of militarism,
however, is not just the normal pride of belonging to a well
organised force, but an exaggerated sense of remoteness and of
superiority over the outside world in all aspects, so that those which
the military do not undertake are considered to be things not
worthwhile for society as a whole. It is normally found in the army,
rather than in the other armed forces. Navies, vital to, and therefore
of vast weight in, the politics of Britain, the United States, Portugal,
Greece, Argentina, Brazil and Chile, have in general acted symbolically through their admiralty establishments, rather than from
actual physical strength, since ships once at sea were effectively out

of touch with domestic affairs. Air forces had little independent weight before 1945, and remain critically dependent on land bases for refuelling. The army formed the ultimate defence in most other countries, and being land-based and stationed usually close to the capital, could exercise all their power if they chose to do so, and in fact frequently did. They were, after all, equally open to the influence of politicians anxious to obtain their support.[16]

Military militarism, then, tends to arise in one of two sets of circumstances. The first is when, for whatever reason, their ambitions become extended to the point of becoming conterminous with the limits of the ambitions of the state itself; that is to say, when the whole end, existence and pride of the state is seen by them to be the concern of the army and the army alone. (Such was the case in Imperial Germany, or in Japan after the Meiji restoration, both ambitious to become 'Great Powers' in the fashion that a rather oversimplified view of European history had taught them was the approved method.[17] This was to wage wars of imperial expansion, and the view was oversimplified because it was not necessary in fact to wage war with any real vigour in order to succeed, but only to give the impression of doing so.)

The alternative situation is when the military feel that they have been betrayed by the civilians – as in the United Kingdom under Lloyd George,[18] in France following the disaster of 1940,[19] or in Egypt after the humiliation of 1948, when their government accepted the Anglo-Egyptian Treaty, and their forces were so conspicuously and ridiculously ineffective against the apparently amateur army of the nascent state of Israel.[20] This can lead to the assumption that the army should take over the state to regain its position, as did José Antonio Primo de Rivera in Spain following its military defeat at the Riff in North Africa (1923); to a long-term process of military politicisation, as in Egypt before 1952; or to an effort by the military to provide alternative bases for 'grandeur' as in Egypt with Israel in 1970, or in France with Algeria in 1958.

Civilian militarism is something rather different. It may afflict either the élite or the mass of the society, or in extreme cases both. It is a nationalist pride in crude power – in Vagts's words 'Self-immolation on the altar of violence'[21] – a feeling that the army is well-deserving of the state, and should be rewarded with the unconditional adhesion of the population on whose behalf it fights. This state of mind, a vital prerequisite of total war in modern states dependent for their deployment of force on conscript armies, has great drawbacks even then.

There have, of course, in every age been people who are exceptionally bellicose. There are thousands more who like vicarious excitement. There are also, in modern times, millions more who in times past have taken part in military service or training; of these some join the ranks of the armchair strategists and others (despite the evidence of their eyes) would be prepared to think the efficiency of a state could be improved by its militarisation. It may not be just nostalgia, of course, for it all depends on what aspect of civilian life they are using for comparison.

Civilian militarism goes beyond approval of the military or even beyond applause. It implies extremism in its support, being more militaristic than the soldier in the front-line. The unlovely action of women pinning white feathers on men in civilian clothes in the First World War is civilian militarism.

The emergence in military situations of the civilian as military leader, strategic planner or even tactician, is another form. The military leader chosen as civil head of state or of government is a third. Acquiescence or cheerful support of dictatorship, aggressive war, concentration camps and so forth, that is a fourth.

Examples of the civil leader as soldier occur normally in time of war. Thus Churchill, Roosevelt and Stalin all assumed military expertise they had not got, though not surprisingly each was, on occasion, right to over-rule more specialist advice in the light of political strategy.[22] Fortunately, their chief opponent had even less knowledge, not solely because of his own inadequacies but also from the struggles of his lieutenants, though the nominal leader of Japan was a sailor and a military appointee.

But so far after every war but one (the First World War) the United States has chosen as president a military hero; in time of peace, therefore, the habits of times of war continue.[23] In major crises the military virtues are those sought for – the willingness to make quick decisions and the zest for action. But in day-to-day matters, it seems clear that military training is regarded as an essential part of citizenship for a political aspirant. The incidence of civilian militarism however is variable, and though it depends greatly on time and historical circumstance, it clearly has an important relationship to the society in which it is found and hence to that society's political system. S.E. Finer argues that it will vary as between liberal democracies, developing states, or the Communist regimes.[24]

In a developing country the perceived emergency implies a strong tendency towards the adoption of democratic Caesarism. The prevalent form of militarism is military. The forces in such countries – whether in Asia, Latin America or Africa – have a pride in their prowess which does not necessarily derive from recent combat, as, in many cases, for geographical or other extraneous reasons, the opportunity has not arisen. Until recently, however, the fact of independence implied an important historic role for the forces. They had the role of guardians of the state thrust upon them, in their opinion, because they saw themselves as the ones who had given birth to it. Secondly, the forces in those countries – primitive as they might appear in the light of modern technological innovations – have an important claim to the principal reservoir of technological expertise within them. Their capacity for force is quite high enough, for the rifle as a marksman's weapon has not improved substantially in the last fifty years and the aeroplanes and machine-guns of the Second World War were quite good enough to kill more people than form the entire population of any African country but Nigeria. But it is the developments ancilliary to these that matter.

The chief aim of education in developing countries tends to be towards the well-qualified specialist. The shortage is so great that the scientist must be given precedence over the technician, while the technicians are so scarce that the military can easily monopolise them. The services need medicine, communications, engineers, surveyors, and they have to supply them for themselves. The example of the US Corps of Engineers, and the way in which the provisions of Congress on the delimitation of land were actually carried out by the bowie knife, the Colt 45, the telegraph, the heliograph and coils of barbed wire, or the role of the soldier in developing north-west India and modern Pakistan, Iraq and Egypt, has its parallels in the Amazonas region of Brazil today. Here the army maintains communications, surveys geographical formations, watches for infiltrators, and teaches civics classes by turn. In Brazil, and in Ecuador, Bolivia and Peru too, the army is often the sole agency of government apparent to the tribesmen, who see it as the agency of miracles in an inscrutable mixture of condign punishment for misdeeds and sudden cures of sick children and animals.[25] And the military of developing countries have been viewed as the chief agency of national unity (Yugoslavia) or even of revolution (China).

In consequence, the defence ministers of such states are in a particularly strong political position, which they do not fail to take advantage of as often as they might. The opposite situation, of course, may be found in the liberal democracies. There the military have been subordinated to the civilian power because of the pro-fessionalisation made necessary by technical advances. This pro-fessionalism removes the military from the community in a way equivalent to that in which the conditions of service overseas on behalf of an expanding power have removed them in a physical sense. Such remoteness, of course, goes far to end military interference in government. No one would expect, however, that it would be totally removed.

The liberal democracy finds that the military operates at once as the largest consumer of finance and as the most powerful lobbyist. Since Elizabethan times the navy has exercised a powerful influence on politics in Britain, and its maintenance and development have been key issues. But in modern times the sophistication of weapons makes the forces dependent on a range of specialist services of little relevance to civilian needs, while its vast weapons procurement needs call into play the typically 'modern' preoccupation with economics and the organisation of state production for defence needs. The rivalries between needs, especially between land, sea and air, do however act against one another in the call on political resources.

The communist state is in a middle situation. Most communist states are underdeveloped in an economic sense, and so their armed services can be expected to follow the behaviour patterns appropriate to this situation. However the role of the military as the major power in retaining the communist party in power in nearly all of them is anomalous. As an élite caste the military cannot hope to displace the communist party in power, because the hegemony which it claims is backed up by a capacity for paramilitary force and rendered more powerful by the ability to exercise the state's right to socialise even within the caste itself, and the schismatic effects of the political police. It can, however, hope to displace individual leaders if they fail to give it due credit and budgetary support. An interesting example is the intervention of Marshal Zhukov in the USSR who positively supported Khruschchev against the 'anti-party group' in June 1957, and was duly rewarded with a place in the Politburo. He was demoted in October 1957 on charges of 'Bonapartism', and of using his position to weaken party primacy within the military.[26]

Militarism in the liberal democracy, therefore, tends to be predominantly a civilian attribute, while in the communist state it can be either military or civilian.

In his analysis of military intervention in politics, S.E. Finer first of all notes that its occurrence depends on both the *opportunity* and the *disposition* to intervene. Many forces have the opportunity, but not all have the disposition, and the relationship between the two is a complex one.

Secondly, he argues, intervention can take place on any one or more of four *levels*. All armed forces act as a *lobby*. Many armed forces have secured virtual independence from civilian control, and assert an independent *voice in executive decisions*, in extreme cases through the formation of a separate military Cabinet. Intervention by direct military action is commonly used to *displace* civilian governments (or even military ones) through the real or implied use of force. Only rarely, as in Ghana (1982) or Brazil (1964), do the armed forces choose to *supplant* civilian government completely.[27]

Finer relates these levels of intervention broadly to types of what he terms 'political culture'. This presents obvious difficulties. Military intervention differs considerably over time in any one country; in 1964, for example, Chile as a democratic presidential state choosing its leaders in competitive elections in a highly aware literate society, would have been regarded as a country of high political culture; by 1974 it was under military dictatorship and all political expression had been suppressed. It seems, therefore, that 'political culture' is the product of military intervention (and other factors) rather than the reverse. Moreover it is difficult to see how such a general and imprecise concept can be measured with accuracy.

Other of the now extensive literature on the military role in politics has focused on the nature and origins of the armed forces themselves, and their relationship to the society in which they serve. In Nigeria, for example, the military takeover of 1966 owed much to the persistence of tribal consciousness in the army. To argue, as some writers have done, that the military act only as the armed wing of a tribe, or indeed of a class, is, on the other hand, to under-estimate the profound importance of the institution to soldiers. The majority of armies are dominated by a relatively small, professionally-trained officer corps, whose largely middle-class recruits are drawn from a wide area, and hence are bound together primarily by institutional ties. It is through the service as an institution, moreover, that they obtain their access to a system of substantial personal privileges, such as pensions, mortgages, credit, cheap goods, clubs, medical attention, and, above all, government positions, for it is membership of the institution that guarantees at one and the same time the safety of a general standard, and the opportunity through promotion to gain access to much greater rewards. Military intervention in politics is guaranteed by the need to maintain this institutional structure in the face of competing civilian interests; its persistence is due to the complex interrelationship between the three levels of the *social*, *institutional* and *personal* interest of the interveners, such that no one of them can be singled out as *the* cause, nor wholly disentangled from the others.[28]

Despite the serious difficulties the political scientist faces in amassing information about active military personnel in many of the most interesting cases, there is much information available. The need to gather information begins with the pre-recruitment stage in an officer's career. What sort of family background, what sort of education, how he came to be chosen for military service, and from what sector of society, for what reasons he took up arms as a career – all these are questions of great importance, but for most countries we lack documentation on attitudes of individual soldiers to set beside Morris Janowitz's *The American Soldier*.[29] What we can know now is how well integrated they are, what sort of regiments they form, and what sort of training process is standard, what their officers are like in relation to them, and whether they have special relationships with the officers of other armies. We should also know whether they are stationed near civilian communities, and if so what sort of arms they have and how they practise with them, and so forth. For the only states in which the military-civilian relationship can be entirely businesslike are those which have maintained a purely alien army, such as the Turkish Janissaries, or have an entirely alien subject population, such as ancient Sparta or modern South Africa.

In all other cases the relationship is a two-way one. Nationalism in the citizenry gives the military a key to national sentiment in time of crisis. But the military pay for having an alert militarised populace by becoming subject to the tides and currents of an informed opinion, so that they lose their own freedom ultimately to alter governments at will.

Revolution is often associated with military action and inevitably with military alienation. But it is always a strategic process capable of modification in response to tactical needs. It can therefore be averted by governments by approaching it on an entirely military level, and preventing the combination of the elements which are essential to the use of force against an armed opponent.

No revolution can occur successfully unless it has an efficient leader, an adequate number of followers, a cause to fight for, and means to make its numbers effective. Of these four, the easiest to avoid is the last. The classic instance is the case of the troops that marched through Baghdad on the night of 13-14 July 1958 on their way to the Israeli frontier. For the first time in the history of the state of Iraq they were not disarmed before entering the capital, and the result was the dramatic revolution which dethroned the Hashemite dynasty and established the Republic. If the means had not been available, there can be reasonable doubt that this revolution would not have taken place – at least, not in the way that it did.[30]

This poses two questions: When military intervention takes place in politics, how far is this a real expression of popular wishes? Is anomic interest articulation the necessary consequence of the blockage of other channels? As already suggested it has been the peculiar sophistication of the twentieth century that men have been able to devise methods of creating the appearance of support, and so isolating the individual who might wish to express views hostile to them and their political programme. In the real world, if a man finds the country is run by the army, and he dislikes the way it is run, he may join the army and try to become a general, or he may take a gun and make for the hills, but he is much more likely to stay at home and mind his own business.

Few people who read the press intensively can fail to be impressed, even in western countries, with what a one-sided picture it presents. When, as in 1967, the news on China comes entirely from Japanese journalists trying to read wallposters in Peking without being seen to look at them we can all see the difficulties. Only the vote, as the 1970 election in the UK showed, can tell, which, if any, of the public opinion polls has made a correct prediction.[31] When there is no vote, or the vote is invalidated by the fact that revolution is the normal method of changing governments or government personnel, we must remember the many years that pass without any such intervention taking place in such a way as to achieve success.

Turbulence as such represents part of a very wide nexus of interactions, which in point of fact may only incidentally be concerned with demands on the government. If people are not orientated to expect things from government they may direct their energies towards getting them from one another, and yet be in general agreement that the government is doing the small minimum they want of it as well as can be expected. Much food for thought in this respect can be found in the table of deaths from domestic group violence given in Russett *et al*, *Handbook of Political and Social Indicators*.[32] Political stability is not the same thing as freedom from violence, and it is not as remarkable a thing as the perspectives of journalism sometimes suggest.

11 Violence and Political Change

The problem of the citizen confronted with a repressive government is one that has been discussed by political philosophers since Plato. The 'right to rebel' has been considered by many to be the ultimate right inherent in the citizens whose lesser civic rights are denied. But it is a different question deciding on what occasion the citizen may legitimately exercise this right, and how he must exercise it to be justified in his actions. The modern heritage on this score is essentially of two different and nearly opposed viewpoints. A great deal depends on the type of justification accepted in any given society. If the citizen is proved wrong after the event it is his life itself that is forfeit.

According to the judgement of St Thomas Aquinas, accepted today in most countries of Catholic heritage, rebellion is justified provided that the rebel can show – after his achievement – that his action was legitimate; that it had involved the use of the minimum possible force by which its ends could be achieved; and that no other resort was open to him.[1] A similar view was held by Islamic writers.[2] According to the view of Locke, however, legitimacy is an attribute fixed before the event. Rebellion is only justified because the government of the day has lost its legitimacy, and the will of the people at large is more exactly represented by its successor. Any action tending to reduce the influence of the people on their own destinies is not legitimate and is to be opposed.[3] This is the view held in Anglo-Saxon countries and their derivates, and the Communist view may be subsumed under it since it sees the overthrow of the bourgeoisie as being pre-ordained by the forces of history, and justified by their previous exploitation of the proletariat.

There is a wide range of anomic activity which is not articulated, the goals of which are not clear in political terms, and which is not so clearly formulated as being within either of these two spheres of justification, if only because, if it does not succeed, it cannot obtain subsequent approval. Indeed any anomic movement which did not aim to strike down the government without delay would probably be suppressed by an efficient government determined to maintain its own power. This shows one of the problems inherent in the study of revolution and rebellion, most of which come back to the basic point that rebellion creates its own legend.

For example, it has long been dogma in conservative circles – following Burke and Carlyle – that the French Revolution of 1789 was an upwelling of primitivism among atavistic plebeians. To them, mobs of dirty illiterates delighted in destroying a social order too educated and complicated for them to understand. Recently, the detailed research of the historian George Rudé among the papers of the Paris Sections has shown that crowd composition in the street demonstrations was principally drawn from the educated artisan class.[4] There are other legends of equal importance, the Marxist one of the Paris Commune of 1871 as the rising of a self-conscious proletariat is another.

The reason for the myth, in the case of a successful revolution, is to support the legitimacy claim of the new government, and in the case of an unsuccessful rebellion, to justify the action taken as a deviation from the prevailing norms of society. All systems of political thought except the anarchist agree that if a government is legitimate it has the 'right' to suppress those who use force against it. Where violence is 'normal', then the use of force against violence is also 'normal'.

There is a further assumption which has come increasingly to the fore in recent years: this is the assumption that political and social change in the motivation of rebellion are bound up together. We are concerned here primarily with political change: change in government or in regime by the use of violence by members of the citizenry. This may or may not be an act which is a prerequisite of deep reaching social change. It is the assumption both of the Marxists and of the American school of sociologists (represented by Pettee, Edwards, Brinton and Chalmers Johnson among writers on revolution) that it is, and that in fact only movements involving such change qualify for the glorious title of revolution.[5] Few periods in history qualify for such acclaim as we have already seen, but those of England (1640-59), America (1774-89), France (1789-95), Mexico (1910-20), Russia (1917-29), China (1911-27, 1949-78?) and Cuba (1959) would be fairly generally recognised, with the additions of perhaps the Dutch (1584), the Turkish (1923) and one or two others.[6]

The supposed interrelationship is not a logical assumption. The only assumption that can be made about the consequences for political revolution is that it has a minimal relationship to social

change, according to Occam's Razor ('Entities must not be multiplied except in necessity'). Many political revolutions occur and
have no important social consequences even though successful,
since many clearly do not seek to obtain them. These activities
which we call palace revolutions, *coups*, etc., can be regarded as
being within the norms of society and certainly not as spectacular
breaks in its continuity. If we make such an assumption with the
so-called great revolutions we do so on social not political grounds,
and we therefore are talking of changes similar to the Meiji restoration in Japan, or the Rise of the Gentry in Tudor England, in
which the element of violence and of the political is seen very
differently.

SUB-REVOLUTIONARY VIOLENCE

It is possible to identify at least three types of anomic political
activity which can be classified as sub-revolutionary violence.

First of all, there are demonstrations. These are anomic groupings of people moved by a single common interest, controlled either
by their own agreement or by leaders, with a limited target of
applying pressure to part or whole of the political system and a fairly
low level of accompanying violence, at least in the early stages.
They may occur anywhere within the territorial limits of the state,
but should they occur in the capital the pressures themselves can be
sufficient to bring down governments and even topple regimes – as
in France in 1830 and 1848.

Demonstrations, however, must be distinguished from riots.
These are uncontrolled movements of frustrated opinion, indis-
criminating in target, and in modern times associated with urbani-
sation. The *jacquerie*, the rural equivalent, in modern states lacks
equivalence in force terms, being removed from the centres of
power except around the capital. Riots show great differences in
their political effects. In Greece in 1965 extensive riots took place,
but had no result in terms of change of government or regime,
though they took place in Athens. The riots of 1967 in the United
States were equally ineffective, while in Colombia in 1948 the
capital was out of control for three days of unrestrained violence
and looting without the President yielding to it. On the other hand a
mob lynched President Villaroel of Bolivia in the course of a riot in
1946, while others killed more than 400,000 people in Indonesia
after the abortive Communist *coup* of 1966, enabling the armed
forces to by-pass and ultimately depose Sukarno.

Thirdly, there is terrorism. Terrorism, in the quite recent past, has been endemic in at least parts of most of the countries of the world. The United Kingdom and Yugoslavia, the two countries at the foot of Russett's table, have both had important terrorist movements within living memory, in both cases associated with nationalist and secessionist aims.[7] The relationship with the lower stages of the anomic hierarchy of force may be clearly seen in the avowed intention of certain organisations to convert the 1960s race riots in the United States into a movement devoted to Black Power.

The nature of terrorism, which may in fact be either spontaneous or organised, is that it is widespread and effective across the political spectrum. Its methods depend on the nature of weaponry in the country, and its articulation as a movement varies with this and the location of its strength. In the past, when weapons were more or less interchangeable with agricultural implements, it was possible for peasants to take their pitchforks and flails and march upon the local 'Big House' to enforce their demands. Nowadays the farm labourer driving a combine harvester is not in a position to do this. But over the greater part of the world peasants still retain the need to use some kind of cutting or slashing instrument as well as firearms in order to stay alive in tropical or semi-tropical conditions.[8] The general opportunities for rural terrorism on a national scale are very much limited also by the intricate nature of the state and modern industrial society.

However, where, as in the United States, there is free sale and distribution of firearms, a new element enters the picture: the possibility of long-term urban violence. Without firearms, this cannot exceed the level of sporadic incidents at weak points in the presence of city government – in dark streets, waste-lots, or deserted buildings not subject to regular police patrol, for example. The introduction of firearms clearly amplifies the possibilities considerably, but it has yet to be proved how far it is actually effective outside closed communities such as those of the Chinese in Hong-Kong or the dwellers in the shanty towns of Caracas.

All these actions fall short of revolution. Revolution is violence *plus* political change: the fall of government or the change of regime. As long as violence falls short of this point it is a means of interest articulation and aggregation, though of a nature in the long run incompatible with the maintenance of ordered government. It corresponds, therefore, to levels of activity within the regular political system: demonstrations being similar in action to pressure groups, riots to the parliamentary aspect of the political party, and terrorism to the mass organisation attempting to build a groundswell of political support. It therefore can be politically significant in application to regular processes as well as those of violence.

This raises the question of how to assess resultant changes in the long term. Any theory of the development of the political system first has to deal with a number of snags. For one there is the problem of identifying the conceptual boundary of the political system in application to the real world. Then there is the problem of delimiting the period within which development is to be considered and its relationship to earlier political formations in the same area. Thirdly, there is the question of how the units of development are to be measured. 'Development' is itself a complex of concepts only some of which can be reduced to expressions in terms of quantifiable indicators. If there is no general agreement what the system is, or how long it has lasted, there is not likely to be much we can usefully say about its development.

This is the problem facing Almond in his essays on developmental theory. As has been shown, he goes some way towards considering the third, avoids the first, and leaves practical application to the reader. Using the concept of revolution used by him elsewhere (e.g. in *The Politics of the Developing Areas*) it seems likely that the major discontinuities, and hence the 'start' and 'finish' of his conceptual systems, are in the major revolutions, in periods of social rather than political change. We have already challenged this concept of discontinuity on the grounds of the prevalence of political change through violence. Now we can also challenge it on the grounds of the prevalence of violence without political change. For if neither violence nor political change is separately the mark of discontinuity in a political system, no combination of the two can effect such a discontinuity. To put it in terms of an example, the French Revolution marks a discontinuity in the history of France, but not in its political system, which continued to exist throughout since it was broken neither by the violence employed nor by the changes of government which occurred during it.

REVOLUTION

If sub-revolutionary violence forms a 'normal' part of the political process, the process of political change that results from it, or from the actual transition between government, may be distinguished from it. Under the umbrella term 'revolution' there are four concepts to be distinguished. First, there is a *process* by which social changes occur, leading towards political change through violence or the convincing threat of violence. Secondly, there is the political *event*, in which a government or regime is actually changed. Thirdly, we can distinguish the *programme* that a post-revolutionary government pursues, which has links with both process and event. Lastly, there is the *myth* of revolution, the symbolic value it holds in the integration of disintegration of the community. The special quality of the myth, which seems to be embodied in the sociologists' concept of social revolution, is that it suggests in aggregate that political order is at once permanent and discontinuous, since it owes its final form to a species of consensus between conservative and radical interpretations.[9]

An integrated model of this kind would probably recognise most usefully the function of revolution in society. It would rest on conflict: the conflict between demands and supports, the conflict between élite (decision-makers) and mass, the conflict, above all, between the political system and the social system as a whole. In the flow pattern of such a model, revolution would form one kind of interaction among the many patterns of positive and negative interchange between these last: the maximisation of demands (or negative inputs) and the minimisation of supports (or positive inputs). All this, however, is to go beyond the scope of this book.

In the political sense, then, revolution is an event primarily, and may be suspected in any violent change of ruler by subjects. There are obviously vast variations in the surrounding events, but in the actual change a certain rigidity is apparent. Certain attributes can be recognised as being important, and can be used therefore for classification.

To begin with the event implies the use of a certain amount of violence by revolutionaries, opposed on occasion by a quantity of force on the part of the regime. The fact of success implies that the revolutionary violence has attained a point which we can term the minimum necessary force (MNF). This point is crucial to the differentiation of revolutionary from sub-revolutionary activity. Failure to reach MNF implies the failure of the movement in question: excess over it, it may reasonably by hypothesised, will result in ancillary phenomena in the political or social consequences of the event.[10] After all, those revolutions which have been associated most closely with developed social phenomena have been those in which the government overthrown exercised power at so low a level that any force used to overthrow it was proportionately almost infinite. The force employed is a measurable quantity, measurable either as the number of troops mobilised or as the number actually deployed at any given moment, multiplied by their capacity to use force and the degree of their spatial concentration.

A revolutionary event must occupy a certain time period. Within this we can distinguish three time phases: a period of *preparation* integral with and related to the social process of disaffection; the *action* itself, which we may term the assault phase; and a period of *consolidation* with the promulgation of the post-revolutionary programme. The nature of the assault period is the determinant of the transition itself, and the duration of it – usually brief – is a second criterion for classification. The reason is that the superiority of power to be obtained by the revolutionary force has to be effective during this period, or, more specifically, during a period, termed the critical time, which in a successful revolution falls wholly within this period. Beyond the conclusion of the assault phase, it should be noted, the use of force is no longer directed specifically at the defeated government, but as in the case of any other government of whatever age, against all possible and probable enemies of the new regime.

A third attribute is the level on which force is deployed, that is to say the geographical space over which the action takes place. This action must be related to the force available if MNF is to be achieved, and the option may exist for initiating hostilities on either of two levels, or on any level, depending on resources. In order of power required, revolutionary action may be directed against the executive, the government, the capital or a province. Each brings its particular hazards.

The immobilisation of the *executive* requires speed and secrecy of planning, but the least actual force; and of the *government* involves a number of personnel, some of whom are of little importance, but others of whom have authority without formal rank. These have to be rapidly and accurately located and captured, and synchronisation of action becomes a major consideration if reinforcements are not to become a hazard. Failure to do so results in the sort of consequences that followed the breakdown of the plot to overthrow the government of Abraham Lincoln, which was successful only in so far as it resulted in the death of Lincoln himself.[11]

A movement directed at securing control of the *capital* involves a number of considerations, but that of force is obviously most important. Since it assumes that a complete superiority of force will be achieved in the key administrative area of a country, which will not be challenged in the critical time by forces brought in from the provinces, it is the form normally favoured by military movements. It is effective because it gains control of the area from which the people at large expect leadership, and that on which the communications net is centred.

The seizure and exercise of governmental functions in a *province*, which requires the most force of any type of revolution, is intended to put pressure on this area indirectly. It can therefore start with small beginnings, but depends on remoteness from the centre of power to attract superior forces before government troops arrive to engage it. It can then hope, if the government does not yield, to strike at the capital and put it out of action directly.

For theoretical reasons, the Marxist writers on revolution advocate movements in which large-scale mobilisation occurs of the masses. In the form of peasant guerrilla movements, advocated by Mao Tse-tung and Che Guevara,[12] these have been successful in China and Cuba through the direct pressure leading to the collapse of central resistance. In China this was aided by the debilitation of the government after eight years of war against the Japanese, and the power vacuum left by the Japanese surrender. This latter factor was largely responsible for the success in 1945 of the Communists in Vietnam, and the followers of Sukarno in Indonesia, their government being established in each case before the return of the colonial power and thus able to provide a geographical base for guerrillas' resistance to reconquest.[13] In Cuba, the guerrilla war formed the pretext for a massive urban uprising. Since the Marxists have traditionally been opposed, also on theoretical grounds, to the *coup*, they have laboured under the necessity of maintaining unusually high force levels in their attempts to gain power. Lenin himself was prepared to adopt the *coup* as an opportunistic short-cut, however, with outstanding success.[14] It was the fact that the Cuban revolution occurred in an area that was already acquainted with revolutionary movements on all levels which pointed up its regularities, and made possible the assimilation of Marxist revolutions to a general theory.

It should be added, however, that difficulties lie in the way of precise application of force analysis (even retroactively) which have nothing to do with the type advocated, but are purely practical. Information about troop numbers and movements is classified information, and by the time security has been lifted, the recollections of witnesses may be unable to rectify the propaganda versions of numbers engaged. In any case, actual numbers are rarely used, vague expressions such as 'regiments', 'companies', 'detachments' being capable of multiple interpretations, even assuming that they were regular formations up to their roster strength. It is for this reason that Lewis F. Richardson chose to set the precedent of measuring the impact of violent events in terms of 'magnitude'. The magnitude of an event is simply the total number of casualties caused by it, as measured on a simple logarithmic scale.[15]

The typology generated for revolutionary events by a matrix of these three attributes of force, duration and level may usefully be compared with most useful of the sociological taxonomies of revolution – that of Chalmers Johnson.[16] It is a derivation from the tradition combining social and political phenomena in an essentially organic concept. The classification is of six phyla identified by a range of criteria, among which, for example, Johnson distinguishes from one another millenarian rebellion, a religious movement which may or may not achieve political ends, *Jacobin* Communist revolution, a social/political nexus involving egalitarianism, and militarised mass insurrection, involving long-term and conscious pursuit of goals by military methods engaging a substantial sector of the population, that is to say, as opposed to a *coup*.

While, therefore, the Johnson typology incorporates criteria of ideology, achievement, numbers and participation, it does not offer a complete matrix, and there are great difficulties in making use of it for exact statement. Its value lies in its perception of the social background of revolution, and the essential unity of forms of violent political change.

What sort of statements can this analysis enable us to make on the nature of actual revolutions? First of all, there is from observation alone no clear link between economic development and the absence of violence in politics, though it is clear that there is some link. Comparison on the one hand between Argentina and Uruguay indicates that a highly developed agricultural country, backed by a substantial industrial complex with money to spend on social and other services, does not necessarily enjoy peaceful politics, or even civilian government. Comparison on the other between Chile and Mexico suggests that it is not necessary to have a large-scale social revolution in order to achieve equality and social justice. Personalities in power are very important, as the destruction of civilian rule in Chile after 1973 demonstrates.

The presence of violence, however, imposes its own necessities. In particular, given the need to adapt to changing times, military intervention all too easily becomes essential where it is normal. Otherwise the operation of a system in which political change is achieved substantially by violent means cannot be continued in face of the non-participation of the monopolists of the means of coercive force. Contrary to the impression that violence is a sign of instability, governments seem to change sometimes more and sometimes less frequently in countries in which violent politics is the norm. It does not seem to make much difference in either case how the change is achieved provided that it is seen to have occurred. A dictator who changes his Cabinet frequently may fulfil the desire for new faces as effectively as the process of frequent elections in other countries, and the value of federalism where it operates, or elective local government where it does not, must at least partly be the facility it offers for frequent lesser changes and the channeling of the impulse into manageable form. But evidently not all states value leadership changes, preferring to demonstrate one leader of accepted skills or outstanding personal qualities, such as Mao, Nasser or Kenyatta.

Thirdly, we must observe that the impulse towards violence results in frequent and fairly simple *coups*, sometimes following one another in a sequence. The 'Great Revolutions', as Lyford P. Edwards named them, such as the French, English and Russian, and even in some states the American, were composed in part of *coups*. As we have already discussed, the relationship between these *coups* and social reform is contradicted on both sides, but on sequential grounds Haiti, Panama and the Dominican Republic all offer equally dramatic examples without the social change.[17]

The difference is often attributed to a particular combination of social circumstances, which impelled into power a set of moderate social reformers who succeeded in arousing expectations and making the burden of the past intolerable, without at the same time taking steps sufficient to satisfy resultant demand. But moderate reform does not necessarily result in the rise and successful accession to power of extremists; it may, and often does, result in a counter-*coup* by irate conservatives. Besides, history abounds with examples in which moderate reform satisfied demands of a potentially revolutionary character: the passage of the Great Reform Act in Britain in 1832 was one.

Even if extremists accede to power, they need not necessarily follow their first reprisals with that organised reign of terror, of which Iraq and Egypt are recent cases in point.[18] Both involved the presence of a possible external alien enemy, however. Cases in which terror has been resorted to have significantly been correlated with the great weakness of the internal opposition, but external enemies have acted to exacerbate suspicion that this weakness was feigned. The numbers however are small, and the suspicion remains that the revolutionary by nature expects to find hostility, and if he does not tends to create it in order to justify his philosophy of violence. There is, after all, the temptation to extend an apparently easy (because successful) method of achieving power into a means of maintaining it.

There must also be taken into account the panic reaction of people who do not wish to be 'liberated' from the traditional ways that they know, which, after all, are basically the means by which they have been taught to survive. In such circumstances even leaders may be nervous about unpredictable changes of opinion.

Finally, therefore, we must consider the ways in which revolutions can be said to be institutionalised. When we do so, we speak not of the process or the event, but of the programme and the myth of revolution. Both are established as permanent essentially by the passage of time. There are no specifically 'revolutionary' institutions, only institutions designed to carry out the revolutionary programme, and the routinisation of these is the process of state formation itself. All modern states contain institutions owing their origin to a revolutionary event and a new programme.

The nature of the new system-balance however depends on the forces it brings into unity or counterpoise. This in turn is necessarily dependent on the social milieu on the initiation of the revolutionary process. The precise form depends on the number of major interest sectors within the ruling élite. If there are only one or two, turbulence remains almost inevitable for the future, while a multiplicity brings the problem of coalition against the possible independence of the instruments of power, for example, the army or the police. A tripartite division seems very nearly ideal.[19] A strong tradition of personalism in the ruling élite can lead to the overwhelming desire for a Bonaparte, the most dramatic form of the democratic Caesar, but otherwise the routinisation of charisma seems to be less a feature of post-revolutionary times than the routinisation of concepts. Individual action can still play an important part, however, in the acceptance of forces and the way in which the rise of new ones is received.

On the other hand, the similarity between post-revolutionary times and primitive politics must not be overstressed. This recollection of the past is dominant in the minds of those establishing the new government. It is their concept of what a government should be. Those who rebel against it are as always few compared with those who seek guidance on forms and precedents. But the event of revolution is only of marginal importance in creating this problem; its myth obscures the lesson that in every age governments are continually evolving to meet new challenges with new responses.

12 Government Versus Politics

In the course of this book we have tried together to examine the principal features of modern governments. We have sought to discern regularities between them and within them. From time to time we have come up with propositions about human behaviour in certain situations. By way of conclusion, it seems time to consider just what these propositions, and others like them, really mean.

Clearly in our study of human political behaviour we are not confronting propositions with the inflexible regularity of the so-called Laws of Nature. There is scarcely a rule of politics that is not broken successfully at one time or another, and there is no reason to suppose that there are in fact any that cannot be broken. All statements in the social sciences are statements of probability, and that probability never actually reaches one. It always falls short, by ever such a small amount as maybe, but it falls short nevertheless. Consequently, any statement about human behaviour can be true only for individuals in groups at the most, and can tell us nothing about the certainty of action by a single individual.

It is salutary to remember that philosophically it is impossible to *prove* even that the so-called Laws of Nature are themselves true.[1] It is, indeed, probable that the regularities which we detect in our own surroundings of the near universe are in fact only local expressions; the underlying principles of nature may well be considerably more complex. Nevertheless, they do have a value, in that they serve as practical guides for action. And this is the point of our discourse here, to illustrate in what ways it is possible to understand the motivation of politicians and to make reliable predictions of their most likely courses of action, together with the probable consequences of alternative courses of action or inaction. Even if it is true that a politician may break all the rules of politics, as we understand them, and get away with it, nevertheless to say this is to say that there are rules that do apply to the majority of cases. The validity of these rules is of course in no way proved by the exceptions, but neither, on the other hand, is their invalidity, because the fact is that we simply cannot guarantee that the environment in which our observations take place remains sufficiently constant for us to be sure that our laws are valid, it is only the circumstances that have changed.

In retrospect, therefore, it seems as if the great debate about predictability in the social sciences has been largely misplaced. In a trail-blazing book of great significance Peter Winch asserted that there was no possibility of developing a predictive science in the social sciences,[2] and his view was widely held by others of his period. As can be shown, the highest sophistication of probability theory in itself is not an adequate substitute for this ability to predict.[3] However, since political structures are determined by human beings it is still possible, and in many ways rewarding, to regard them as operating not according to Laws of Nature but to man-made rules which those skilled in such matters can learn and hence predict, in the sense in which an individual participating in a game necessarily learns and predicts the moves of his opponents. In this sense the ability to play the game efficiently depends on the ability to anticipate the moves of all relevant players, at least to the point at which the likelihood of any given move and its consequences may be accurately assessed.

It is tempting to think of this game as being played by government versus opposition; tempting, but misleading. It is tempting for the reasons stated above, namely that the human mind naturally likes clear-cut divisions between being and not being. It is misleading because, as we have seen also, a government need not in fact have any significant opposition. What it always has is both a positive and negative relationship with the social system of which it is the directing agent.[4] This relationship is positive in the sense that the government, by regulating and directing the social system, has the capacity to make it more productive. It is negative in the sense that in order to do so it needs to withdraw resources from the system which might be employed otherwise in productive activity.

It has been traditional to represent the relationship between the government and the social system in terms of a contract between the individual citizen and the government. The philosophers who used this device were, of course, well aware that the contract of which they spoke was not a real historical event, but rather a concept designed to explain a social relationship. Equally theoretical is the explanation of those philosophical anarchists who held, and indeed still hold, the view that government is imposed upon society by force or fraud. Certainly government is something given, not consented to, in so far as the relationship to any individual citizen is determined before that citizen reaches the age of maturity, and the process of maturation is indeed guided and regulated by the state. To this extent, the citizen's consent is engineered. Nor could it be said in any real sense that the mere act of coming of age involved an applied contract between the citizen and the government he finds in office on that day, though it might reasonably be argued that acceptance over a period of time implied such consent, and many writers on the subject of consent have held that negative consent is so implied and registered.

The question is, however, to what extent does the citizen have any opportunity to change matters? As one of a very large number of citizens his power is limited to that proportion of the total social mass which is signified by his ability to vote, or in those societies in which this is not possible otherwise to express his political wishes. It is even further limited by the fact that there is no very clear evidence that the majority of human beings in fact wish to change this state of affairs. Even when it is suggested to them that they would wish to change it, in the main they do not seek to do so, and this is not satisfactorily explicable either by the process of their education, or by the suggestion that they regard the operation, as opposed to the institution of government as morally sanctioned. It appears, rather, that the acceptance of government is psychologically determined in that the actions of it fulfil important needs felt by the individual in a recognisable form, and in some ways substitute therefore for social structures which have been encountered as an earlier state of existence.

We have already seen how the anthropologists term the act of replication as a process of modelling the greater upon the lesser. In this way they see social structures embodying the principal features of society as they are understood at the level of the simplest family or small band. If they are correct, and there seems good reason to think that they are within the structure of traditional societies with which they habitually deal, then we may expect political institutions within these societies to be built up of a combination of horizontal and vertical links forming structures each within a defined boundary and each enjoying a determined relationship with one another. These structures, combining in greater or lesser extent the principle of hierarchy with the principle of equality are combined to form all other forms of government. And from these basic forms of government, as we have seen already, there have grown up in a slow process of historical evolution those elaborated structures of government which today exist and are clearly continuing to evolve in new ways in fulfilment of needs not previously seen and towards goals not yet accurately formulated.

174 Politics, Power and Revolution

That this process of evolution has taken place largely as a result of trial and error reflects the lack of systematic knowledge available to the majority of constitution builders in the past, and in particular the limitation of each to the perimeter of a single society. The makers of the American Constitution were unusually fortunate in the breadth of the knowledge upon which they could call, but then they performed their act of Constitution-making at a point in historical time when it was possible for an educated man to know most of what was to be known about the world, and at a time when the systematic learning of the Renaissance had not yet become dissipated. They were, moreover, consciously creating a Constitution not merely for a single country but, as they saw it, for a new world. Few modern Constitution makers have been so ambitious, and none of them has been, perhaps, so successful.

What these thinkers above all demonstrated was an awareness of a significance of basic structural relationships. The institutions which they used were only those with which they were already familiar, and which they had learnt to use themselves over a period of many years, and indeed decades. They did not experiment with the then modern notion of faction or as we would now term it party, for example. It would not probably have occurred to them to do so, but in retrospect we can see that it was a prudent move in so far as the dynamics of the large group situation which a mass party and a mass following entail are substantially different from those of the small groups upon which they built their basic institutions.

It is often said, and with some truth, that this is because they distrusted the people. It is, on the other hand, certain that they distrusted the government. They distrusted government because to them governments were dangerous. And if governments are dangerous it is not because they are remote sinister impersonal forces, it is because they are made up of people. All people are dangerous to one another, and it is precisely because the majority of people throughout the ages have recognised that the smallest tear in social fabric spells danger – potentially fatal – to the individual human being who happens to be caught in it, that so many of them have been prepared to accept unattractive or authoritarian governments.

This is however a counsel of despair and, besides, it is the counsel of ignorance. In so far as politics can be regarded as a necessary process for the protection of the individual against the government upon which he relies, it is in his interests to take a positive rather than a negative view to his relationship with it. For if he does not take an interest in it, he has no assurance that it will not take an interest in him.

Notes

CHAPTER 1

1. Aristotle, *Ethics*, I, i, 1094a, cited in *The Politics*, trans. and ed., Ernest Barker (Oxford, Clarendon Press, 1968), p.354.
2. W. G. Runciman, *Social Science and Political Theory* (Cambridge, Cambridge University Press, 1963), pp. 2-3.
3. William W. Howells, 'The meaning of race', and Theodosias Dobzhansky, 'Race equality', in Richard H. Osborne (ed.), *The Biological and Social Meaning of Race* (San Francisco, W. H. Freeman & Co., 1971), pp. 5-6, 13 ff.
4. Modified from Max Weber, *The Theory of Social and Economic Organization* (New York, The Free Press, 1965), p.154.
5. Joseph Frankel, *International Relations* (Oxford, Oxford University Press, 1964), p.13, regards the definition as unchanged since Jean Bodin (1576).
6. Ibid., pp. 28, 126, 156.
7. Figures from *Statesmans' Year Book*, 1981 (London, Macmillan, 1981).
8. Johan Galtung, 'The structural theory of imperialism', *Journal of Peace Research*, (1971) VIII, No. 2, p.81.
9. Henry Valen and Stein Rokkan, 'Norway; conflict structure and mass politics in a European periphery', in Richard Rose (ed.), *Electoral Behavior, A Comparative Handbook* (New York, Free Press, 1974), p.315.
10. As e.g. Andrew H. Whiteford, *Two Cities of Latin America, A Comparative Description of Social Classes* (Garden City, N.Y., Doubleday Anchor, 1964).
11. Communication to VI Congress, International Political Science Association, Brussels 1967; cf. Ludwig Neundörfer (ed.), *Atlas sozial ökonomischer Regionen Europas* (Frankfurt a.M., Soziographisches Institut an der Johann Wolfgang Goethe-Universität, 1961).
12. Arthur S. Banks and Robert B. Textor, *A Cross-Polity Survey* (Cambridge, Mass., The MIT Press, 1963).
13. Peter Calvert, *A Study of Revolution* (Oxford, Clarendon Press, 1970).
14. Gabriel A. Almond and Sidney Verba, *The Civic Culture* (Princeton,

Princeton University Press, 1963).

15.   'Cybernetics' comes from the same Greek root (*gubernetes*— steersman) as 'government' and means 'the science of steering'. Norbert Weiner, *Cybernetics* (Cambridge, Mass., the MIT Press, 1967), p.11.

16.   Robert A. Dahl, *Modern Political Analysis* (Englewood Cliffs, N.J., Prentice-Hall, 1964), p.9.

17.   Gabriel A. Almond, 'Introduction: a functional approach to comparative politics', in G. A. Almond and James S. Coleman, *The Politics of the Developing Areas* (Princeton, N.J., Princeton University Press, 1960), p.13.

18.   D. Mack Smith, *Italy, A Modern History* (Ann Arbor, University of Michigan Press, 1959), pp.27. 192-210, 390.

19.   i.e. 'the actually existing powers and forces in a country' – Ferdinand Lassalle, *Verfassungswesen* (1862), cited in Bertrand Russell, *German Social Democracy* (London, Allen & Unwin, 1965), p.52. See also K. C. Wheare, *Modern Constitutions* (Oxford, Oxford University Press, 1951), pp. 1-3.

20.   As collected in Leslie Wolf-Philips (ed.), *Constitutions of Modern States* (London, Pall Mall, 1968), p.182 ff. For other Constitutions, S. E. Finer, *Five Constitutions: Contrasts and Comparisons* (Hassocks, Harvester Press, Harmondsworth, Penguin, 1979), and Amos J. Peaslee (ed.), *Constitution of Nations*, 3 vols, (The Hague, Martinus Nijhoff, 1968).

21.   Douglas V. Verney, *The Analysis of Political Systems* (London, Routledge, 1961), p.18, citing J. A. Hawgood, *Modern Constitutions since 1787*, pp. 145-6.

22.   Charles-Louis de Secondat, Baron de Montesquieu, *The Spirit of the Laws*, trans, Thomas Nugent, intro. Franz Neumann (New York, Hafner, 1966), book XIV, p.221 ff.

23.   Jean-Jacques Rousseau, *The Social Contract and Discourses*, trans. and intro. G. D. H. Cole (London, Dent, 1958), pp. 163 ff. ('A discourse on the origin of inequality'.)

CHAPTER 2

1.   Konrad Lorenz, *On Aggression* (London, Methuen, 1966).

2.   Jacob Bronowski, *The Ascent of Man* (London, BBC Publications, 1973); W. B. Emery, *Archaic Egypt* (Harmondsworth, Pelican, 1961), pp. 44-5, 60, record wars under the First Dynasty.

3.   John Dollard, Leonard W. Doob, Neal E. Miller, O. H. Mowrer and Robert R. Sears, *Frustration and Aggression* (New Haven, Yale University Press, 1939), and Ted R. Gurr, *Why Men Rebel* (Princeton, Princeton University Press, 1970) p. 24ff.

4.   Julius Fast, *Body Language* (London, Souvenir Press, 1971) pp. 25-7, 33-44, 50ff.

5.   Robert Ardrey, *The Territorial Imperative, a personal inquiry into the animal origins of property and nations* (London, Collins, 1970), pp. 97ff, 128-9. cf. J. H. Crook, 'The nature and function of territorial aggression', in

Ashley Montagu (ed.), *Man and Aggression* (New York, Oxford University Press, 1973) p. 183ff.
6.   Boris Goldenberg, *The Cuban Revolution and Latin America* (London, Allen & Unwin, 1965) p. 227.
7.   Peter Farb, *Man's Rise to Civilization, as shown by the Indians of North America from Primeval Times to the Coming of the Industrial State* (New York, Avon, 1968) pp. 257-9.
8.   J. B. Bury, *A History of Greece to the Death of Alexander the Great* (London, Macmillan, 1956) 3rd edn rev., pp. 74-5.
9.   Desmond Morris, *The Naked Ape* (New York, Dell, 1969); see also his *The Human Zoo* (New York, McGraw Hill, 1969); and cf. David Pilbeam, 'An idea we could live without; the naked ape', in Montagu, *op.cit.*, p.110 ff.
10.   Lionel Tiger, *Men in Groups* (London, Nelson, 1969) p.xiii.
11.   Elaine Morgan, *The Descent of Woman* (London, Corgi Books, 1974).
12.   Lucy Mair, *Primitive Government* (London, Penguin Books, 1962).
13.   Lawrence Krader, *Formation of the State* (New York, Prentice Hall, 1968) p.29ff.
14.   M Fortes and E. E. Evans Pritchard (eds), *African Political Systems* (Oxford, Oxford University Press, 1963); see esp. preface by A. R. Radcliffe Brown.
15.   ibid., 'Introduction', pp. 4-5.
16.   Margaret Mead, *Male and Female* (Harmondsworth, Penguin Books, 1962).
17.   E. E. Evans Pritchard, *The Nuer, a Description of the Modes of Livelihood and Political Institutions of a Nilotic People* (Oxford, Clarendon Press, 1940), pp. 5-6.
18.   Erwin I. J. Rosenthal, *Political Thought in Mediaeval Islam, an Introductory Outline* (Cambridge, Cambridge University Press, 1962) pp. 3-4.
19.   Dennis Bloodworth, *Chinese Looking Glass* (Harmondsworth, Penguin Books, 1969), pp. 325-7.
20.   Emery, op.cit., pp. 47, 69.
21.   David P. Henige, *The Chronology of Oral Tradition, Quest for a Chimera* (Oxford, Clarendon Press, 1974), p.4.
22.   Evans Pritchard, op.cit., pp.163-4, 172 ff.
23.   Walter Ullmann, *A History of Political Thought, the Middle Ages* (Harmondsworth, Penguin Books, 1965), p.207, demonstrates that the first break with this idea was due to Marsiglio of Padua.
24.   Roy. A. Rappaport, *Pigs for the Ancestors; Ritual in the Ecology of a New Guinea People* (New Haven, Yale University Press, 1968), p.3.
25.   F. G. Bailey, *Strategems and Spoils* (Oxford, Basil Blackwell, 1969), pp. 32-3.
26.   Aristotle, *The Politics,* E. Barker (ed.), (Oxford, Clarendon Press, 1968) V,ii, 1312, p.243.
27.   See C. J. Friedrich, *Tradition and Authority* (London, Pall Mall, 1972), pp. 14-15, 47-8.
28.   Max Weber, *The Theory of Social and Economic Organization* (New

York, Free Press, 1964), pp. 132, 324 ff.
29.   Sir David Lindsay Keir, *The Constitutional History of Modern Britain, 1485-1951* (London, A & C Black, 1957, 5th edn), p.63.
30.   Douglas V. Verney, *The Analysis of Political Systems* (London, Routledge, 1961), p.3.
31.   Georgina Masson, *A Concise History of Republican Rome* (London, Thames & Hudson, 1973), p.16.
32.   Geoffrey Gorer, *Africa Dances* (London, Penguin Books, 1945), pp. 116-18.
33.   Masson, op.cit., pp.16-17.

CHAPTER 3

1.   Morton R. Davies and Vaughan A. Lewis, *Models of Political Systems* (London, Pall Mall, 1971), pp. 22-3.
2.   Evon Z. Vogt, *Zinacantan, a Maya Community in the Highlands of Chiapas* (Cambridge, Mass., Belknap, 1969), ch.24, p.582 ff. See also Richard Rose, *Governing without Consensus, an Irish Perspective* (London, Faber, 1971), pp. 27, 31.
3.   John H. Herz, *International Politics in the Atomic Age* (New York, Columbia University Press, 1959), p.64.
4.   An example of this approach is Peter Wales, *Elements of Comparative Government* (London, Duckworth, 1967).
5.   As in Talcott Parsons and Edward A. Shils (eds), *Towards a General Theory of Action* (New York, Harper, 1962), pp. 54-5.
6.   G. A. Almond and J. S. Coleman, *The Politics of the Developing Areas* (Princeton, N.J., Princeton University Press, 1959) p.17.
7.   As in Karl Deutsch, *The Nerves of Government, Models of Political Communication and Control* (New York, the Free Press, 1966).
8.   ibid., pp.90, 106.
9.   Peter Calvert, 'The dynamics of political change', *Political Studies*, XVII, no.4, December 1969.
10.   Aristotle, *The Politics*, trans and ed. E. Barker (Oxford, Clarendon Press, 1968). p.113 ff.
11.   Bernard Diedrich, *Trujillo, the Death of the Goat* (London, Bodley Head, 1978), p. 248.
12.   Robert A. Dahl, *Modern Political Analysis* (Englewood Cliffs, N.J., Prentice-Hall, 1964), p.26 ff.
13.   Robert A. Dahl, *A Preface to Democratic Theory* (Chicago, University of Chicago Press, 1964), pp. 84-7.
14.   Leonard Schapiro, *Totalitarianism* (London, Pall Mall & Macmillan, 1972), p.18.
15.   Graham T. Allison, *Essence of Decision; Explaining the Cuban Missile Crisis* (Boston, Little-Brown, 1971), p.5.
16.   Bernard Crick, *Basic Forms of Government; A Sketch and a Model* (London, Macmillan, 1973), pp. 74-81.

17.   Jean Blondel, *Comparing Political Systems* (London, Weidenfeld & Nicolson, 1973), p.40.

18.   Douglas V. Verney, *The Analysis of Political Systems* (London, Routledge, 1961), p.3.

19.   ibid., p.57 ff.

20.   John Locke, *Two Treatises on Government*, ed. P. Laslett (Cambridge, Cambridge University Press, 1964), p.383.

21.   Dahl, *Modern Political Analysis*, p.35 ff.

22.   Joseph Frankel, *The Making of Foreign Policy; an Analysis of Decision-Making* (London, Oxford University Press, 1963), pp. 17-19.

23.   Parsons and Shils, *op.cit.*

24.   J.L. Talmon, *The Origins of Totalitarian Democracy* (London, Mercury Books, 1961).

25.   G. A. Almond and G. Bingham Powell, *Comparative Politics, a Developmental approach* (Boston, Little-Brown, 1966).

26.   Max Weber, *The Theory of Social and Economic Organization* (New York, Free Press, 1965), pp.346 ff.

27.   S. Eisenstadt, *The Political Systems of Empires* (New York, Free Press, 1963), p.4.

28   Peter Calvert, *Revolution* (London, Pall Mall & Macmilan, 1970), pp.40, 43-4.

CHAPTER 4

1.   The slogan 'The Medium is the message' used by Marshall McLuhan is a misleading statement of the proposition 'The message is limited by the medium.' See his *Understanding Media, The Extensions of Man* (New York, Signet, 1964), p.23 ff.

2.   George A. Miller, *Language and Communication* (New York, McGraw Hill, 1963), p.6.

3.   Konrad Lorenz, *On Aggression* (London, Methuen, 1966) pp. 149-51.

4.   David Butler (ed.), *Elections Abroad* (London, Macmillan, 1959), p.261.

5.   Anthony Nutting, *No End of a Lesson, The story of Suez* (London Constable, 1967), p.21; Hugh Thomas, *The Suez Affair* (London, Weidenfeld, 1966), p.22.

6.   Leo Huberman and Paul M Sweezy, *Cuba, Anatomy of a Revolution* (New York, Monthly Review Press, 1968), p.152, who foresaw, but dismissed, the need for the CP to assume this role.

7.   Colin Cross, *The Liberals in Power, 1905-1914* (London, Barrie & Rockliff with Pall Mall, 1963), pp. 18-19.

8.   For Chile see *The Economist*, 20 November 1971. For the Peruvian Press Law of 1970 see *The Times*, 20 January and 10 February 1970; for the case of Cuba, see Boris Goldenberg, *The Cuban Revolution and Latin America* (London, Allen & Unwin, 1965), pp.202-4.

9.   Denis McQuail, *Towards a Sociology of Mass Communications* (New York, Collier-Macmillan, 1969), p.71 ff.

10.   John C. Condon, Jr, *Semantics and Communication* (New York, Macmillan, 1966), p.9.
11.   Goldenberg op.cit. p.107.
12.   Martin Albrow, *Bureaucracy* (London, Pall Mall, 1969), p.99.
13.   Ernest S. Griffith, *The American System of Government* (London, Methuen, 1965, 4th edn), pp. 101-2.
14.   Theodore White, *The Making of the President, 1964* (London, Jonathan Cape, 1965), p.366.
15.   J. R. Pierce, *Symbols, Signals and Noise, The Nature and Process of Communication* (London, Hutchinson, 1962), pp.25, 29; Condon, op.cit., p.51; see also Miller op.cit., p.257.
16.   See also Richard L. Merritt, *Systemic Approaches to Comparative Politics* (New York, Rand McNally, 1970), pp. 152-3.
17.   On semantic variation in social attitudes see H. J. Eysenck, *Psychology and Politics* (London, Routledge, 1963).
18.   Basil Bernstein, *Classes, Codes and Control*, 4 vols (London, Routledge, 1973-6.) This does not imply acceptance of Bernstein's thesis of the class origins of such codes.
19.   Hong Yung Lee, *The Politics of the Chinese Cultural Revolution; a Case Study* (Berkeley, University of California Press, 1978).
20.   Cf. Nick Bosanquet and Peter Townsend (eds), *Labour and Equality; a Fabian Study of Labour in Power, 1974-79* (London, Heinemann, 1979), pp. 7-8.
21.   Donald E. Weatherbee, *Ideology in Indonesia; Sukarno's Indonesian Revolution* (New Haven, Yale South East Asia Studies, Monograph Series, no.8), gives examples.
22.   Charles E. Osgood, George J. Suci and Percy H. Tannenbaum, *The Measurement of Meaning* (Urbana, University of Illinois Press, 1957), p.25.
23.   R. Díaz Guerrero, *Psychology of the Mexican, Culture and Personality* (Austin, University of Texas Press, 1975), p.89 ff.
24.   Robert C. North *et al.*, *Content Analysis* (Evanston, Northwestern University Press, 1963); Ithiel da Sola Pool (ed.), *Trends in Content Analysis* (Urbana, University of Illinois Press, 1957).

CHAPTER 5

1.   The treatment in this chapter is based on Douglas V. Verney, *The Analysis of Political Systems* (London, Routledge, 1961), supplemented by D. W. Brogan and D. V. Verney, *Politics in the Modern World* (London, Hamish Hamilton, 1963), with substantial modifications introduced both to bring the material up-to-date, and to conform with the general treatment.
2.   Crane Brinton, *The Anatomy of Revolution* (New York, Vintage Books, 1952) discusses these.
3.   Carl Leiden and Karl M. Schmitt, *The Politics of Violence; Revolution in the Modern World* (New York, Prentice-Hall, 1968), discuss these.
4.   Walter Ullmann, *A History of Political Thought, the Middle Ages* (Harmondsworth, Penguin, 1965), pp. 12-13, terms belief in the Middle

Ages in the will of the people the 'ascending thesis', in contrast to the 'descending thesis' attributing royal authority to the will of God.

5. Walter Starkie, *The Road to Santiago* (London, John Murray, 1957), p.124.
6. Max Farrand (ed.), *The Records of the Federal Convention of 1787*, rev. edn, (New Haven, Yale University Press, 1966); the reference was, however, to the power of the Justiciary.
7. G. Bruun, *The Enlightened Despots* (New York, Holt, 1929).
8. Douglas Verney, *The Analysis of Political Systems* (London, Routledge, 1961), p.18; see also John A. Hawgood, *Modern Constitutions since 1787* (London, Macmillan, 1939), pp. 145-6.
9. As adapted over time; see Richard E. Neustadt, *Presidential Power* (New York, Signet, 1964).
10. Martin C. Needler, *Latin American Power in Perspective* (Princeton, Van Nostrand, 1963).
11. Robert I. Rotberg, *Haiti, the Politics of Squalor* (Boston, Houghton Mifflin, 1971), p.232.
12. *The Annual Register of World Events* (henceforth cited as AR) 1973, p.94. Martin Weinstein, *Uruguay, The Politics of Failure* (Westport, Conn., Greenwood Press, 1975), pp. 132-3.
13. Federico G. Gil, *The Political System of Chile* (Boston, Houghton Mifflin, 1965), p.208, AR 1973, pp.64, 70.
14. Montesquieu, *The Spirit of the Laws*, trans. Nugent (New York, Haffner, 1966), book XI, ch.4, p.151: 'Of the Constitution of England'.
15. Verney, op.cit., p.39 ff.
16. François Bourricaud, *Power and Society in Contemporary Peru* (New York, Praeger, 1970), p.270; Philip Cerny, 'The new rules of the game in France', in Philip G. Cerny and Martin A. Schain, *French Politics and Public Policy* (London, Methuen, 1980) p.32.
17. The Swedish government removed the last vestiges of political authority from the king in 1975 (AR 1975, p.151); cf. Brogan and Verney, op.cit., p.83.
18. AR 1975, p.253 ff.
19. J. J. Rousseau, *The Social Contract and Discourses*, trans, G. D. H. Cole, (London, Dent, 1958), pp.20, 22-30.
20. John Locke, *The Second Treatise of Government*, ed. J.W. Gough (Oxford, Basil Blackwell 1956), pp. 49-50, 95-8; John Stuart Mill, *Considerations on Representative Government*, ed., Carrin V. Shields (Indianapolis, Bobbs Merrill, 1958), pp. 102-3 (ch. VII).
21. William Kornhauser, *The Politics of Mass Society* (Glencoe, Ill., The Free Press, 1959).
22. J. L. Talmon, *The Origins of Totalitarian Democracy* (London, Mercury Books, 1961).
23. G. A. Almond and J. S. Coleman, *The Politics of the Developing Areas* (Princeton, N.J., Princeton University Press, 1960), p.17.
24. Thomas Hobbes, *Leviathan, or the Matter, Forme and Power of a Commonwealth, ecclesiasticall and civil* (Oxford, Blackwell, 1957), pp.121-2. Verney, op.cit. p.60.

25. R. S. Milne, *Government and Politics in Malaysia* (Boston, Houghton Mifflin, 1967), pp. 14-16.
26. A. A. Afrifa, *The Ghana Coup* (London, Cass, 1966).
27. F.L. Carsten, *The Rise of Fascism* (London, Methuen, 1967), pp. 152-5.
28. C. W. Previté Orton, *The Shorter Cambridge Mediaeval History* (Cambridge, Cambridge University Press, 1952), p.992.
29. Hugh Seton-Watson, *The East European Revolution* (New York, Praeger, 1956), pp. 167-71, quoted in Alvin Z. Rubinstein, *Communist Political Systems* (Englewood Cliffs, N.J., Prentice Hall, 1966), p.38 ff.
30. Herbert L Matthews, *The Yoke and the Arrows* (London, Heinemann, 1958), pp. 76-7.
31. William S Stokes, *Latin American Politics* (New York, Thomas Y. Crowell Co., 1959), pp.302; 385 ff., discusses this form, whose name is derived from Laureano Valenilla Lanz, *Cesarismo democrático* (Caracas, Empresa El Cojo, 1919).
32. Ghita Ionescu, *The Politics of the European Communist States* (London, Weidenfeld & Nicholson, 1967), pp.16, 20.
33. See also Francois Fejtö, *A History of the People's Democracies*, (Harmondsworth, Penguin Books, 1974).
34. John N. Hazard, *The Soviet System of Government*, 3rd edn, (Chicago, University of Chicago Press, 1964), p.221, appendix.
35   Frederick C. Barghoorn, *Politics in the USSR* (Boston, Little-Brown, 1966), p.148.
36. V. I. Lenin, 'What is to be done?' in *Selected Works*, (Moscow, Foreign Languages Publishing House, 1967), I. p.97 ff.
37. Text in S. E. Finer, *Five Constitutions: Contrasts and Comparisons*, (Hassocks, Harvester Press, Harmondsworth, Penguin Books, 1979).
38. Hazard, op.cit., pp.221-2, 223.
39. ibid., p.245.
40. Arnold J. Heidenheimer, *The Governments of Germany*, 3rd edn (New York, Crowell, 1971), p.265 ff.
41. Rubinstein, op.cit., p.202-3; see also his 'Yugoslavia's opening society', *Current History*, XLVIII, March 1965, p.149.
42. Joan Robinson, *The Cultural Revolution in China* (Harmondsworth, Penguin, 1969), pp. 32 ff., 122-3.
43. *The Sunday Times*, 19 February 1978.
44. Edward González, 'Castro and Cuba's new orthodoxy', in *Problems of Communism*, XXV January-February 1976, p.1.
45. Boris Goldenberg, *The Cuban Revolution and Latin America* (London, Allen & Unwin, 1965), pp.267-8.

CHAPTER 6

1. G. A. Almond and J. S. Coleman, *The Politics of the Developing Areas* (Princeton, N.J., Princeton University Press, 1960) p.33 ff.
2. The word was coined in 1893 by Emile Durkheim and its English

equivalent by his translator, George Simpson; see *The Division of Labor in Society* (New York, Free Press, 1964), p.ix.

3. Almond and Coleman, op.cit., p.34.
4. Peter Calvert, 'Revolution, the politics of violence', *Political Studies*, XV, no.1. February, 1967, p.1.
5. Almond and Coleman, op.cit. p.45.
6. William Kornhauser, *The Politics of Mass Society* (Glencoe, Ill, the Free Press, 1959). pp.92-3.
7. Almond and Coleman, op.cit. pp.9-10, 17.
8. Robert A. Scalapino and Junnosuke Masumi, *Parties and Politics in Contemporary Japan* (Berkeley, University of California Press, 1962), p.4ff.
9. Giovanni Sartori, *Parties and Party Systems, A Framework for Analysis* (Cambridge, Cambridge University Press, 1976), pp. 3-13, discusses the emergence of party from faction.
10. OED — the etymologies are disputed; see also Encyclopaedia Britannica, 13th edn. s v 'Whig'.
11. W. W. Pierson and Federico G. Gil, *Governments of Latin America* (New York, McGraw Hill, 1967), p.340 ff.
12. Maurice Duverger, *Political Parties* (London, Methuen, 1959), rev. edn, p.64.
13. ibid., p.1.
14. See John D. Lees and Richard Kimber (eds), *Political Parties in Modern Britain, an Organizational and Functional Guide* (London, Routledge, 1972), p.81.
15. Duverger, op.cit., pp.36-40.
16. Jerry F. Hough, *The Soviet Union and Social Science Theory* (Cambridge, Mass., Harvard University Press, 1977), p.126. The figure of 5.8 per cent as at 1 January 1973 represented, as Hough points out, 8.9 per cent of the (eligible) adult population.
17. Sartori, op.cit., p.254-5.
18. AR 1975, pp. 82-3.
19. Sartori, op.cit., p.230 ff., calls them 'hegemonic' parties.
20. Sigmund Neumann, *Permanent Revolution; Totalitarianism in the Age of International Civil War* (London, Pall Mall, 1965), p.158.
21. Sartori, op.cit., pp. 280-2. Since he wrote, Spain offers an example of an exception that however, as he points out, will not of itself refute the rule.

CHAPTER 7

1 A. J. Milner, *Elections and Political Stability* (Boston, Little-Brown, 1969), pp. 3-4.
2. Jean-Jacques Rousseau, *The Social Contract and Discourses*, trans, G.D.H. Cole (London, Dent, 1958), p.23; see also P. H. Partridge, *Consent and Consensus* (London, Pall Mall, 1971), p.36.
3. Duncan Black, *The Theory of Committees and Elections* (Cambridge, Cambridge University Press, 1958), pp. 69-72, 218-19.

4.   F. M. Cornford, *Microcosmographia Academica, Being a Guide for the Young Academic Politician* (London, Bowes & Bowes, 1970), pp. 14-16.
5.   Black, op.cit. pp. 206-7; the issue was the construction of the New Belfry.
6.   J. B. Bury, *A History of Greece to the Death of Alexander the Great,* 3rd edn. (London, Macmillan, 1956), p.349.
7.   On the Polish election of 1958 see D. E. Butler (ed), *Elections Abroad* (London, Macmillan, 1959), pp. 170-1. On Soviet elections see L.G. Churchward, *Contemporary Soviet Government* (London, Routledge, 1975), ch.7. pp. 103 ff.
8.   William S. Stokes, *Latin American Politics* (New York, Thomas Y. Crowell Co., 1959), pp. 344-6.
9.   Black, op. cit., pp. 156-85.
10.   Jorgen Scott Rasmussen, *The Liberal Party, a Study of Retrenchment and Revival* (London, Constable, 1965), p.41.
11.   *The Times Guide to the House of Commons, February 1974* (London, Times Newspapers Ltd, 1974), p.30.
12.   Peter G. J. Pulzer, *Political Representation and Elections in Britain* 3rd edn. (London, Allen & Unwin, 1975), pp. 4, 97, 98.
13.   Butler (ed.), op.cit., pp. 232-4. See also Gwendolyn M. Carter, *The Politics of Inequality: South Africa since 1948* (London, Thames & Hudson, 1958), ch.5.
14.   Milnor, op.cit., p.43.
15.   *The Times Guide to the House of Commons, February 1974.* p.266.
16.   Milnor, op.cit., pp.41-2
17.   Richard E. Feinberg, *The Triumph of Allende, Chile's Legal Revolution* (New York, Mentor Books, 1972), pp. 162-3.
18.   Butler, (ed.), op.cit. p. 33.ff.
19.   *The Times*, Monday, 13 March 1978.
20.   *The Times,* Monday, 20 March 1978.
21.   Gordon E. Baker, *The Reapportionment Revolution* (New York, Random House, 1966).
22.   Milnor, op.cit., pp.49-52.
23.   Joan Rydon, 'Electoral methods and the Australian party system, 1910-1951', *Australian Journal of Politics and History*, II, November 1956, p.82.
24.   *The Report of the Hansard Society Commission on Electoral Reform,* June 1976, pp. 29-30.
25.   Enid Lakeman, *How Democracies Vote, a Study of Majority and Proportional Electoral Systems* (London, Faber, 1970), p.90 ff. It should be noted that for Lakeman the term 'majority' includes 'plurality'.
26.   ibid., pp. 93-7; see also Douglas W.Rae, *The Political Consequences of Electoral Laws* (New Haven, Yale University Press, 1967), pp. 31-4. In both places the alternative formula employing the numerical sequence 1.4,3,5,7 . . . proposed by Sainte-Laguë and used in Sweden and Norway since 1952, is explained also.
27.   Peter Campbell, *French Electoral Systems and Elections since 1789* (Hamden, Conn., Archon Books, 1965), pp. 112-23; and his 'Remarques

sur les effets de la loi électorale francaise du 9 mai 1951', *Revue française de science politique* I, October-December 1951, p.498.

28.   Benjamin Akzin, 'Israel Knesset', *Israel Yearbook* 1967 (Tel Aviv, 1967), p.79, cited in Milnor, op.cit., p.85.

29.   *Hansard Society*, pp. 49-51, appendix I.

30.   Lakeman, op.cit., p.196.

31.   Maurice Duverger, *Political Parties* (London, Methuen, 1959), pp. 245-52. Duverger is very hesitant, and it is significant that in the best example then given of the multiplicative effect – the UK – the situation has changed markedly since his data were first recorded in 1951. Giovanni Sartori, *Parties and Party Systems* (Cambridge, Cambridge University Press, 1976), p.95, rejects the Duverger 'laws' out of hand.

32.   Lakeman, op.cit., pp.103, 265; *Hansard Society*, loc.cit.

33.   Lakeman, op.cit., pp. 105 ff.

34.   ibid., pp. 137-9.

35.   Vernon Lee Fluharty, *Dance of the Millions; Military Rule and the Social Revolution in Colombia, 1930-1956* (Pittsburgh, University of Pittsburgh Press, 1957), pp. 99-101.

36.   Bernard Diedrich, *Somoza and the Legacy of US Involvement in Central America* (London, Junction Books, 1982), pp. 153-7.

37.   Richard Gott, *Guerrilla Movements in Latin America* (London, Nelson, 1970), p.67; Thomas and Marjorie Melville, *Guatemala _ Another Vietnam?* (Harmondsworth, Penguin, 1971), pp. 204-6.

CHAPTER 8

1.   Vilfredo Pareto, *Works,* ed. S. E. Finer (London, Pall Mall, 1965).

2.   See C. A. Gibb (ed.) *Leadership* (Harmondsworth, Penguin, 1969), which reprintes R. M. Stodgill, 'Personal factors associated with leadership: a survey of the literature', *Journal of Psychology,* XXXV, 1948, p.35.

3.   R. B. Cattell and G. F. Stice, 'Four formulae for selecting leaders on the basis of personality', *Human Relations*, VII, 1954, p.493.

4.   Martin Albrow, *Bureaucracy* (London, Pall Mall & Macmillan, 1970).

5.   Rt Hon. Sir Edward Bridges, 'The Reforms of 1854 in retrospect', in William A. Robson, (ed.), *The Civil Service in Britain and France* (London, Hogarth Press, 1956), p.25.

6.   Brian Chapman, *Police State* (London, Pall Mall & Macmillan, 1970), p.16.

7.   Max Weber, *The Theory of Social and Economic Organization* (New York, Free Press, 1965), pp. 333-4.

8.   I have been unable to trace the original source of this well-known saying.

9.   Sir Ivor Jennings, *Cabinet Government* (Cambridge, Cambridge University Press, 1951), pp. 297, 306.

10.   Emmeline Cohen, *The Growth of the British Civil Service, 1780-1934* (London, Allen & Unwin, 1941), pp. 22-44, esp. p. 37.

11.   C. Northcote Parkinson, *Parkinson's Law, or the Pursuit of Progress*

(London, John Murray, 1958), pp. 5-14.

12.   H. H. Gerth and C. Wright Mills, *From Max Weber, Essays in Sociology* (London, Oxford University Press, 1946), pp. 198, 215.

13.   But see Peter Blau and Otis Dudley Duncan, *The American Occupational Structure* (New York, John Wiley, 1967); see also J. LaPalombara, (ed.), *Bureaucracy and Political Development* (Princeton, Princeton University Press, 1963) and F. Morestein Marx, *The Administrative State* (Chicago, Chicago University Press, 1967).

14.   F. F. Ridley and J. Blondel, *Public Administration in France* (London, Routledge, 1964), pp. 24-27, 31.

15.   C. K. Allen, *Law and Orders* (London, Stevens, 1947), p. 76 ff., George W. Keeton, *Trial by Tribunal* (London, Museum Press, 1960).

16.   Frank Stacey, *Ombudsmen Compared* (Oxford, Clarendon Press, 1978).

17.   Fred W Riggs, *Administration in Developing Countries* (Boston, Houghton Mifflin, 1964).

18.   R. E. Wraith and E. Simpkins, *Corruption in Developing Countries* (New York, Nortin, 1965).

19.   Graham T. Allison, *Essence of Decision: Explaining the Cuban Missile Crisis* (Boston, Little-Brown, 1971).

20.   ibid., pp. 78-95; see also Chester Barnard, *The Function of the Executive* (Cambridge, Mass., Harvard University Press, 1938); and James March and Herbert Simon, *Organizations* (New York, Wiley, 1958) for basic concepts.

21.   Allison, op. cit., pp. 162-80; see also Richard E. Neustadt, *Presidential Power*, (New York, Signet, 1964).

22.   Allison, op.cit., p. 176, quoting Don K. Price.

23,   ibid., p. 162 n.

24.   This model will be expanded further in my forthcoming work on presidential image-making in the United States.

25.   Orrin E. Klapp, *Symbolic Leaders; Public Dramas and Public Men* (Chicago, Aldine Press, 1964), pp. 42 ff.

26.   Geraint Parry, *Political Elites* (London, Allen & Unwin, 1969), p.31.

27.   C. Wright Mills, *The Power Elite* (New York, Oxford University Press, 1956).

28.   Compare the British equivalent, the 'Establishment', as in Hugh Thomas (ed)., *The Establishment* (London, Anthony Blond, 1959).

29.   Leslie Wolf-Philips (ed.), *Constitutions of Modern States* (London, Pall Mall, 1968), p.210.

30.   He was included in the transitional provision of being a citizen when the Constitution came into effect.

31.   Wolf-Philips, op.cit., p.153.

32.   Robert Michels, *Political Parties: a Sociological Study of the Oligarchical Tendencies of Modern Democracy* (New York, Dover Publications, 1959), p.390

33.   ibid., p.378.

34.   Parry, op.cit., pp. 115, 139.

35.   Peter Calvert, *The Concept of Class; An Historical Introduction* (London, Hutchinson, 1982).

36.   Gerth and Mills, op.cit., p.180 ff., esp. pp. 186-7.

CHAPTER 9

1. Niccoló Machiavelli, *The Prince and the Discourses,* intro. Max Lerner (New York, Random House, 1950), pp. 414-15.
2. Patrick Anderson, *The President's Men* (New York, Doubleday Anchor, 1968), pp. 474-5.
3. Merrilee S. Grindle, *Bureaucrats, Politicians and Peasants in Mexico* (Berkeley, University of California Press, 1977), pp. 46-7.
4. Frederick C. Barghoorn, *Politics in the USSR* (Boston, Little-Brown, 1972), pp.180-2.
5. F. A. Lumley, *The Republic of China under Chiang Kai-shek; Taiwan Today* (London, Barrie & Jenkins, 1976), p. 63.
6. Herbert L. Matthews, *The Yoke and the Arrows* (London, Heinemann, 1957) described Franco's rule after the first twenty-five years. On Salazar at the end of his rule – see Antonio de Figueiredo, *Portugal: Fifty Years of Dictatorship* (Harmondsworth, Penguin Books, 1975).
7. On De Gaulle, as an ageing leader see Alexander Werth, *De Gaulle* (Harmondsworth, Penguin Books, 1965), p.9.
8. Phillis Auty, *Tito; A Biography* (London, Longman, 1970).
9. C. P. Fitzgerald, *Mao Tse-tung and China* (London, Hodder & Stoughton, 1976).
10. Jane Marceau, 'Power and its possessors', in Philip G. Cerny and Martin A. Schain (eds.), *French Politics and Public Policy* (London, Methuen, 1980), p.53.
11. Anderson, op.cit., p. 134 ff.
12. Bernard Diedrich, *Somoza and the Legacy of US Involvement in Central America* (London, Junction Books, 1982). pp. 83, 107, 139.
13. AR 1976, p.91.
14. Alex Inkeles, *Social Change in Soviet Russia* (Cambridge, Mass., Harvard University Press, 1968), p.217.
15. Nancy Mitford, *The Sun King* (London, Hamish Hamilton, 1966), p.63.
16. HRH the Duke of Windsor, KG, *A King's Story* (London, Cassell, 1951), pp. 142-3.
17. Theodore Sorenson, *Kennedy* (London, Hodder & Stoughton, 1965), p. 517.
18. *The Times,* Saturday, 14 July 1962.
19. *Congressional Quarterly Weekly Report,* XXI, no. 43, 27 October 1973.
20. Joan Robinson, *The Chinese Cultural Revolution* (Harmondsworth, Penguin Books, 1968).
21. Robert J. Alexander, (ed.), *Aprismo; the Ideas and Doctrines of Victor Raúl Haya de la Torre* (Kent State University Press, 1973), pp. 13-14.
22. AR 1978, p.74.
23. D. J. Goodspeed, *The Conspirators; A Study of the Coup d'Etat* (New York, Viking Press, 1962), pp. 24-5.
24. Mervyn Matthews, *Privilege in the Soviet Union; a Study of Elite Life-Style under Communism* (London, Allen & Unwin, 1978).

25.   *Encyclopedia Britannica,* 14th edn. (1973), XXII, p. 762.
26.   C. H. Haring, *The Spanish Empire in America* (New York, Oxford University Press, 1952), p.100.
27.   *The Times,* Wednesday, 14 November 1973.
28.   William S. Stokes, *Latin American Politics* (New York, Thomas Y. Crowell Co., 1959) pp. 393-4.
29.   F. R. Cowell, *Cicero and the Roman Republic* (Harmondsworth, Penguin Books, 1956), p. 175.
30.   A. Andrewes, *The Greek Tyrants* (London, Hutchinson, 1958), p.20.
31.   A. Curtis Wilgus, *South American Dictators in the First Century of Independence* (New York, Russell & Russell, 1963), pp. 65, 261.
32.   On Bolivarian thought see W. W. Pierson and Federico G. Gil, *Governments of Latin America* (New York, McGregor Hill, 1967), p. 124 ff. and Stokes p. 228; as well as J. L. Salcedo-Bastardo, *Bolivar, a Continent and its Destiny* (Richmond, The Richmond Publishing Co. Ltd., 1978).
33.   F. F. Ridley and J. Blondel, *Public Administration in France* (London, Routledge, 1964), pp. 40-1.

CHAPTER 10

1.   The reference is to Thomas Hughes, *Tom Brown's Schooldays*
2.   James Cramer, *The World's Police* (London, Cassell, 1964).
3.   ibid., p.292.
4.   Frank Gregory, *Protest and Violence; the Police Response* (London, Institute for the Study of Conflict, 1976), p.4.
5.   Cramer, op.cit. pp.403-5.
6.   Brian Chapman, *Police State*, (London, Pall Mall, Macmillan, 1970), p. 15 ff.
7.   The literature on the CIA is now extensive but by the nature of its subject highly tendentious and so untrustworthy. See, *inter alia,* David Wise and Thomas B. Ross, *The Invisible Government* (London, Jonathan Cape, 1965); Allen Dulles, *The Craft of Intelligence* (London, Weidenfeld, 1964); Philip Agee, *Inside the Company; CIA Diary* (Harmondsworth, Penguin, 1975); Haynes Johnson, *The Bay of Pigs* (London, Hutchinson, 1965).
8.   See Peter Calvert, 'The dynamics of political change', *Political Studies,* XVII, No. 4. December 1969
9.   David Easton, *A Framework for Political Analysis* (Englewood Cliffs, N.J., Prentice-Hall, 1965), p.122.
10.   G. A. Almond and J. S. Coleman, *The Politics of the Developing Areas* (Princeton, N.J., Princeton University Press, 1980), p.7: 'claims for the employment of legitimate compulsion.'
11.   Simon Wolin and Robert M. Slusser, *The Soviet Secret Police* (New York, Praeger, 1957).
12.   Anthony Short, *The Communist Insurrection in Malaya, 1948-60* (London. Frederick Muller, 1973), pp. 285-91; Wang Gung-wu (ed.), *Malaysia* (London, Pall Mall, 1966).
13.   John Coast, *Some Aspects of Siamese Politics* (New York, Inter-

national Secretariat of the Institute of Pacific Relations, 1953, mimeo.)
14.   Jacques Delarue, *The Gestapo* (New York, Morrow, 1964).
15.   Alfred Vagts, *A History of Militarism, Civilian and Military* (London, Hollis & Carter, 1959).
16.   On Brazil, see Alfred Stepan, *The Military in Politics; Changing Patterns in Brazil* (Princeton, N.J., Princeton University Press, 1971).
17.   Gordon A. Craig, *The Politics of the Prussian Army, 1640-1945* (Oxford, Oxford University Press, 1955).
18.   C.E. Callwell, *Field-Marshal Sir Henry Wilson, His Life and Diaries* (London, 1927).
19.   Alexander Werth, *France 1940-1955* (London, Robert Hale, 1956).
20.   Muhammad Neguib, *Egypt's Destiny* (Garden City, N.Y., Doubleday, 1955).
21.   Vagts, op.cit., p.22.
22.   ibid., pp. 463-9.
23.   The exception was the Great War, 1917-18, in which, however, Herbert Hoover made his name through the organisation of relief work. The consequences of the Vietnam War, 1964-73, have yet to be seen.
24.   S. E. Finer, *The Man on Horseback* (London, Pall Mall, 1962), pp. 86-9.
25.   François Bourricaud, *Power and Society in Contemporary Peru* (London, Faber, 1970), pp. 313-5.
26.   Finer, op.cit., p.108, citing Robert Conquest, *Power and Policy in the USSR* (London, Macmillan, 1961), pp. 338-9.
27.   Finer, op.cit., pp. 70-1.
28.   Peter Calvert, 'The *coup*; a critical restatement', *Third World Quarterly*, I, no. 4. October 1979, p.89, reviewing Edward Luttwak, *Coup d'Etat, A Practical Handbook* (London, Wildwood House, 1979). See also *inter alia*, Michael Howard (ed.), *Soldiers and Governments* (London, Eyre & Spottiswode, 1957).
29.   *Morris Janowitz, The American Soldier* (Glencoe, Ill., The Free Press, 1960).
30.   Finer, op.cit., p.79.
31.   *The Times Guide to the House of Commons 1970* (London, Times Newspapers Ltd., 1970), p.26.
32.   Bruce M. Russett (ed.), *World Handbook of Political and Social Indicators* (New Haven, Yale University Press, 1964), pp. 99-100; see Rudolph J. Rummel, 'Dimensions of conflict behavior within and between nations', *General Systems* (1973): See also Ivo K. Feierabend, Rosalind L. Feierabend and Betty A. Nesvold, 'Correlates of political stability', paper to 1963 Annual Meeting of the American Political Science Association.

CHAPTER 11

1.   A.P. d'Entrèves (ed.), *Aquinas' Selected Political Writings* (Oxford, Blackwell, 1959), pp. 161, 181-5.
2.   Erwin I. J. Rosenthal, *Political Thought in Medieval Islam: An Intro-*

ductory Outline (Cambridge, Cambridge University Press, (1962), p.97.
3. John Locke, *Two Treatises on Government* ed. P. Laslett (Cambridge, Cambridge University Press 1964). p. 202.
4. George Rudé, *The Crowd in History* (New York, John Wiley, 1964),p. 195. ff.
5. Peter Calvert, *Revolution* (Key Concepts in Political Science) (London, Pall Mall & Macmillan, 1970), p.121 ff; George S. Pettee, *The Process of Revolution* (New York, Harper, 1938); Lyford P. Edwards, *The Natural History of Revolution* (Chicago, 1927, reprinted New York, Russell & Russell, 1965); Crane Brinton, *The Anatomy of Revolution* (New York, 1938), reprinted Vintage, 1952), and Chalmers Johnson, *Revolution and the Social System* (Stanford, Hoover Institution Studies 3, 1964).
6. Brinton, op.cit; see also Carl Leiden and Karl M Schmitt, *The Politics of Violence, Revolution in the Modern World,* (Englewood Cliffs, Prentice-Hall, 1968).
7. Bruce M. Russett (ed.), *World handbook of Political and Social Indicators* (New Haven, Yale University Press, 1964), p.100.
8. On 'machetismo' see William S. Stokes, *Latin American Politics* (New York, Thomas Y. Crowell Co, 1959), pp.300-12.
9. Calvert, *A Study of Revolution*, (Oxford, Clarendon Press, 1970), p.4.
10. ibid., p.32.
11. Murray Clark Havens, Carl Leiden and Karl M. Schmitt, *The Politics of Assassination* (Englewood Cliffs, NJ, Prentice-Hall, 1970), p.43.
12. See *The Political Thought of Mao Tse-Tung,* trans. and ed., Stuart Schram (New York, Praeger, 1963), pp. 202-88 and Ernesto Che Guevara, *Guerrilla Warfare* (New York, Monthly Review Press, 1967), p.15.
13. George McTurnan Kahin (ed.), *Governments and Politics of South-East Asia*, 2nd edn. (Ithaca, NY, Cornell University Press, 1964), pp. 392-5.
14. D. J. Goodspeed, *The Conspirators, A Study of the Coup d'Etat* (London, Allen & Unwin, 1962), p. 70 ff.
15. Lewis F. Richardson *Statistics of Deadly Quarrels* (London, Stevens, 1960), pp. 6-7.
16. Johnson, op. cit., see also his *Revolutionary Change* (Boston, Little-Brown, 1966).
17. Calvert, op.cit., p.181ff.
18. Majid Khadduri, *Political Trends in the Arab World; The Role of Ideas and Ideals in Politics* (Baltimore, John Hopkins Press, 1970), p.137 and no.5.
19. See Peter Calvert, 'The institutionalisation of the Mexican Revolution,' *Journal of Inter-American Studies*, XI, no.4, October 1969, p.503.

CHAPTER 12

1. Michael Lessnoff, *The Structure of Social Science, A Philosophical Introduction* (London, Allen & Unwin, 1974), p. 14.
2. Peter Winch, *The Idea of a Social Science and its Relation to Philosophy* (London, Routledge, 1958), p.92.

3.   Lessnoff, op.cit., p.54.
4.   Calvert, 'The dynamics of political change', *Political Studies*, XVII, No.
4. December 1969.

Index

Abbey National Building Society, 93
ability, 135
abuse, 138
Abyssinia, 143, *see also* Ethiopia
accountable, 119, 121, 122
achievement, 72, 121, 168
Act of Settlement, 39
action(s), 89, 125, 154, 166, 171
activists, 96
actor(s), 126–7
administration, 64, 120, 121, 123, 139
administrative apparatus, 132
administrative law, 120, 141
adult education, 64
advisers, 135
adults, 91
aeroplanes, 155
Afghanistan, 32
Africa, 24, 75, 85, 154
aggressive behaviour, 146
aging, 134
agitation, 83
agreement, 99
aggression, 18–20, 23
aggressiveness, 66
agricultural implements, 163
aid, 56
aircraft, 41
air forces, 153
airlines, 85
airports, 72
Alfred, King of England, 32
Algeria, 57, 115–16, 153
alienation, 88
alien enemy, 169
al-Khalifa family, 32
Allende, Salvador, 58, 72, 106
alliance, 8
Allies, 110
Allison, Graham, 124, 125, 126
Almond, Gabriel A, 10, 39–40, 47, 51, 52, 54,
    75, 87, 88, 89, 150, 164
alternative vote, 108
alternatives, 99

al-Thani family, 32
Amazons, 35
ambassadors, 69
ambassadorships, 133
America, 161, *see also* United States of
    America
American colonies, 65
American Medical Association (AMA), 88
American Revolution, 90, 169
Americans, the, 20, 39, 90
Amin, Idi, 143
anarchist, 161, 172
ancien regime, 65
anarchy, 68
Andes, 106
Andorra, 52
Andrae, C.C.G., 111
Angola, 79
Anglo-Egyptian Treaty (1948), 153
Anglo-Saxon countries, 160
Anglo-Saxon legal system, 140
'Anglo-Saxon' police, 147
animal behaviour, 18–25
animals, 155
anomic activity, 160, 162
anomic interest groups, 88–9, 162
'anti-party group', 156
anthropologists, 26–8, 37, 173
'anthropologists' present', 38
anthropology, 17, 67
apartment blocks, 58
apparat, 81—2
apparentement, 110
appeal, 122, 141
appointive office, 133
appointment(s), 135
approaches,
    whole unit, 8–9
    competing power centres, 8
    local community, 9
    standard unit, 9
appropriation, 121
approval, 72
anticipation, 133

Aquinas, St. Thomas, 160
Arab countries, 140
Arabs, Palestinian, 6
Aragon, 68
arbitrators, 29
arbitration, 141
archaeology, 26
Argentina, 107, 110, 114, 139, 152, 168
Argentine Confederation, 142
Argentines, 106, 142
aristocracy, 144
Aristotle, 1, 13–15, 17, 32, 44–5, 47
armed conflict, 32
armed forces, 34, 63, 88, 106, 127, 139, 152–9, 163, 167
army,-ies, 47, 81, 94, 106, 115, 116, 129, 130, 132, 152, 153, 157, 158, 159, 170
arrest, 139, 148
articulation, 92, 163
artisan class, 161
Asia, 75, 154
assassination, 142, 152
assault phase, 166
assembly, 39, 47, 67, 68, 70, 71, 72, 73, 76, 78, 80, 81, 82, 83, 84
assembly, freedom of, 114
associational interest groups, 88, 89, 90, 95
Athens, 162
Athenians, 101
attitudes, 149
Attlee, Clement R, 95
attributes of revolution, 165
aufheben, 63
Australia, 15, 57, 69, 79, 97, 108, 111, 137
  –House of Representatives, 108
  –Senate, 111
Austria, 35, 70, 143
authoritarian states/systems, 52, 74, 179
authority,
  defined, 33, Weberian, 33–4, 35, inherited, 38, 42, 51, 68, 78, 84, 133, 140, 141, 146, 166
autocracy, 45
autocratic regimes, 46
autonomy, 139
Ayub Khan, 50
Aztec Eagle, Order of the, 136

baboons, 25
Baghdad, 158
Bahrein, 32
Bahamas, 79
Bailey, F.G., 31
baker, 55
balance of payments, 85
balance of trade, 86
ballot paper, 71, 102, 104, 108, 112
'ballot stuffing', 116
ballots, 107
bands, hunting, 24–5, 36, 53, 173

banishment, 133, 138
banking, 97
Banks, Arthur, S., 10
banquets, 136
Banzer, Hugo, 138
bar, 100
bargaining, bargains, 2, 30, 74, 125
barracks, 152
bayonets, 80
beggars, 147
behaviour, human, 5, 12–13, 17, 149, 171
Belgium, 15, 55, 69, 110, 140
Berlin Wall, 138
Bhutan, 32
bias, 61
biological replacement, 65
biology, 2, 13, 18
Black, Duncan, 100
Black Power, 163
Black Rod, 77
blank cheques, 81
Blondel, Jean, 46
boards, 118
Bolivia, 50, 116, 138–9, 155, 162
Bolívar, Simón, 143
'Bonapartism', 156
books, 58
Boone, Daniel, 146
boundary, 19, 38, 41, 164, 173
bourgeois, 3, 90, 97
bourgeoisie, 160
branch, 93, 94
branches of government, 78
Brazil, 9, 37, 50, 70, 78, 81, 103, 114, 115, 144, 152, 155, 157
Brezhnev, Leonid, 135
Broederbond, 138
Brinton, Crane, 161
Britain
  see Great Britain
  United Kingdom
British, the, 20
British Empire, 120
British Medical Association (BMA), 88
Brutus, Marcus Junius, 142
budget, 81, 124
Buenos Aires, 142
building techniques, 49
Bulgaria, 80, 82, 143
Bund, 95
bureaucracy, 46, 60, 120, 121, 122, 123, 125, 127, 141
'bureaucratic politics' model, 46, 125
bureaucratic state, 120–1
bureaucrats, 120, 127
Burgundy, 119
Burke, Edmund, 161
business, 127, 150
by-elections, 111, 134
Byzantine Empire, 120

cabbage patch, 86
cabinet(s), 45, 71, 78, 85, 118, 122, 125, 135,
    137, 157, 168
cabinet, 135
cadre party, 94
Caesar, C. Julius, 142
Caithness & Sutherland, 104
Cambodia, 34, 139
campaign, 137
Canada, 15, 69, 79, 104
candidates, 99, 101, 102, 103, 106, 107, 110,
    111, 112, 113, 114, 115, 128, 134
candidato unico, 103
cantonments, 152
capabilities, 40, 44
Cape Colony, 109
capital (of a state), 78, 147, 153, 158, 162, 166,
    167
capitalist, 11, 83
Caps (Sweden), 91
Caracas, 163
career, 121, 134, 135, 158
Caribbean, 23, 44
Carlyle, Thomas, 161
carnivores, 24–5
cars, 136
Carter, Jimmy, 135
Cassius Longinus, Gaius, 142
cast, 126
castes, 88
Castro Ruz, Fidel, 57, 65, 85
Castro Ruz, Raúl, 135
casualties, 167
catch-phrases, 65
categories, 47, 118
Catholic countries, 160
caucus, 77, 93, 94
cause, 158
cell, 94
Central African Empire, 102
Central America, 70, 100
Central Intelligence Agency (CIA), 149
centre, 8–9, 69, 93, 97
centre parties, 110
ceremonial, 72
cetecea, 55
Chad, 6
chairman, 69, 82, 85, 100, 101
Chamorro, Pedro Joaquín, 115
change, 81—2, 83, 119, 123
channel, 54
channels of participation, 76, 159
charisma, 33, 95, 135, 170
charismatic authority, 33, 117
Charlemagne, 32
checks and balances, 53, 72
chemistry, 2
chief, 27
'Chiefs', 125
children, 58, 133, 136, 155

Chile, 58, 72, 81, 106, 114, 115, 139, 152, 157,
    168
China, 22, 28, 67, 69, 76, 82, 84, 135, 138, 139,
    155, 159, 161, 167
    Chinese Empire, 133
    Republic of China, 134
Chinese, the, 3, 28, 64, 120
choice, 81, 98, 99, 100, 102, 114, 116
Christ Church, Oxford, 101
Christian Democratic Party (Chile), 72
Churchill, Winston Leonard Spencer, 95, 154
church organisations, 100
Cicero affair, 152
circulation of elites, 130
cities, 22, 23, 36, 77, 102, 106, 163
citizen(s), 35—6, 56, 59, 78, 87, 101, 114, 120,
    121, 122, 128, 132, 133, 140, 147, 148, 154,
    158, 160, 172, 173
city states, 6
civics, 64
civil servants, 120, 123
civil service(s), 45, 88, 119, 133
civil war, 34, 77, 139, 140
civilian(s), 153
civilian government, 168
civilian organisations, 130
Clarendon, Constitutions of (1164), 14
class(es), 38, 88, 130–1, 136, 157
classification, 10, 44, 46, 47, 75, 90, 92, 93, 165,
    166, 168
clientele, 92
Clifford, Clark, 135
climate, 17
clothing, 38
clubs, 157
coalition(s), 16, 74, 78, 103, 106, 110, 170
code(s), 54, 57, 63–5, 146
code law, 140, 145
Code Napoléon, 120, 140
coercion, 43, 44, 81, 83, 133, 168
cofradías, 100
Coleman, James, S., 39–40, 47, 54, 74, 89
collaborationists, 123
collective, 102
collective farms, 22
collective leadership, 84
collective responsibility, 78–9, 82
Colombia, 97, 115, 138, 143, 162
colonial power, 167
colonies, 79
colonisation, 79
combat, 154
committee(s), 2, 69, 70, 71, 76, 77, 82, 84, 100,
    101, 118, 140, 150
Committee of Public Safety (France), 69
Committee on State Security (KGB), 149, 151
common law, 63, 121
Commonwealth, 121, 140
communes, 22
communication(s), 44, 54–66, 120, 149, 155,
    166

Communist Party, 74, 81, 84, 85, 95, 102, 135, 156
Communist systems/states, 64, 78, 81–5, 97, 115, 138, 140, 154, 156
Communists, 74, 84, 93, 110, 160, 162, 167
community,-ies, 19, 90, 97, 100, 145, 146, 150, 152, 155, 165
companies, 167
comparative politics, 4, 5, 6, 37, 39, 61, 63, 74, 87, 89, 90, 130
competing power-centres, 46
competitive examination, 102
competitive parties, 45, 50
competitive systems, 75, 90
compromise(s), 69, 71, 74, 77, 78, 79, 80, 85, 99, 101
concentration, 165
concentration camps, 154
concierge, 58
Conciliar government, 122, 123
Condorcet, Marie-Jean-Antoine-Nicolas Caritat, Marquis de, 104
confederation, 8, 48
conference, 62
conflict, 19, 39, 69, 72, 74, 85, 130, 165
congress, 39, 69, 72, 77, 80, 81, 106
congressional districts, 107
Congress Party (India), 96
Connally, Governor John, 135
conquerors, 27
consensus, 75, 99, 165
consent, 34, 101, 173
consequences, 165
Conservative Party (Nicaragua), 97
Conservative Party (UK), 93, 105, 107
conservatives, 169
consolidation, 166
conspiracy, 115
constabulary, 147
constituencies, 104, 107, 108, 109, 110, 111, 112
constitution, 'real', 14–15, 78, 174
Constitution(s), written, 14–16, 69, 106, 141
Constitution of the United States (1787), 39, 68, 70, 128, 174
Constitution of the USSR,
   1936: 15, 47, 82, 84, 85
   1977: 69, 83, 85
constitutionality, 71
content, 63
contest, 92
contestants, 112
Continental Congress (US), 65
'Continental' police, 147–8
contract, 172
contractual relationship, 121
control, 40, 83, 121, 132, 133, 134, 145, 156
Convention (France), 65
'Convention Theory', 47, 67–9, 76, 82–3
convergence, 158

conversation, 58
conversion functions, 40
Cook, Capt. James, 27
co-option, 133, 134, 135
Cornforth, John, 101
corporations, 49
corruption, 124
Corsica, 145
cost, 141
council(s), 118, 122
Council of the Indies (Spain), 122
councillor(s), 56
counter-terrorist activities, 151
counties, 147
county councils, 39
coup, 71, 73, 119, 124, 151, 152, 162, 167, 168, 169
courts, 39, 120–1, 132, 140, 141, 150
cows, 30
credit, 157
Crick, Bernard, 46
crime, 19
criminals, 137, 147
crisis, 72, 97
critical time, 166
critics, 126
Croats, 84
cross-national comparisons, 66
Crockett, Davy, 146
Cromwell, Oliver, 147
crowd composition, 161
crown, 63
Cuba, 23, 57, 59, 65, 68, 69, 70, 85, 114, 135, 148, 161, 167
Cuban missile crisis, 124
cultural society, 102
Cultural Revolution; Great Proletarian, 22, 76, 84, 158
culture, 6
cumulative vote, 108
currency, 85
cybernetic(s), 41, 54
cyclical majority, 101
Cyprus, 139
Czechoslovakia, 80, 84

Dahl, Robert, A., 45
Dahomey (Benin), 35
dams, 72
'dark horse', 101
data, 150
deadlines, 125
debate, 77, 101
decision(s), 39, 41, 75, 78, 87, 98, 100, 101, 117, 120, 122, 123, 124, 125, 141, 154, 156
decision-makers, 44, 59, 62, 66, 87, 127, 150, 165
decision-making, 46, 57, 73, 79, 87, 94, 123, 124, 125, 138, 150
Declaration of Independence, 65

decolonisation, 139
defeat, 126
defence, 156
defensive capacity, 83
defence ministers, 155
delegates, 82
delegation, 119
demands, 39, 40, 42, 43, 52, 59, 85, 87–98, 132,
    165, 169
democracy, 11, 44, 45, 48, 49, 50, 74, 77, 82,
    96, 102, 113
Democratic Caesarism, 81, 85, 154, 170
democratic-monarchical dimension, 46
Democratic Party (US), 72
democratic state(s)/societies, 52, 126
demonstrations, 60, 152, 162, 163
demotion, 133, 138
Denmark, 110, 111
denunciation, 138
despotic monarchies, 68
département, 110, 148
departments, 72, 133
detachments, 167
detention, 138, 139
Deutsch, Karl, 41
developing countries, 123, 154
development, 12, 16, 48–51, 79, 89, 90, 123,
    164
developmental model, 150
deviation, 82, 83
dezhurnaya, 58
d'Hondt system, 109, 110, 111
    see largest average system
diachronic perspective, 16
dictator(s), 142, 144, 168
dictatorship, 6, 11, 44, 132, 142–4, 154, 157
differentiation, 89
dignitaries, 102
dinner, 100
direct communication, 85
diplomas, 121
direct democracy, 47
direct structure, 93–4, 96
direction, 63
direct speech, 55, 56
disaffection, 166
disagreements, 125
disaster, 72
discipline, 121
discontent, 58
discontinuities, 164
discussion, 91
disintegration, 165
dismissal, 133, 137–8
disposition, 156
disputes, 132
distortion, 61
distribution functions, 152
district, 102
divine right, 34

Djilas, Milovan, 82
doctors, 88
Dodgson, Charles L., 101
dollar, 85
Dollard, John, 19
domestic group violence, 159
Dominican Republic, 15, 169
dolphins, 55
dramatic conventions, 126
Droop, H.R., 112
dualism, 51–2
dues, 95
duel, 145
duration, 166, 167
Duvalier, Dr. François, 71, 81
Duverger, Maurice, 92, 94

earthquake, 34
Easton, David, 60, 87, 150
Ecole Polytechnique, 143
economic development, 89–90, 94, 168
economic modernisation, 49
economic necessity, 88
economic power, 130
economies, 12, 14, 16, 26, 46, 83, 97, 156
economies of scale, 49
Ecuador, 50, 78, 155
education, 57, 112, 128, 129, 131, 146, 155,
    157, 173
Edwards, Lyford, P., 161, 169
Edward, Prince of Wales, 137
efficiency, 69, 154
egalitarian, 82
egalitarianism, 168
Egypt, 57, 67, 115, 140, 153, 155, 169
Egypt, ancient, 19, 28, 120
Eisenstadt, S., 51
elders, 143
elected leader, 118
election(s), 2, 39, 50, 59, 71, 75, 76, 85, 98, 99,
    102, 105, 106, 107, 108, 109, 113, 114, 116,
    140, 144, 157, 168
election rigging, 113
elective office, 134
elector(s), 110, 111, 115
Electoral College, American, 13
electoral process, 115
electoral system, 92, 98, 99, 111, 113, 114, 118
electorate, 70, 99, 103
electors, 101, 102, 107, 116
elements of revolution, 158
élite(s), 60, 61, 117, 127—30, 134, 137, 138, 139,
    141, 144, 150, 153, 156, 165, 170
Elizabeth I, Queen of England, 146
Elizabeth II, Queen of the United Kingdom,
    32
El Salvador, 45
emergency powers, 72
emergency-ies, 132, 141
empire, 35, 71

Emperor, 103
employment, 122
Enabling Act, 80
encapsulated society, 37–8
encapsulation, 31
Encyclopaedists, 104
engineers, 155
energy, 38
England, 9, 32, 35, 57, 63, 67, 76, 112, 147, 161, 162
English (language), 14, 63, 66, 127
English Civil War/Revolution, 68, 169
environment, 37, 41–2, 54, 59, 60, 61, 62, 172
Environment, Department of the (UK), 64
equality, 168, 173
errors, 62
Ethiopia, 32
espionage, 149
esteem, 124, 126
ethnic groups, 88
etiquette, 145
ethology, 18
Europe, 23, 28, 32, 34, 45, 46, 49, 50, 67, 83, 90, 91, 92, 96, 97, 113, 120, 122, 129, 136, 141, 143, 147, 150
European Economic Community, 8
Evans-Pritchard, E.E., 27
event, revolutionary, 165, 167, 170
evidence, 125
evolution, 65
examination, 121, 139
examining magistrate, 140
exclusion, 64
execution, 133, 139
executive, 48, 69, 71, 78, 80, 81, 82, 84, 140, 156, 166
executive committee, 82
Executive Committee (China), 85
Executive Council (Yugoslavia), 84
executive power, 40, 47, 84
exile, 138–9
expenditure, 81
expertise, 154
explanation, 126
exploitation, 83
external aid, 119
external attack, 43
extractive processes, 150
extremists, 169
face-to-face communication, 59, 60, 62
'factored' problems, 124
factory, 102
faction, 90, 91, 95, 174
Falange, 80
family, 87, 88, 119, 135, 142, 158, 173
farmers, 55
fasces, 137
fasci di combattimento, 151
Fascist parties/movements, 94, 95, 115
Fatherland Front (Bulgaria), 80

fatigue, 100
fear, 64
Federal Bureau of Investigation (FBI), 149
federal government, 73, 77
federalism, 48, 73, 168
federal state/system, 48, 77, 84, 92
federation, 8
federative power, 47
feedback, 41, 59, 65
Feldsicherheitspolizei (FSP), 151
female, 128
femininity, 146
feminists, 27
feud, 145
feudal authority, 51
feudal states, 52
Few, the, 44–5, 48, 49
finance, 93, 156
Finer, S.E., 154
fines, 133
Finland, 26, 70, 110
firearms, 129, 163
First World War, 139, 154
flag, 63
flats, 58
fleets, 85
flight, 64
'floating voters', 105
flood, 34
Florida, 108
focus of power, 71, 73
followers, 158
food, 22–23, 27, 38, 94
food gatherers, 23
food surplus, 23
football, 75
force, 5, 32–3, 38, 43, 71, 98, 132, 139, 145, 146, 153, 158, 160, 161, 162, 165, 166, 167, 172
force analysis, 167
foreign attack, 152
forms, 150
Fortes, Meyer, 27
fortune, 119
Fourth of July, 63
fox, 19
'foxes', 129
France, 7–8, 15, 16, 20, 32, 70, 79, 93, 103, 106, 109, 110, 119, 120, 123, 128, 135, 136, 139, 140, 141, 143, 147, 153, 161, 162, 164
–First Republic 35, 67, 73
–Third Republic 16
–Fourth Republic 16
–Fifth Republic 73, 107
–colonial Empire, 71, 140
–Constitution of 1791, 77
–National Assembly, 92, 107, 110
–Constitution of 1958, 115
Francia, Dr. José Caspar Rodríguez de, 142
franchise, 91, 93

Franco Bahamonde, Francisco, 132, 135
free elections, 112, 113, 114
free selection, 121
French, the, 20, 35, 80
French languge, 63
French Revolution (1789), 68, 75, 140, 142, 161, 164, 169
Friedrich, Carl, J., 45
friends, 135, 142
frontiersman, 146
frontier troops, 151
frustration, 19
function(s), 13, 16, 71, 75, 76, 119, 165
'fused' decision-making, 123
future-directed, 98

gain, 41
Gaitán, Jorge Eliecer, 115
Galtung, Johan, 8
game, 30, 126, 172
Gandhi, Indira, 73
garages, 58
gardeners, 86
gardens, 30, 36, 58
gatekeepers, 60, 150
Gaulle, Charles de, 135
Gauguin, Paul, 17
Gaullist(s), 93, 110
Gemeinschaft, 95
general codes, 63
general theory of revolutions, 167
general will, 74, 99
Geneva, 82
geography, 16
Georgia (USA), 135
German Communist Party (KPD), 115
German language, 63
German Socialist Unity Party (SED), 80
Germany, 6, 32, 46, 79–80, 84, 128, 143, 153
Germany, East (German Democratic Republic), 57, 80, 84, 138
Germany, West (German Federal Republic), 8, 9, 56, 57, 69, 110–11, 115, 123
–Bundestag, 110–11
Gesellschaft, 95
Ghana, 15, 79, 157
Gibraltar, 108
goals, 124, 160, 168, 173
goats, 30
Golden Condor, Order of the, 136
Golden Fleece, 136
goods, 81, 157
goose, 55
gorillas, 25
gossip, 134, 150
Gournay, Jean Claude Marie Vincent de, 120
governed, 1
government
  defined, 1, 5
  origins 18 ff. 10, 16, 34, 42, 51, 52, 53, 54, 76, 91, 98, 137, 157

government(s), 33, 42, 43, 56, 58, 59, 61, 64, 67, 68, 71, 72, 73, 74, 76, 77, 78, 83, 84, 85, 86, 94, 97, 105, 111, 113, 114, 115, 117, 118, 119, 122, 124, 126, 127, 130, 132, 133, 134, 135, 136, 137, 141, 142, 149, 150, 151, 152, 155, 156, 158, 159, 160, 161, 162, 163, 164, 165, 166, 167, 168, 170, 171, 172, 173, 174
Governmental Politics model, 125
governor, 94, 106
Grau San Martín, Ramón, 59
Great Britain, 6, 7, 15, 16, 20, 35, 39, 64, 66, 69, 70, 71, 77, 79, 88, 91, 93, 97, 103, 105, 106, 108, 121, 123, 128, 136, 137, 139, 141, 146, 147, 152
Great Leap Forward, 22
Great Patriotic War, *see* Second World War
'Great Powers', 153
Great Reform Act, 39, 169
Greece, 32, 110, 143, 152, 162
Greece, Ancient, 15
Greek (language), 23, 142
Greeks, 102, 142
group(s), 82, 101, 117, 118, 120, 128, 129, 174
group syntality, 118
Guatemala, 110, 115, 136, 139
guerrilla movements, 167
Guevara de la Serna, Ernesto 'Che', 167
guilt, 140–1
Guinea, 79
gun fight, 146
gunsight, 41
Gurr, Ted, 19
Guyana, 110
gypsies, 143

hair, 25
Haiti, 70, 71, 81, 169
Hamilton, Alexander, 128
handbills, 58
hands, 137
Hare System, 111
  see also single transferable vote (STV)
Hare, Thomas, 111
harvest, 51
Hashemite dynasty, 158
Hats (Sweden), 91
Hawaii, 70
Haya de la Torre, Victor Raúl, 138
head of the family, 29
headman, 94
head of government, 62, 72, 82, 150, 154
head(s) of state, 32, 70, 72, 73, 77, 79, 82, 84, 154
heads, counting of, 99, 100
hearings, 141
heckling, 57
hegemony, 96, 156
Henige, David P., 28
hereditary factors, 131

heredity, 102
Henry VIII, King of England, 34
hierarchy-ies, 45, 94, 121, 124, 125, 150, 173
historical bureaucratic state, 51, 52, 120
historicism, 12
history, 2, 10, 16, 44, 160
Hitler, Adolf, 46, 79, 84, 95, 133, 143, 151
Hobbes, Thomas, 18, 68
Hong Kong, 163
honours, 133, 136–7
Hood, Robin, 146
Horse, 19
hostility, 66, 96
household, 119
Household Finance Corporation (HFC), 93
householders, 86
House of Commons (UK), 77, 101, 106
House of Lords (UK), 101
houses, 58
housing, 38
human beings, 173–4
human nature, 100
Hungary, 46, 82, 143
hypothesis, 11

Iceland, 70
'ideal types', 33, 73, 122
ideas, 92
ideology, 46, 50, 64, 66, 92–3, 97, 168
Illinois, 109, 116
illiteracy, 50
illiterate, 92, 116
'Imperial Presidency', 73
imports, 97
imprisonment, 114, 133, 139
income, 58, 129
incremental change, 125
incumbents, 38
independence, 83, 96, 156
India, 69, 73, 78, 89, 96, 100, 139, 155
'Indians', 125
Indians, Brazilian forest, 38
indicators, 164
indirect rule, 79
indirect structure, 93–4
individual, 47, 81, 83, 87, 90, 94, 101, 117, 118,
    119, 120, 122, 125, 129, 138, 147, 159, 173
Indonesia, 162, 167
industrial disputes, 141
industrial state/society, 91, 163
infiltration, 149
information, 55, 56, 61, 90, 124
inheritance, 51
initiation, 94
ink, 58
input, 13
input(s), 39–40, positive and negative 41–3;
    52, 59, 60, 62, 117, 150, 165
input control, 42, 150
Inquisition, 82

institution(s), 16, 76, 84, 85, 141, 157, 170, 174
institutional interest groups, 88, 89, 95
institutionalised revolution 170
integration, 165
intellectual(s), 129
intelligentsia, 129, 131
interest(s), 42, 75, 79, 88, 119, 123, 157, 162,
    170
interest arbitration, 42
interest aggregation, 40, 75, 90, 91, 163
interest articulation, 40, 75, 90, 91, 93, 159,
    163
interest groups, 76, 87–90
    –latent, 87, 88
interference, 61
international influences, 42
international law, 138
international relations, 6, 37
interpretations, 165
'intraputs', 41, 87
intrigue, 152
invasion, 34
Ionescu, Ghita, 81
Iran, 32, 67, 68, 114, 139
Iraq, 158, 169
Ireland, 30, 70, 90, 111, 112, 121, 147
    –Daíl, 112
Irish, 148
Islamic thought, 28
Islamic writers, 160
Isle of Wight, 28
Israel, 35, 69, 95, 110, 153
Israel, ancient, 25
issue(s), 100, 125
Italy, 14, 16, 46, 70, 110, 117, 140, 143
Ivory Coast, 79

Jaca, 68
Jacobin Communist revolution, 168
Jacobins, 74
Jackson, Andrew, 133
jacquerie, 162
jamming, 61
Janowitz, Morris, 158
Japan, 32, 34, 68, 69, 108, 153, 154, 162
    –Diet, 108
Japanese, 159, 167
Jews, 143
job, 125
job satisfaction, 124
Johnson, Chalmers, 161, 168
Johnson, Lyndon B., 60
journalists, 134
judges, 140
judicial power, 40, 47–8
judiciary, 45, 140
junta, 45
jury, 140
justice, 141
Justicialist party (Argentina), 96

Justizstaat, 120

Kennedy, John Fitzgerald, 136, 137
Kenya, 139
Kenyatta, Jomo, 169
Khomeini, Ayatollah, 139
Khrushchev, Nikita S., 156
kin groups, 28, 88
king(s), 32, 142, 147, 152
Kinship, 28
Kissinger, Dr. Henry, 128
Komsomol, 102
Kornhauser, William, 74, 90
Kuwait, 32

Labour Party (UK), 93, 105
lag, 41
Lakeman, Enid, 111
land, 106
Land, Lander (GFR), 110, 111
Land Rover, 94
language, 6, 10, 55, 57, 63, 64
largest average system, 109
largest remainder system, 109
Lassalle, Ferdinand, 15
Latin, 142
Latin America, 85, 92, 93, 113, 135, 138, 140, 148, 154
law(s), 29, 30, 32, 39, 48, 102, 120, 121, 122, 132, 139–41, 145, 146, 147
law, international, 7
Laws of the Indies, 140
laws of nature, 3, 171, 172
laws of politics, 172
lawyers, 33, 39, 102, 139
lay assessors, 148
leaders, 95, 97, 117, 118, 119, 124, 129, 134, 154, 156, 158, 162, 169
leadership, 117, 118, 120, 129, 166, 169
leading role, 126
lecture room, 21–2
left-wing, 92, 107
legal, 121, 122
legal-rational authority, 33–4, 117
legal requirements, 114
legal restraints, 141
legality, 121
legal systems, 140
legends, 146
Legion d'Honneur, 136
legislative power, 39, 47
legislature, 45, 71, 81, 82, 103, 106
legitimacy, defined, 33; 34, 75, 143, 160, 161
Lenin, Vladimir Il'ych, 83, 134, 148, 167
leopard-skin chiefs, 29
levée en masse, 35
level (of revolutionary action), 166, 167
levels of force, 146
levels of government, 1, 6, 94
levels of military intervention, 156

levels of participation, 76
liberal-authoritarian dimension, 46
liberal democracies, 45, 154, 155, 156
Liberal Party (Nicaragua), 97
Liberal Party (UK), 58, 93, 105
Liberia, 70
liberty, 65, 114
Liechtenstein, 52, 92
life style, 59
light, 123
limited vote, 108
Lincoln, Abraham, 166
lineage, 32, 51, 68
linkage, 90
lions, 24
'lions', 129
list systems(s), 103, 109, 111
lists, 111
literacy, 57, 157
literati, 129, 131
Lloyd, J Selwyn B., 137
Lloyd George, David, 153
lobby, 156
lobbyist, 156
local authorities, 64, 78
local government, 62, 76, 78, 168
Locke, John, 47, 74, 160
logarithmic scale, 167
London, 134
lot, 101
Lorenz, Konrad, 18—19
Louis IX, King of France, 32
Louis XIV, King of France, 136
Louis Napolean, 103
loyalty, 78
Luang Pibulsongkhram, 151
Luxemburg, 52, 70, 110
Lydian, 142

Machiavelli, Niccolò, 133
machine guns, 155
machinery, 49
Macmillan, Harold, 137
Magna Carta, 39
magnates, 119
magnitude, 167
maize, 23
majority, 72, 74, 75, 78, 100, 103, 104, 105, 106, 107, 108, 113
Malauan Emergency, 151
Malaysia, 69, 79, 151
male, 127, 128
male dominance, 24
mandarinate, 133
Malta, 111
manpower, 124
manipulation, 115
Many, the, 44–5, 48, 49
Mao Tse-tung, 82, 84, 135, 167, 169
Mapai (Israel), 95

martial law, 147
Marx, Karl, 3, 12, 22, 27, 53, 92, 130–1
Marxism, 12
Marxism-Leninism, 64, 85
Marxists, 161, 167
Maryland, 9
mass(es), 67, 150, 153, 163, 165, 167, 173, 174
Massachusetts, 9
mass communication, 46, 57–8
mass meeting, 57
mass party, 46, 91, 93, 94, 96
mass production, 49
mating, 25
mayor, 106, 148
means, 158
measurement, 2
media, 72
Medici, 33
medicine, 3, 155
meeting(s), 2
Meiji Restoration, 153, 162
Members of Parliament (MPs) 56, 77, 94, 104, 128
membership, 94, 96, 109, 114
memoranda, 59
men, as resources 30; voting age, 92; 99, 146
Méndez Montenegro, Mario, 115
method, 4–5
'Method of Marks' 101
mercy, 141
merchants, 27
Metropolitan Police (London), 147
metacommunication, 58
Mexico, 66, 67, 68, 70, 97, 103, 110, 128, 129, 134, 135, 136, 161, 168
Mexico City, 22
Michels, Roberts, 127
middle ages, 144, 147
Middle East, 71
'middle ground', 105
militarisation, 154 militarised mass insurrection, 168
militarism, 152—4
military, 67, 71, 85, 119, 124, 129, 143, 144, 151–9, 168
military commanders, 102
military installations, 73
military intervention, 155–7, 166, 168
military leader, 154
military regiments (s), 71, 72, 124
military service/training 36, 154
military threat, 142
militia, 132, 148
militia-structural party, 94
milkman, 55
Mill, John Stuart, 74
Mills, C. Wright, 127
millenanan rebellion, 168
Milnor, A.J., 105
minimum necessary force (MNF), 165

minister(s), 70, 122, 148
ministry, 70, 119
minorities, 105
minors, 127
'mixed' constitutions, 45, 74
mixed (electoral) system, 110
mixed systems, 73
mobilisation, 67, 167
mobilised systems, 52
model, 165
moderates, 169
modernisation, 48–51
modernising oligarchy, 50
Mollet, Guy, 57
Monaco, 52
monarcj(s), 39, 68, 70, 119, 136
monarchies, 32, 45, 68, 76, 136, 141, 143
money, 43, 85, 121, 123, 129, 168
Montesquien, Charles-louis de Secondat, Varon de, 17, 27, 72
Morocco, 79
Morris, Desmond, 23–4
mortality, 134
mortgages, 157
Moslem, 116
motorist, 56
motorways, 85, 86
movement, freedom of 114
Mozambique, 79
multi-functional model, 123
multi-Party systems, 97, 98, 111
Mussolini, Benito, 14, 46, 80, 143, 151
mutation, 78
myth, 161, 165, 170

Napoleon I, Emperor of the French, 143, 170
Napoleon III, Emperor of the French, 143
Napoleonic Wars, 148
Nasser, Gamal Abd-el, 169
nation, 31, 36, 86
nation state, 31, 36
National Front (Czechoslovakia), 80
National Association for the Advancement of Colored People (US), 88
National Farmers Union (UK), 88
national interest, 126
nationalism, 158
nationalists, 163
Nationalist parties, 105
Nationalist Party (South Africa), 105
National People's Congress (China), 85
National People's Power Assembly (Cuba), 85
national security, 141
National Socialist German Workers Party (NSDAP), 95
natural-born citizen, 128
natural disasters, 42, 43
natural products, 49
natural sciences, 2, 3, 12
navy,-ies, 152, 156

needs, 173
Nehru, Jahwaral, 96
Nepal, 32
nature, state of, 17
Nauru, 7
network, 61
Netherlands, 35, 68, 69, 70, 110, 140, 161
Neundörfer, Ludwig, 9
'new class', 82
New South Wales, 111
New Spain, 122
newspapers, 58
newsprint, 58
New York City, 55
New York State, 9
New Zealand, 15, 56, 79, 104
Nicaragua, 67, 71, 97, 102, 115, 135
Nicholas I, Tsar of all the Russias, 148
Nigeria, 15, 79, 155, 157
Nixon, Richard M., 73, 128, 135, 137
nobles, 68
noise, 61
nomination, 114
non-associational interest groups, 88, 89, 95
non-Communist, 87
non-competitive systems, 75, 90, 97
non-élite, 128
'non-Western' systems, 75, 90
Nordic countries, 70
norm(s), 146, 161
North Africa, 71, 153
North American Indians, 18
Northcote-Trevelyan reforms, 120
Northern Ireland, 89, 93, 112
Norway, 70, 110
Nuer, 27, 29
numbers, 168
nursery rhymes, 146

obedience, 34
objections, 125
objectives, 124
Obote, Milton, 139
obligations, 121
Occam's Razor, 162
occupation, 58, 114, 121, 129
occupational groups, 88
official, 121, 122
office (of state), 101, 102, 103, 119, 121, 128, 132, 133, 134, 135, 138, 142, 143, 144
officer corps, 157
officers, 94, 157—8
officials, 65, 82
oil wells, 85
Olduvai Gorge, 24
oligarchy, 45, 49, 50
ombudsman, 123
One, the, 44–5, 48
one man rule, 76–7, 142
one party states, 81, 97, 98

opinion, 103, 138, 158
opponents, 92, 97, 114, 135, 138, 139, 142, 158
opportunity, 156
opposition, 110, 114, 137, 139, 169, 172
opposition parties, 96, 103
oppositionless stage, 81
optics, 123
organic body, 60
organic remains, 26
Organisational Process model, 124–5
organisations, 73, 89, 90, 91, 93, 124, 125, 126, 127, 130, 143, 149, 163
organisations, supranational, 7
outer Mongolia, 82
output(s), 39–40; positive and negative, 41–3; 59, 61, 62, 117, 150
outlaws, 146
overcrowding, 19, 21–2
overload, 61
'overlords', 122
ownership, 83, 121
Pakistan, 50, 96, 155
palace revolutions, 162
Panama, 169
panchayats, 100
Paraguay, 114, 142
paramilitary forces, 132, 151–2, 156
Pareto, Vilfredo, 117, 127, 129, 130
Paris, 109, 110, 134, 147
Paris Commune (1871), 161
parking, 149
Parkinson, C. Northcote, 122
Parliament, 35, 39, 69, 70, 77, 78, 80, 134
parliamentary states/systems, 47, 69–70, 72, 73, 78–80, 82, 106
Parry, Geraint, 130
participation, 64, 74, 75—8, 84, 85, 96, 98, 168
party, parties; political, 46, 50, 67, 75, 76, 77, 80, 81, 83, 87, 90–8, 99, 102, 103, 104, 106, 107, 109, 110, 111, 115, 127, 134, 156, 163, 174
pass laws, 149
patriarchal authority, 51, 52
patrimonial authority, 51, 52
patronage, 96, 133, 135
pattern maintenance, 40
peacock, 55
peasants, 163, 167
Peking, 159
penalty, 146
pensions, 56, 121, 133, 135, 157
people, persons, 30, 31, 36, 55, 58, 59, 60, 67, 68, 70, 74, 85, 91, 93, 98, 104, 120, 127, 128, 134, 142, 143, 148, 149, 160, 174
People's Commissariat for Internal Affairs (NKVD), 151
People's Courts, 140, 148
People's democracies, 45, 50
perceptions, 66
performance, 126

period, 164
periphery, 8–9, 69, 93, 97
Perón, Juan Domingo, 96
personalities, 95, 118
Peru, 50, 58, 73, 115, 136, 138, 143, 155
pestilence, 34
Pétain, Philippe, 79
Pettee, George S., 161
phases of revolution, 166
Philippines, 70
philosophers, 4, 172
philosophies, 92
philosophy, 2
physics, 2
physiology, 13
pictorial material, 57
pigs, 30, 36
plan(s), 83, 125
Plato, 53, 160
players, 126, 172
plays, 126
plebeians, 161
plebiscite, 103, 143
plurality, 103, 104, 106, 107
Poland, 46, 80, 82, 103
police, 46, 56, 88, 132, 141, 146–51, 163, 170
Police Nationale (France), 148
police power, 121
police state, 149
policy,-ies, 59, 60, 62, 72, 99, 100, 106, 124, 125, 141
Politburo, 82, 100, 125, 138, 156
political action, 89
political activism, 114
political anthropology, 27
political appointees, 133–4
political asylum, 138
political behaviour, 10, 17, 171
political change, 53, 161, 163, 164, 168
political concepts, 65–6
political communication, 40, 54, 66, *see also* communication(s)
political culture, 69, 157
political development, 89–90
political democracy, 49, 50
political education, 63
political life, 97
political mobilisation, 52
political obligation, 86
political opinions, 59
political order, 165
political organisation, 76, 115
political parties *see* party, parties: political
political philosophers, 74, 100, 160
political philosophy, 17, 27
political process, 76, 90, 91, 94, 98, 137, 164
political recruitment, 40
political revolution, 161, 162
political science, 2–3, 4, 11, 92, 119
political scientists, 2, 4, 8, 11, 61, 104, 157
political socialisation, 40, 131, 146
political stability, 159
political sympathies, 58
political system(s), defined 38; 37, 39, 42, 44, 47, 48, 49, 50, 51, 52, 54, 67, 74, 87, 133, 138, 139, 150, 162, 164, 165
political thought, 161
political unification, 8
politicians, 2–3, 16, 66, 95, 117, 153, 171
politics, defined, 1; value, 5; 10, 23, 26–7, 38, 41, 42, 44, 75, 76, 89, 96, 97, 98, 99, 118, 129, 157, 168, 171–4
polity, 89
Polizeistaat, 121
polling booth, 102, 116
polling stations, 116
polo, 75
polyarchies, 45
Polybius, 53
poor, 51
popular support, 43
Popular Unity (UP) (Chile), 106
popular will, 69
population, 26, 96, 133, 149, 150, 153, 168
population growth, 42
populist, 93
Portsmouth, 28
Portugal, 135, 143, 152
poster(s), 58
position, 122
postmen, 56
post-revolutionary times, 170
Powell, G. Bingham, 40, 51, 52
power, 32, 33, 34, 38, 42, 48, 51, 52, 68, 70, 71, 72, 73, 75, 81, 83, 84, 87, 95, 105, 114, 116, 119, 120, 122, 125, 127, 128, 129, 130, 131, 132, 133, 134, 136, 138, 142, 150, 153, 155, 161, 162, 165, 166, 167, 168, 169, 170, 173
'power élite', 127
power resource extraction, 42–3
power resources, 38, 42, 69, 133
powers, 39, 72
praesidium, 45, 134
pre-Constitutional order, 141
predictive models, 44
Prefect, 148
prejudices, 102
pre-mobilised modern systems, 52
preparation, 166
presidency, 80, 81
president, 39, 45, 62, 70, 71–3, 81, 82, 84, 103, 106, 123, 128, 136, 154
presidential elections, 103, 105
Presidential Medal of Honor, 136
presidential state(s)/systems, 47, 69, 73, 77, 78, 79, 80–1, 82, 84, 107, 128, 136, 157
'President's Rule', 73
press, 159
press conference, 62, 78
pressure groups, 45, 50, 75, 88, 163

priesthood, 83
priests, 51, 102
primary election, 107–8
primates, 21, 23—4, 25
prime minister, 34, 39, 85, 128, 137
primitive communism, 27
primitive government, 26
Primo de Rivera, José Antonio, 153
prince, will of the, 122
printing press, 58
primitive society, 27–8, 38, 119
prism, 123
prismatic model, 123
prison, 56
private aspect, 122
private secretary, 123
privileges, 157
Privy Council (UK), 122
probabilities, 3
probability theory, 172
'problem solving' leader, 118
procedures, 124, 150
process, revolutionary, 164, 170
production, 83, 97, 130, 156
professional men/groupings, 88, 114
professionalism, 64, 155
programme, 165, 166, 170
programs, 125
proletarian internationalism, 64
proletariat, 3, 74, 90, 131, 160, 161
promises, 86, 96
promotion, 121, 132, 133, 134, 157
propaganda, 57, 167
property, 22, 91, 148, 149
proportionality, 107, 110, 111
proportional systems, 108
prosecution, 150
protectorates, 79
proverbs, 146
province(s), 65, 102, 142, 166–7
Prussia, 35
psychologists, 18, 66, 117, 118
psychology, 18
public, 61, 98, 122, 126
public order, 148
public buildings, 85
public opinion, 56
	–polls, 159
public prosecutor, 150
punishment(s), 33, 41, 51, 133, 137–9, 150, 155

Qatar, 32
Quakers, 100
qualifications, 127
qualities, personal, 169
Quetzal, Order of the, 136
quota, 109, 112–13

rabbits, 22
race, 128–9
race riots, 163

radical-conservative dimension, 46
radio, 55, 57, 85
Rado Cairo, 57
railway users, 86
railway carriage, 21–2
Ralliement du Peuple Francais (RPF), 110
Raleigh, Sir Walter, 146
rank(s), 121, 133, 136, 166
Rappaport, Roy, 30
rat, 19
rational, 122, 124, 125, 126
'Rational actor' model, 124
reapportionment, 107
rebel, 160
rebellion, 160, 161
receiver, 54, 55
Rechstaat, 120
recounts, 104
recruitment, 95, 96
red deer, 21
Red Guards (China), 76
referendum(-a), 76, 115
reform, 169
'refracted' decision-making, 123
refuse collectors, 56
regime, 134, 139, 141, 147, 161, 162, 163, 164, 165
regiments, 36, 158, 167
region, 110, 130
regional autonomy, 48
regional centres, 97
regional strongholds, 97
regulative processes, 150
reign of terror, 69, 169
relations, 142
relay, 54
religion, 6, 34, 89, 90, 128
Renaissance, 174
replication, 31, 173
representation, 67, 68, 69, 111
representative democracy, 75
representatives, 74, 98, 100, 102, 110, 112
republic, 136, 142, 143, 158
Republican Party (US), 72, 105
republican regimes, 46
Republican Security Companies (CRS), 148
republics, 32, 73
reputational criteria, 62
research design, 11
residence, 149
resources, 30, 39, 97, 136, 150, 156, 166, 172
responsibilities, 119, 147, 148, 149
restricted codes, 63–5
retainers, 135
reticence, 125
retirement, 133
returning officer, 112
revolution(s), 34, 65, 67, 85, 140, 151, 158, 159, 161, 163, 164–70
revolutionaries, 165, 169

revolutionary change, 83
reward(s), 51, 96, 133, 136, 138, 157
Rhine, 35
Richard II, King of England, 80
Richardson, Lewis, F., 167
Riff, 153
rifle, 155
Riggs, Fred, 123
rights, 114, 120, 141, 144
'right to rebel', 160
right-wing, 92
Riksdag (Sweden), 73
riots, 60, 162, 163
Rise of the Gentry, 162
ritual, 19–20, 31
ritualisation, 146
roads, 72, 146
Robespierre, Marie-Maximilien Isidore de, 74
Rodrigo the Cid, 32
Röhm *putsch*, 151
Rokkan, Stein, 9
roles, 1, 126, 150, 151, 155
Romania, 82
Rome, 80
Rome, ancient, 15, 35–6, 74, 137, 142
Roosevelt, Franklin, D., 95, 154
Rosas, Juan Manuel de, 142
rotation in office, 133, 134
Rousseau, Jean-Jacques, 17, 27, 74
routines, 124, 125
Rudé, George, 161
Rugby football, 146
rule-adjudication function, 40, 48, 71, 141
rule-application function, 40, 45, 47, 70, 71, 150
rule-enforcement, 150
    see rule application
rule-making function, 40, 45, 47, 71
rulers, 44, 50, 68, 74, 80, 94, 119, 123, 133, 141, 142, 165
rules, 30—1, 32, 39, 125, 141, 171, 172
ruling élite 130, 132
rumour, 134
Russett, Bruce, M., 159, 163
Russia, 67, 68, 97, 161
    see also Soviet Union
Russian Revolution, 148, 169
Russians, 148

sacrifice, 86
Sakharov. Aleksandr, 56
Sala, 123
salaried officials, 120
salaries, 121, 126
Salazar, Antonio de Oliveira, 135
'salient' leader, 118
sanction(s), 5, 41, 133, 137, 150
San Marino, 52
Sartori, Giovanni, 95, 96, 98
satisficing, 125

Saudi Arabia, 32
Scandinavian countries, 123
scarcity, 42
scenarios, 125
school board, 109
Schutz Staffeln (SS), 151, 152
science, political science as 2–3
scientist, 155
Scotland, 32, 104, 112, 123
screening process, 60
script, 126
seamen, 27
search, 124
seats, 105, 107, 108, 109, 110, 111, 112, 113
secessionist(s), 163
second ballot, 106
Second World War, 50, 97
secrecy, 2, 121
secretaries, 72–3
secret police, 148, 149–51
sects, religious, 88
secularised city states, 52
security, 148, 149, 167
security guard, 58
segregation, 149
Seine, 148
Sejm (Poland), 103
self-criticism, 84
self-employed, 114
semantic space, 66
semantics, 65–6
seniority, 77, 121
separation of powers, 45, 77
sequence (of *coups*), 169
Serbia, 139
    see also Yugoslavia
Serbs, 84
servants, 119
servomechanism(s), 54, 62, 64
settlement, 102
Seville, 122
school, 64
sexes, 5
Sforza, 32
Shanghai, 22
shanty towns, 163
shell, 41
Shils, Edward, B., 49–50
Sicily, 145
signal, 54, 61, 62
signs, 58
Sihanouk, Prince Norodom, 34, 139
simple majority
    see plurality
sinecure, 136
single member second ballot system, 111
single member single ballot system, 104–5, 110
single non-transferable vote, 108
single-party systems, 96, 97
    see also one-party states

single transferable vote(STV), 111–13
situation, 118
skill(s), 129, 169
Slovenes, 84
small groups, 78, 117–18, 120, 174
    see also groups
social change(s), 67, 106, 161, 162, 164
social class, 129
'social closure', 128–9
Social Contract, 64
social control, 139
social environment, 61
social fabric, 174
socialisation, 61, 145
social justice, 168
social order, 97, 161
social pressures, 114
social reformers, 169
social relationships, 37
social revolution, 165, 168
social science(s), 129, 172
social standing, 58, 131
social structures, 12, 14, 79, 173
social systems, 34, 42, 79, 132, 165, 172
socialism, 84
socialist, 11, 83
socialist countries/states, 58, 78
society-ies, 16, 37, 38, 41, 42, 62, 63, 74, 81, 82,
    87, 89, 90, 91, 98, 100, 105, 111, 116, 119,
    120, 127, 128, 136, 139, 145, 146, 147, 158,
    161, 165, 172, 174
sociologists, 165
sociology, 2
'sociometric' leader, 118
soldier(s), 63–4, 80, 116, 118, 154, 157, 158
Solon, 142
solution, 100
Solzhenitzyn, Alexander, 138
Somoza Debayle, Anastasio, 135
Somoza, José, 135
sophistication, 89
Somozas, 71
South Africa, 15, 57, 78, 104, 111, 114, 138,
    149, 158
 – Senate, 111
South America, 70
sovereignty, 6, 32–3, 34–5, 73
Soviet Motherhood, Hero of, 136
Soviet Union, 7, 9, 22, 46, 47, 56, 58, 64, 82–4,
    87, 95, 97, 100, 102, 114, 115, 129, 134,
    135, 136, 138, 139, 148, 149
soviets, 82, 102
Spain, 32, 34, 80, 82, 122, 132, 135, 136, 140,
    143, 153
Sparta(n), 129, 158
Special Branch (UK), 149
specialist knowledge, 102
speech, freedom of, 114
speeches, 66
'spoils system', 133

Sri Lanka, 69
stable government, 84
staff, 59, 119, 120, 121, 124
Stalin, Josef V., 15, 22, 46, 82, 95, 154
standard operating procedures, 125
state
    defined 6, comparing 7–10, Greek 13–14,
        primitive 26, 28, 29, as systems 37, 45, 47,
        58, 74, 75, 78, 79, 83, 85, 91, 119, 120, 122,
        132, 133, 138, 142, 143, 145, 146, 147, 148,
        149, 150, 152, 153, 156, 162, 163, 170
state monopoly, 58
statements, 66
states (of the U.S.), 39, 77, 106, 116
statesmen, 117
statistical indicators, 63
status, 38, 62, 81, 129, 131, 136
status quo, 59, 61, 65
Statute of Westminster, 39
stories, 146
strategy, 154
stratum,-a, 129, 131
street, 58
strength, 97
stress, 63
strike-breaking, 152
strikers, 149, 152
structure(s), 1, 13, 67, 75, 82, 85, 92, 93, 96,
    118, 119, 132, 140, 141, 173
students, 59, 118, 149
Sturma b teilugen (SA), 151
subjects, 165
sub-revolutionary violence, 162, 164, 165
sub-Saharan Africa, 71
subsidies, 42–3
subsystem autonomy, 48
subsystems, 37, 48, 51
succession, 95, 119
successors, 119, 144
Suez, 57
suffrage, 92
Sukarno, President, 162, 167
superiors, 121, 122
superpowers, 45
supplementary estimates, 81
support(s), 40–1, 42, 43, 52, 59, 62, 75, 85, 93,
    98, 99–116, 138, 150, 154, 159, 165
supporters, 133, 135
Supreme Court, 39, 107
Supreme Soviet, 82, 102
surplus, 112–13
surveyors, 155
surveys, multi-country, 9–10
Sweden, 70, 73, 91, 110
Swiss chocolate, 86
Swiss lakes, 26
Switzerland, 92, 110
synchronisation, 166
system, 13, 133
system maintenance, 132

systems analysis, 13

Taiwan, 134
talents, 135
Talmon, J.L., 50, 75
Tanzania, 78, 139
task(s), 118, 119, 124
Tasmania, 111
taste, 58
taxation, 43
taxes, 41, 42–3
Tchambuli, 27
tea, 100
teachers, 88
technical qualifications, 121
technical training, 121
technician, 155
technological expertise, 155
technological innovation, 65
teeth, 23–4
Tel Aviv, 110
telephone(s), 56
television, 55, 57, 58, 62, 77, 85
term, presidential, 71
territorial space, 21
territoriality, 20–3
territory, 145
Terror (France), 69
terrorism, 163
Texas, 116, 135
Thatcher, Margaret, 122
Thailand, 151
time, 100, 127, 166, 170
'time of troubles', 51
Tito, Josip Broz, 84, 135
Textor, Robert B., 10
thieves, 149
third party, 105
Tiger, Lionel, 24
tigers, 24
time, 16–17, structuring 31; 124, 141
Tönnies, Ferdinand, 95
Tokyo, 22, 55
Tonga, 94
Tontons Macoutes, 81
Tories, 91
totalitarian states, 45–6
totalitarian democracy, 50, 75
totalitarian oligarchy, 50
totalitarianism, 46, 49
town(s), 9, 25, 58, 68
trade organisation, 114
trade unions, 77, 88, 102, 114
traditional authority, 33–4
traditional élites, 128
traditional oligarchy, 50
training, 94, 129, 154
transactions, 30
transition, revolutionary, 166
transitional elites, 128

transmitter, 54
Transport House, 93
tribal consciousness, 157
tribe(s), 27, 28, 29, 30, 31, 37, 52, 53, 157
tribunals, 123, 141
troops, 80, 165, 167
tropical conditions, 163
Truman, Harry S., 95
truths, 92
turbulence, 159
Turkey, 67, 68, 97, 110, 158, 161
tutelary democracy, 50
two-party systems, 97
tyrant, 142

Uganda, 139, 143
Ukraine, 9
umpire, 31
unanimity, 99, 100, 103
Union of Soviet Socialist Republics (USSR), 7, 156
  see also Soviet Union
Union Republics (USSR), 47, 102
Unionist Party (N. Ireland), 93
unitary state, 73
United Kingdom, 15, 32, 38, 59, 73, 95, 101, 104, 105, 107, 109, 111, 114, 128, 153, 159, 163
United Nations, 7, 47
United States of America, 7, 9, 13, 14, 22, 38, 39, 48, 49, 56, 62, 63, 66, 67, 68, 69, 70, 71, 72, 77, 88, 90, 91, 97, 103, 104, 105, 106, 107, 108, 109, 111, 115, 116, 121, 122, 128, 133, 134, 135, 136, 137, 139, 140, 146, 152, 154, 162, 163
  – Congress, 155
  – House of Representatives, 137
United Workers Party (Poland), 80
universe, 171
university-ies, 77, 100, 112, 140
urban violence, 163
urbanised, 112
Uruguay, 72, 114, 139, 168

vagabonds, 147
Vagts, Alfred, 152
Valen, Henry, 9
value, 75
value judgement, 48
values, 64, 66, 145, 146
Vatican City State, 52
vegetarian, 23–4, 25
Velasco Alvarado, Juan, 58
Venezuela, 9, 15
Verba, Sidney, 10
Verney, Douglas V., 15, 47, 67
Versailles, 19, 63
Victorians, the, 53
Vietnam, 167
Vietnam War, 137

Villa, Pancho, 129
village, 102
Villaroel, Gualberto, 162
violence, 67, 89, 145, 153, 159, 160–1, 162, 163, 164, 168, 169
visual communications, 57–8
Visconti, 33
vizier, 119
vocabulary, 63, 65
voice communications, 57, 60
volume, 63
voluntary bodies, 88
vote(s), 36, 71, 76, 85, 92, 100, 101, 106, 107, 109, 110, 111, 112, 113, 114, 159, 173
voting, 76
 – in public, 115
voting machine, 115

wages, 64
Wales, 9, 112, 123
wall poster, 76, 159
war, 19, 25, 28, 34, 36, 67, 129, 133, 141, 149, 153, 154
warfare, 151
Washington, D.C., 134, 135
wealth, 83, 129
weapons, 152, 163
weapons procurement, 156
Weber, Max, 33—4, 51, 73, 117, 121, 122
Weimar Constitution, 84
Weimar Republic, 111
West Indies, 128

West Saxons, 28
'Western' systems, 75, 90, 96
Westphalia, Treaty of, 6
wheat, 23
Whigs, 91
White House, 135
will of the people, 34
William the Conqueror, 32
Wilson, J. Harold, 64
Wilson, Thomas Woodrow, 128
Winch, Peter, 172
Winchester, Statute of (1285), 147
Wine Growers Association (France), 88
'withinputs', 41, 87
wolves, 24
women, 27, 30, 35, 92, 127, 146
words, 55, 63, 64
work, 114
workers' democracy, 84
working people, 83, 84
writing, 57
written communications, 59, 60

yachtsmen, 86
youth, 145
Yugoslavia, 78, 84, 135, 143, 155, 163

Zaire, 79
Zhukov, Marshal Gregory K., 138, 156
zoning, 22
Zurich, gnomes of, 38